TRANSFORMING
EXPERIENCE

Other recently published titles in the series include

Elements of Knowledge:
Pragmatism, Logic, and Inquiry
Revised and Expanded Edition
Arthur Franklin Stewart

The Loyal Physician:
Roycean Ethics and the Practice of Medicine
Griffin Trotter

His Glassy Essence: An Autobiography of Charles Sanders Peirce
Kenneth Laine Ketner

Rorty and Pragmatism: The Philosopher Responds to His Critics
edited by Herman J. Saatkamp, Jr.

Genuine Individuals and Genuine Communities: A Roycean Public Philosophy
Jacquelyn Ann K. Kegley

The Continuity of Peirce's Thought
Kelly A. Parker

The Philosophy of Loyalty
New Paperback Edition
Josiah Royce

Intensity: An Essay in Whiteheadian Ontology
Judith A. Jones

The Relevance of Philosophy to Life
John Lachs

TRANSFORMING

EXPERIENCE

John Dewey's
Cultural Instrumentalism

Michael Eldridge

Vanderbilt University Press
Nashville and London

This publication is made from high-quality paper that meets the minimum
requirements of American National Standard for Information Sciences—
Permanence of Paper for Printed Library Materials. ∞

Library of Congress Cataloging-in-Publication Data
    Eldridge, Michael.
        Transforming experience : John Dewey's cultural instrumentalism /
    Michael Eldridge. -- 1st ed.
            p.   cm.
        Includes bibliographical references and index.
        ISBN 0-8265-1307-7. -- ISBN 0-8265-1319-0 (pbk.)
        1. Dewey, John, 1859-1952. 2. Instrumentalism (Philosophy)
    I. Title.
    B945.D44E43 1997
    191--dc21   97-45427
                                             CIP

Manufactured in the United States of America

In memory of
Ralph W. Sleeper

CONTENTS

❖

❖

PREFACE

URING THE TIME the initial draft of the manuscript that was to
become this book was under review for publication, I accompanied
my wife to Atlanta. While Sue was attending her conference, I worked
in Emory University's library. Also, since I was to be on campus, I arranged
to have lunch with Emory philosopher Jim Gouinlock, who, once he learned
of my project, wanted to know what it was about. Always before when
someone would ask, I would reply, "Dewey wrote an immense amount over
a very long time. He was active well into his eighties. The collected works
comprise thirty-seven volumes in the edition published by Southern Illinois
University Press. Well, I am trying to make sense out of all this. I am trying
to summarize Dewey's project." But in replying to the knowledgeable questions of a respected Dewey scholar (and in reflecting later on what I had
said), it became clear to me just what my take on Dewey was. I realized that
my version of Dewey was both more pragmatic and more secular than that
of others.

This is not what I had set out to do. Originally I had wanted to write a
book that would summarize his project *and* "save Dewey whole." I was going
to show how Dewey's philosophy fit together, forming a coherent whole. This
had been the promise of a paper that I had read at the Eastern Division
meeting of the American Philosophical Association in 1985; finally, in 1993,
I began to complete that program. Santayana and others who had tried to
split Dewey up were wrong; the integrity of Dewey's work could be shown.

But the book did not turn out as planned. I did discover what unifies
Dewey's thinking—his effort to increase the intelligence of our practices.
But in so doing I found myself deconstructing his religious proposal. Much
to my surprise, I found myself siding with Sidney Hook on the issue with
which he had disagreed with Dewey when he was helping Dewey prepare
the manuscript that was to be published as *A Common Faith*. Hook questioned the wisdom of Dewey's use of the term *God* to refer to the process
whereby large ideals interact with actual situations. I now found myself

ix

agreeing with Hook. I also found myself doing something I thought I would never do. In the APA paper I had argued that Richard Rorty was but the latest in a long line of interpreters who had split Dewey up. Now, like Rorty, I was deconstructing a piece of Dewey's thinking. Also, like Rorty, I thought I was saving what is important.

Clearly, what I have saved is much more than what Rorty has retained. But, as robust as my Dewey is, he is thinner than the original. I know from many interchanges with Dewey scholars in person, on the Internet, and in nonelectronic correspondence that some think I have trimmed too much. But I have long been convinced that loyalty to Dewey is not to be found in adherence to everything he wrote. I had never thought that saving Dewey whole required one to preserve and harmonize everything he had ever written. That would be impossible. Dewey changed his mind on many matters over the course of his long philosophical career. He could be stubbornly persistent in his thinking, but he could also subject it to criticism. Indeed, he thought philosophy *was* a form of criticism.

Dewey's religious proposal comprises only a small part of what he wrote. In contrast, his efforts to make our practices more satisfying by using the resources present in our continually developing culture are pervasive in his writings. His cultural instrumentalism—that is, his recommendation to transform experience by means of experience—provides the focus for his lifework. This book attempts to make sense out of and justify this claim.

The one who initially encouraged me in the effort to save Dewey whole was Ralph Sleeper. He was present at the 1985 APA session, quickly initiated a correspondence with me the next month, and continually nudged me at annual meetings of the Society for the Advancement of American Philosophy to get on with my project. I am very grateful for his encouragement, wit, and criticism. No doubt, if he were alive today he would find something worth challenging, as well as amusing, in what I have written.

I would like to express gratitude to Queens College for the opportunity while there to complete the first part of the initial draft. I am particularly grateful to Catherine Haselden--teacher, writer, lawyer, and colleague--and to Rosemary Arneson and her staff at the library for helping me locate materials that were not in the library's limited collection.

Since the fall of 1995 I have been fortunate to teach on a continuing basis at the University of North Carolina at Charlotte. I am grateful to the chair of the Department of Philosophy, Bill Gay, the members of the department, and the secretary, Vicki Griffith, for their hospitality and support. One of the members of the department, Steve Fishman, has a long-standing interest in Dewey, and he recently coauthored an innovative book on

Dewey's educational approach. Steve's knowledge, intensity, curiosity, and integrity, both philosophical and personal, as well as our shared interest in Dewey, are much appreciated.

Also during this period of time I have been a regular participant on the Dewey electronic discussion list (jdewey-l@vm.sc.edu), initially managed by Todd Lekan, to whom those of us in the electronic Dewey community will be forever grateful, and now ably continued by Tom Burke. Many a time something worked out in the manuscript got summarized and tried out in this forum, many of whose subscribers are both very knowledgeable and insightful about things Deweyan.

Many people have kindly consented to read various parts or versions of the evolving manuscript. These, not all of whom liked what they read, include Tom Alexander, Doug Anderson, Randy Auxier, Gary Calore, Vincent Colapietro, Michael Donovan, Larry Hickman, John Lachs, John J. McDermott, Steven Rockefeller, Pat Shade, Beth Singer, and John Stuhr. The efforts of those who took the time to comment in writing are much appreciated. A historian and former colleague at Queens College, Charlie Reed, painstakingly worked through several chapters, attempting to improve the prose. Another historian, then at Queens but now of Yale University, Glenda Gilmore, asked helpful questions regarding a very early version of chapter 2.

But none has been a more attentive and thoughtful reader than Ellen Haring. Her philosophical perspective and good writing sense have been very helpful, as have her long-standing friendship and support.

I am thankful to Charlene Haddock and Hans Seigfried for their hospitality, philosophical exchanges, and professional support.

Larry Hickman, as director of the Center for Dewey Studies, has also assisted me on more than one occasion in tracking down references or supplying me with material. He and his staff have responded promptly, graciously, and professionally to my every request. Everyone who works with the Dewey material is in debt to Larry's predecessor, Jo Ann Boydston, for editing *The Works of John Dewey*. I am particularly grateful for the textual commentaries.

I am grateful to Morris Library, Southern Illinois University at Carbondale, for permission to quote from one of Dewey's letters, as well as to the Center for Dewey Studies, which holds the literary rights. In two instances I made use of material that I had previously published. I am grateful to the *Transactions of the Charles S. Peirce Society* and Texas A&M University Press for permission to use this material. I am particularly grateful to Peter Hare for publishing in the *Transactions* the essay to which Robert Westbrook responded. I learned much from this.

Everyone associated with Vanderbilt University Press has been splendid. I appreciate their courtesy, wit, and professionalism. Herman Saatkamp, Jr., as the general editor of The Vanderbilt Library of American Philosophy, has been encouraging, attentive, and resourceful. The Press's director and staff have skillfully and patiently guided me as a novice through an intimidating process.

My wife has been alternatively (and appropriately) patient and impatient during the long process that produced this book. We are both glad that it is done and can now get on with our lives. I will always be grateful to her for the opportunity she permitted me to pursue and finally settle questions about Dewey that had long gone unanswered by me—or answered partially and unsatisfactorily. If others benefit from the results of my questions, then the pleasure of the effort is increased.

Transforming Experience

I

❖

INTRODUCTION
DEWEY'S LIFELONG EFFORT

*If basic problems can be settled only where they arise, namely, in the
cultural conditions of our associated life; if philosophy is fundamentally a criticism which brings to light these problems and gives them the
clarity that springs from definite formulation; and if after formulation
philosophy can do no more than point the road intelligent action must
take,—then the greatest service any particular philosophical theory
can render is to sharpen and deepen the sense of these problems.*
>   —Dewey, "Experience, Knowledge and Value: A Rejoinder" (LW
>   14:89)[1]

*In the last analysis . . . philosophy for Dewey stands for a method of
cultural interpretation, evaluation and criticism, a study and creation
of cultural meanings.*
>   —Thomas M. Alexander, *John Dewey's Theory of Art, Experience,
>   and Nature: The Horizons of Feeling*[2]

IN "THE NEED FOR A RECOVERY OF PHILOSOPHY" (1917) John Dewey
suggested that pragmatism had been welcomed by some because "it was
taken as a sign that philosophy was about to surrender its otiose and
speculative remoteness" (MW 10:42). A few pages later occurs the declaration that is often regarded as signaling Dewey's distinctive approach to philosophy: "Philosophy recovers itself when it ceases to be a device for dealing
with the problems of philosophers and becomes a method, cultivated by
philosophers, for dealing with the problems of men" (MW 10:46). Rather
than continuing to speculate about matters of concern only to philosophers,
Dewey urged a program of public philosophy. He thought philosophy would
come into its own when it paid attention to human problems by improving
the intellectual tools used by humans to resolve their problems.

DEWEY'S PROJECT

The basic notion of Dewey's instrumentalist version of pragmatism is this: Thinking is not something apart from our lives; it is a very effective way to secure our interests. Thinking, despite its occasional pretensions that it is above it all, is really a tool for solving problems, human problems, and philosophy's role is to develop this tool.[3] But the part philosophy is asked to play is not one dimensional. Sometimes the philosophical role calls for a logician, sometimes a cultural critic.[4] In either case philosophizing for Dewey will be characterized by a critical attentiveness to the way we actually think. The techniques used and their intellectual outcomes will be reviewed, assessed, and, as needed, reworked by the philosopher (in direct or indirect collaboration with others). Philosophy's role can range from specific points in logic to tensions in society to great issues of cultural import.[5] Not that every philosopher will range as widely as did Dewey, but each one, he insisted, needs to understand that ultimately the *philosophical* objective is to assist in the resolution of human problems.

In 1914, three years before he published "The Need for a Recovery of Philosophy," Dewey had begun the transition from prominent academic philosopher and educator to public philosopher through his articles in *The New Republic*.[6] But in the 1920s and 30s he was to become even better known through several major books, reports on his travels to China and elsewhere, efforts to start a third political party, and the chairing of a commission to consider charges brought against Leon Trotsky.

In the fall of 1939, then, at the end of Dewey's most productive years as a publicly engaged philosopher, it is understandable that his eightieth birthday was marked by not one event, but four. Groups of all sorts, reflecting his varied concerns, honored Dewey. A brief review of these events and groups provides a glimpse of the range of Dewey's interests. The first event was the publication on his birthday, October 20, of *The Philosophy of John Dewey*,[7] a collection of descriptive and critical essays with a rejoinder by Dewey, a brief biography edited by his daughter Jane, and a sixty-five-page bibliography. The second event was a dinner and conference held on Dewey's birthday and the following day, sponsored by the Progressive Education Association and several other organizations, including the American Civil Liberties Union.[8] The third event, on October 22, was a second meeting held by the Conference on Methods in Philosophy and the Sciences. The presentations made at this meeting were published, along with Dewey's address at the October 20 dinner, as a second volume of essays, *The Philosopher of the The Common Man: Essays in Honor of John Dewey to Celebrate his Eightieth Birthday*.[9] Finally, according to *The New York Times*, the American Philosophical Association held an unusual joint meeting of the Eastern and Western divisions "in honor of Dr. Dewey's birthday" (December 24, 1939, p. 11). Presiding at the annual dinner, noted the *Times*, was William Pepperell Montague, Dewey's longtime colleague at Columbia University.[10]

In introducing Dewey, Montague praised him for having practicalized intelligence. Given Dewey's concern with human needs and the usefulness of intelligence, one might think that he would have appreciated a colleague's praise, but his reply to this intended compliment showed that he did not. We learn of the exchange from Charles Frankel's account, which was published almost three decades later. Frankel had been both an undergraduate and a graduate student in philosophy at Columbia University during Dewey's last years there as an emeritus professor. Later Frankel became a professor of social and political philosophy at Columbia, served in the State Department, and was the founding director of the National Humanities Center. Frankel was in his second year of graduate study at Columbia, where he was also employed as a lecturer[11] when the events of the story took place. Here is Frankel's retrospective account: "When Dewey was eighty, he engaged in a debate, at a meeting of the American Philosophical Association, with his old friend and Columbia colleague, William Pepperell Montague, in the course of which Montague complimented him for his lifelong effort to practicalize intelligence. Dewey replied quietly but firmly that Montague was taking a narrow, inbred view—a philosopher's trade-union view, he implied—of what he, Dewey, had tried to accomplish. His effort had not been to practicalize intelligence but to intellectualize practice."[12]

Montague's mistake, from Dewey's perspective, was to judge that Dewey began with intelligence and then tried to make it practical. Dewey regarded thinking as an activity that was a part of—not apart from—our interactions with one another and the world. Dewey thought thinking was the aspect-become-means of action by which we discern and modify the connections in cognitive and noncognitive experience.[13] Therefore, Dewey did not have to make intelligence practical. All he had to do was develop the intelligible connections present in experience. I make it sound easy. But notice that it was a colleague who had missed the verbally slight but all-important difference in Dewey's approach.

Briefly, Dewey's "lifelong effort" to promote "intelligent action"[14] can be understood to be one that recommends that we begin with what he took to be the pervasive problem in our society—the split between the successful methods of modern science and technology for transforming experience and the older, premodern values associated with morality, religion, and traditional philosophy. Dewey thought this debilitating division was but a manifestation of a more general problem, the problem of existence and value. Our inherited ways of knowing and doing are inadequate to the task of relating existence and value, or, as he sometimes put it, actual and ideal. If one began, however, with our actual practices and sought to make them more effective, judging them not by some set standards but by desired and actual consequences, one could overcome these standing cultural divisions. Therefore, I take Dewey's proposal that we make our present beliefs, attitudes, and institutions more intelligent than they would otherwise be as the organizing aim of what he did. This, like much in Dewey, is not very dramatic. It can easily be trivialized. But by keeping it constantly in mind one can avoid many errors in understanding what he was doing.

Interpreters often refer to Dewey's famous comment about dealing with "the problems of men" rather than "the problems of philosophers," then proceed to focus on what Dewey had to say about the latter. But if we are to understand Dewey's project we must keep the focus on his effort to cultivate methods for dealing with human problems and explore the conceptual implications of this policy. One such implication, which I will discuss later in this chapter and even more fully in the last chapter, is his secular orientation. It is no accident that Dewey both advocated intelligent practice and opposed supernaturalism, for he was making use of the resources within culture to criticize culture. He continually recommended that we reconstruct existing situations, using the possibilities in our current practices to remake them in more satisfying ways. Old solutions encounter new difficulties, providing us with opportunities to develop new resolutions. "In its large sense," Dewey observed in *Liberalism and Social Action* (1935), "this remaking of the old through union with the new is precisely what intelligence is" (LW 11:37).

To be sure, Dewey had much to say about a host of philosophers' problems, but one should not mistake bulk for overall purpose. Dewey found himself quite often arguing with his fellow philosophers, but he did so in an effort to shift attention to human problems and their resolution. It is important to realize that, although Dewey could be a resourceful, persistent polemicist for his philosophical views, the point of his arguments was not so much to win philosophical converts as to better society and the lives of its members. Dewey wanted, above all, for his contemporaries to become more intelligent in how they lived so that they could live better. His philosophizing was subordinated to this purpose. Failure to keep this straight can lead one to read him as either an ineffective social-political activist or an advocate of a philosophical position, pragmatism or instrumentalism, that can serve as a comprehensive theory for a way of life, a "philosophy." Dewey did not want to make philosophers into pragmatists or instrumentalists so much as he wanted philosophers and nonphilosophers alike to be intelligent, or, as he also often put it, scientific and democratic. Dewey did not offer a distinctive, competing way of life. He argued, as a pragmatist or instrumentalist, that we should fully embrace and develop the values and techniques of science and democracy. It was not that he uncritically accepted modern society. But he did think that these particular developments within his—and our—society should be embraced and critically developed.

One has to read Dewey's carefully constructed and often qualified prose patiently to understand his view. Although Dewey seldom wrote succinctly or expressed himself completely in any one place, his prose is crafted more than it appears to be. The meaning is there for one to grasp, particularly when one reads the text in question with related ones. But one does have to work to comprehend Dewey's prose and the project he is proposing. Despite the apparent plainness of the prose, the philosophy is not on the surface. But there is a distinctive, carefully worked out, if evolving, Deweyan project that we can identify, then use to criticize some of Dewey's many specific proposals about an astonishing range of topics. It is highly significant that Dewey's thinking was neither static nor amorphous. He was constantly rethinking what he thought. But through the many decades of his active philosophizing and various reconstructions one can discern a fairly tight, coherent project.

My Project

Making practice more intelligent than it would otherwise be is not all that Dewey did, but by keeping the focus on this project we can understand much of what Dewey was about and even correct some of his more specific proposals, notably the religious one found in *A Common Faith*.

Like Thomas M. Alexander, I want to identify what is central in Dewey. In the introduction to his major book on Dewey, Alexander writes, "The primary task of this work, then, is to undertake a systematic thinking-through of Dewey's philosophy. Instead of providing a survey of the numerous topics of his thought, such as his ethics, his theory of inquiry, his views on education, and so on, I propose to investigate what I consider to be the central, guiding thought in his philosophy: the aesthetic dimension of experience" (xiii). But I part company with Alexander when he makes his last assertion. I do not take the "aesthetic dimension of experience" as the "guiding thought" of Dewey's philosophy. Without denying the significance of what Alexander takes to be central, I focus on Dewey's instrumentalism. Alexander continues, "It is the thesis of this book that the best approach to what Dewey means by 'experience' is not to be gained by focusing primarily on the theme by which Dewey is generally known, his 'instrumentalism,' but instead by looking at experience in its most complete, most significant, and most fulfilling mode: experience as art."[15]

The conflict with Alexander is lessened when one reflects on the last phrase, "experience as art," for the gap between art and intelligent action is narrow for Dewey, if not nonexistent. Indeed, Alexander writes later in the book, in the chapter "The Art of Experience": "*An* experience embodies intelligently controlled action; it leads to involvement with the subject matter through care. To create this, the artist must take on both the role of maker and viewer and integrate these activities so that they control his action" (207). To do justice to Dewey, one must hold together what he has to say about experience and intelligence. Alexander works more with the former, I with the latter. But the burden is on any Deweyan interpreter to overcome any distinction that threatens to turn into a dualism.

Also lessening the conflict between Alexander and me is that my understanding of Dewey's instrumentalism is not what Alexander fears—reading Dewey as "a proto-postivist who sought to reduce meaning to scientific procedure" (xiv). I recognize the significance of the "artistic-esthetic" in Dewey (the phrase is Dewey's; see LW 8:56) and will attempt to avoid proto-positivist reductionism by understanding his instrumentalism as being culturally implicated. I think Alexander oversimplifies the matter in asserting that Dewey's instrumentalism was "built to serve a far more general theory of experience" (xiv), but I share his misgivings about a stand-alone instrumentalism. Indeed, I describe Dewey's philosophy as a *cultural* instrumentalism in order to emphasize Dewey's situating of thought within society and history. Besides, Dewey's instrumentalism relies on cultural products. His is not primarily a theory about tools; it is a theory about the significance for action of intellectual tools (see MW 11:7 and LW 10:294). Therefore, I agree with Alexander that "it is the very possibility for experience to take on . . . satisfying quality which determines the evaluation of so much of our ordinary experience as unfulfilling, fragmented, problematic, or meaningless. If human experience reached its possible limits in mindless routine or disconnected activity, not only would Dewey's aesthetics be superfluous but his instrumentalism as well" (184). But I can acknowledge the conceptual significance of the aesthetic for Dewey and still maintain that the organizing focus of Dewey's lifelong project was his concern for intelligent action.

Alexander's book thus goes in a different direction than mine. He deals ably with aesthetics and metaphysical issues; I focus more on Dewey's social, political, and religious philosophy. Yet, like Alexander, I attempt to be inclusive in my understanding of Dewey. If I fall short without utterly failing, this book can be read as a complement to Alexander's work. If I succeed, it can be read as a more adequate expression of Dewey's core project, one that builds on much fine Dewey scholarship published in the last decade or so.

Some have paid attention to a particular facet of Dewey's thought (Larry Hickman to that on technology or Tom Burke to that on logic) or dealt with his thought historically (Alan Ryan). Some are both historical and focused on some aspect of his thought (Robert Westbrook on his politics, Tom Alexander on his aesthetics and metaphysics, Ralph Sleeper on his logic and metaphysics, Raymond D. Boisvert on his metaphysics, Steven C. Rockefeller on his religion, and Jennifer Welchman on his early and middle ethics). J. E. Tiles and James Campbell have attempted to deal with Dewey's thought as a whole. Tiles usefully relates Dewey to the concerns of analytic philosophy, offering a fresh perspective of Dewey's work; Campbell calls attention to Dewey's social orientation. Boisvert's just-published book, *John Dewey: Rethinking Our Time* (New York: State University of New York Press, 1998), is a brief, intentionally "expository rather than critical" introduction to Dewey's thought (4). But Boisvert succeeds, where many have failed, in presenting Dewey in the thinking and language of our time rather than simply paraphrasing him. James Gouinlock also considers Dewey's thought as a whole, but his focus is on Dewey's moral philosophy.[16] None of these, however, attempts what I do: to identify and elaborate Dewey's core project, intelligizing practice as that which drove his philosophic efforts.

In a way, I am taking an un-Dewey-like approach. I am attempting to be conceptual about a philosopher who often preferred to treat problems and specific areas of philosophy in a historical manner, avoiding a systematic approach. Thus many of the authors cited in the preceding paragraph are more faithful to Dewey's own situation and historical approach than I am. In calling attention to his effort to intelligize practice and showing how this effort makes sense of much, if not all, of what he wrote, I risk the systemization that he avoided. My aim, however, differs from Dewey's. Whereas he was trying to transform our experience in intelligent ways by means of his cultural instrumentalism, I am trying to understand this instrumentalism.

Dewey was, of course, not unaware of the unity of his philosophy, but he did not himself present his thought in a single, comprehensive work or ordered series. Rather, his preferred style was that of addressing issues in an almost ad hoc way. He allowed current events and public concerns to play a role in the selection of his topics.[17]

Dewey was neither a hierarchical nor a linear thinker, and one does undue violence to his work by organizing it in such a fashion. Although I risk being more conceptual than some Deweyan interpreters, my presentation is less orderly than some would like. Also, because of the experiential character of Dewey's philosophy, I use events in Dewey's life to understand his core project. So this study is both historical (but not a narrative) and conceptual. It is also expository. I continually ground my interpretations in what Dewey wrote.

The book is organized in six chapters. In the first substantive one, chapter 2, "Intelligent Practice: Dewey's Project," I provide an initial exposition of his instrumentalism, situating it in his philosophy as a whole. I then broaden and deepen this understanding in the third and fourth chapters, "Transforming Society: Dewey's Cultural Instrumentalism" and "A Transforming Society: Democratic Means and Ends." In these two chapters I draw on both Dewey's life and his work. By carefully spelling out the meaning of his recommended way of life through exposition of texts, criticism of other interpretations, and consideration of cases, I hope to establish the basis for my claim in the final two chapters that Dewey was a resolutely secular thinker, despite his selective use of traditionally religious language.

In chapter 5, "Dewey's Religious Proposal," I show how Dewey presented his secular project in religious language (*faith, piety, God*) but in such a way that it can be translated back into secular discourse without remainder. I do not think that his proposal was entirely successful, for it allowed many to misread him. The pull of the conventionally religious in our culture is such that Dewey's carefully qualified language can be, was, and is readily misunderstood. Nevertheless, his was a noble effort to articulate a novel approach in a manner that could be appreciated by what he took to be his target audience, those who accepted the methods and findings of science but aspired to be religious in a way consonant with modern life.

In chapter 6, "The Secularity of Deweyan Criticism," I focus on the secular character of Dewey's proposal, reinforcing the claims in chapter 5 and unpacking the notion in chapters 2, 3, and 4 that Dewey works from within situations to transform them. His method needs nothing external to the conditions-consequences, means-ends continua present actually or potentially in the interactions that constitute experience.

My strategy, then, is not to defend everything that Dewey wrote, but to concentrate on what I take to be central. Interpreters have long noted that Dewey was a "hedgehog" rather than a "fox," to use Isaiah Berlin's famous dichotomy. But they have not always clearly identified the actual practices that he persistently, relentlessly recommended. Too often they have glibly tossed about the terms he himself used—*science, social intelligence,* and *democracy*—failing to trace out the actual practices to which Dewey took these words to refer. Too often they have simply paraphrased his religious proposal, failing to carefully consider his mildly expressed but implacable opposition to traditional and conventional religions. They neglect to ask how this proposal fits with Dewey's more frequently articulated secular proposal for intelligent action. Too often interpreters of the second chapter of *A Common Faith,* "Faith and Its Object" have been fascinated by Dewey's use of the term *God* and failed to note that the real subject is intelligence. This is a passionate, social, idealizing intelligence, to be sure, but what is actually discussed is what we find everywhere in Dewey, but usually not in religious clothing—the implications of the scientific method for modern living.

For too long too many have mistakenly thought that what Dewey was talking about when he used the terms *faith, piety,* and *God* was—more or less—what other people are talking about when they use these terms. One needs to ask what Dewey meant by understanding *God* as the *"active* relation of ideal and actual" (LW 9:34), particularly when one realizes that Dewey did not use *ideal* to mean perfect or complete, but a "generalized end-in-view" (LW 13:226) and that for Dewey *actual* did not mean that which is fixed—incapable of directed change. It meant what has existed or does exist, but it has changed and will continue to do so. One does not have to look far to realize that the referent for Dewey's "God" and social intelligence is one and the same process. His understanding of the divine, then, turns out to be, say, a historical process, such as the abolition movement, the women's suffrage movement, the development of land-grant universities, or, more recently, the civil rights or environmental movement. But one must not think that there is a guiding personality that has shaped these processes. Rather, they are processes that have resulted from the interaction of values and existing conditions over time—or, perhaps better, the processes are these interactions over time.

In identifying the making of practice more intelligent as the organizing proposal and showing the secular implications of this recommendation, I am able to provide a unity to Dewey's thinking that has eluded other interpreters. Dewey did not happen to recommend a broad, historicized intelligence and an enhanced secularity. Secularity is the condition and enhanced secularity the consequence of his commitment to intelligent action. In the programmatic *Reconstruction in Philosophy* he says, "Experience carries principles of connection and organization within itself" (MW 12:132). Then two pages later he writes, "Aforetime man employed the result of his prior experience only to form customs that henceforth had to be blindly followed or blindly broken. Now, old experience is used to suggest aims and methods for developing a new and improved experience. Consequently experience becomes in so far constructively self-regulative." And, finally, "The very fact of experience thus includes the process by which it directs itself in its own betterment" (134). The point to which my discussion in chapter 5 of his religious proposal is a counterpoint is that, if one persistently and comprehensively thinks through the implications of the Deweyan commitment to intelligent action, one will find, as Dewey did, that one is committed to a cultural instrumentalism, understanding *cultural* to refer not only to the web of practices and meanings in which we find ourselves, but the sort of environment that we cannot transcend. We may be able to modify or even escape a particular culture, but we are in an important sense culturally bound. Thus "cultural" slides over into "secular" in the sense of "belonging to this age."

Secularity was not a reason for despair for Dewey; he celebrated the possibilities of a cultural instrumentalism. It will be the task of this book to show what he celebrated and why he did so. We will come to understand that *cultural* and *instrumental* are not simply juxtaposed in Dewey; they are implicated in one another. His cultural instrumentalism was a deeply secular proposal, one that he thought was liberating; and for him the human condition was full of meaning—provided that humans used the tools available within our secular-cultural situation (or developed new ones from the materials at hand) to realize its possibilities.

2

❖

INTELLIGENT PRACTICE
DEWEY'S PROJECT

The proper business of intelligence is discrimination of multiple and present goods and of the varied means of their realization. . . . The progress of biology has accustomed our minds to the notion that intelligence is not an outside power presiding supremely but statically over the desires and aims of man, but is a method of adjustment of capacities and conditions within specific situations.
—John Dewey, "Intelligence and Morals" (MW 4:44).

JOHN DEWEYS' LIFELONG PROJECT was increasing intelligence, which he understood to be experience deliberatively transforming itself. This is what explains his activities as an academic, a public philosopher, and an educator. He was not just a bundle of diverse roles—political thinker, public figure, philosopher of education, logician, and teacher; these various activities are unified by his project of cultivating intelligence. This project also unifies the central doctrines of Dewey's philosophy relating to the topics of experience, scientific method, and democracy, enabling us to conceptualize and criticize his work.

This unified understanding of Dewey is challenged by the revisionist account of Richard Rorty. His neopragmatic reading of Dewey eliminates or scales back Dewey's metaphysics of experience, his reliance on the scientific method, and his confidence in democracy as an engaged, shared experience.[1] But Rorty's overly eliminative approach is useful, for it enables us to grasp just what is essential in Dewey. By looking briefly in this initial section at what a prominent, well-informed postanalytic philospher tries to distance himself from, we can begin to appreciate what is distinctive about Dewey's approach.[2] I contest Rorty's interpretation of Dewey, but I do so without fully engaging his broader critique. It is sufficient for my purposes

13

to spell out in this chapter what Rorty says cannot be specified—Dewey's call for intelligent action.

RORTY'S CHALLENGE

Robert Westbrook declared, "No one has done more to revive interest in Dewey among American academics than Richard Rorty."[3] Rorty's neopragmatic championing of the historicist and relativist or "good" Dewey over the scientistic and metaphysical or "bad" Dewey has simultaneously brought Dewey back into the intellectual mainstream and angered "paleo-pragmatists," Westbrook's designation for those who have been attempting to extend the classical pragmatists' work, often in opposition to the linguistic turn that Rorty and other leading philosophers have made.[4] I will not here rehearse Rorty's critical appropriation of Dewey or the strong reaction to it among Deweyans, except to call attention to the significance of two Deweyan themes that Rorty rejects—the interactional model of experience and the worth of the scientific method—affirming the value of the insights of Dewey's transformed metaphysics and accepting Rorty's challenge to present a coherent, interesting account of Dewey's "scientific" method.

The Value of a Transformed Metaphysics

Consideration of Dewey's metaphysics of experience is important if one is to understand Dewey, and I will do so in the chapters that follow. A systematic defense of Dewey on this point, however, lies outside the scope of this book, for this would involve me in "the problems of philosophers" in ways that would detract from my focus on his core proposal.[5] But I will be implicitly supporting the Deweyan doctrine in arguing for the integrity of Dewey's project to intelligize practice. I think Dewey was right to think that experience is more than a psychic event; it is a transaction between organisms and their environments that is implicated in our efforts to make our practices more effective. Rorty's view, moreover, still seems infected by the psychic interpretation—experience is a person's thinking-feeling reaction to events. Worthy of notice is what Rorty said in response to Ralph Sleeper and Abraham Edel in an exchange at a 1983 meeting of the Society for the Advancement of American Philosophy: "'Language' is a more suitable notion than 'experience' for saying the holistic and anti-foundationalist things which James and Dewey had wanted to say. This is not because formulating philosophical problems in terms of sentences rather than in terms of psychological processes is 'clearer' or 'more precise,' but simply because the malleablility of language is a less paradoxical notion than the malleability of nature or of 'objects.'"[6] In his notion of experience Dewey attempted to avoid the split between psychic and nonpsychic events. Therefore, Rorty's characterization of Dewey's understanding as one having to do only with "psychological processes" misrepresents Dewey's inclusive theory of experience.

Rorty makes some of the mistakes that paleo-pragmatists are quick to spot in hostile interpretations by others of Dewey's work. Too often he dichotomizes Dewey and fails to understand Deweyan language in the ways specified by Dewey.[7] He does not read Dewey in the context with which many Deweyans are comfortable—the immense body of Dewey's work and the tradition of classical American philosophy, which includes, notably but not only, Charles Peirce, William James, and George Herbert Mead. Rorty's contexts are often those of contemporary analytic and Continental philosophy and the even wider one of contemporary culture, contexts that both distort and illuminate Dewey's thinking. It may be difficult for some to be amused and enlightened by Rorty's playful, provocative, and broadly informed (of philosophy and culture generally) treatment of Dewey, but for those who value Deweyan criticism and the diversity it values I think Rorty's contribution is welcome, provided one keeps it in perspective. As some have pointed out, the disaster that could occur among those whose attention has been seized by Rorty would be mistaking Rorty's reading of Dewey as a faithful representation of what Dewey thought. Rorty rejects realistic readings, ones that regard a text as a machine to be understood by being disassembled. He favors instead Harold Bloom's "strong misreading," in which the critic "beats the text into a shape which will serve his own purpose."[8] Therefore, it would be ironic if one were to take Rorty's interpretation of Dewey as "a faithful representation."

Also ironic is that Dewey's writing, to the extent that it lacks artistry, exemplifies the means-ends problem that Dewey took to be the outstanding problem of all criticism, if not *"the* problem of experience" (LW 1:277 and 310).[9] Rorty thinks a "'metaphysics of experience'" is not needed as a "'philosophical basis' for the criticism of culture."[10] But surely it is helpful to grasp the ways in which Dewey's alleged failures—not just his writing, but also his lack of a political technology, which we shall examine in chapters 3 and 4—and the difficulties of his religious proposal (discussed in chapter 5), are all examples of what he took to be a pervasive problem: effectively relating ideal and actual. If nothing else, Dewey's alleged failures are negative examples of his "metaphysical" analysis. Therefore, the metaphysical insight regarding "the problem of experience," which is the sort of philosophical activity that Rorty would eliminate, turns out to be an illuminating way to understand Dewey's supposed deficiencies and confirms the major problematic identified in his philosophy, a problematic that his proposal to intelligize practice was designed to address.

Dewey thought that there was value in a transformed metaphysics, one that offered functional generic descriptions in the service of cultural criticism. This "thinking at large" (LW 1:33) could be valuable, provided the philosopher realized that his or her ideas were drawn from experience and must be referred back to it. Thinking at large, if done in the service of intelligizing our practices, could be a part of an effective cultural criticism—and not just idle metaphysics.[11] But notice that this large thinking is not, as Rorty charges, foundational; it is contextual. One enlarges one's thinking in order to make it more meaningful and the practices the thinking modifies more effective than they would otherwise be. One does not look for rock bottom; one spreads out from the focus of attention, attempting to situate it in a broader context.

Dewey's Recommended Method

My focus on intelligent practice would seem to involve me in a defense of Dewey on scientific method, requiring me to meet Rorty's challenge to specify something that is less general than a set of recommended habits, but more general than a set of specific techniques. I will do so, but not quite on the terms set by Rorty.

In responding to James Gouinlock's essay in *Rorty and Pragmatism: The Philosopher Responds to his Critics*, Rorty takes the main disagreement to be "the utility of the notion of 'method,'" a "notion" Rorty finds "pretty useless" (92): "If there is an exegetical question at issue between Gouinlock and myself it is whether one can isolate, in Dewey's work, something both wide enough to be 'extended to all problems of conduct' and also narrow enough to have 'formal properties'—something which is both generic enough to be, as Gouinlock says it is, the method of democracy as well as of science, and yet specific enough to be contrasted with other methods that people have actually employed. I do not think one can" (92). He then issues this challenge: "Granted that Dewey never stopped talking about 'scientific method,' I submit that he never had anything very useful to say about it. Those who think I am overstating my case here should, I think, tell us what this thing called 'method'—which is neither a set of rules nor a character trait nor a collection of techniques—is supposed to be" (94).[12]

Dewey did think that philosophers were to cultivate a method for dealing with human problems and that this method had been most fully devel-

oped by science. It is this general method, inclusive of science, that Dewey
thought could be specified. I will set forth, in this chapter and the chapters
that follow, his account of the method of inquiry, a method Dewey regarded
as the activity of intelligence. Dewey's use of this method was wide, as Rorty
charges, but we can specify it. This "method" is not a recipelike set of operations, but it is more than just a vague recommendation to be open to the
future or to experiment. Dewey defined *inquiry* (the directed transformation
of an indeterminate situation into a determinate one) and spelled out its
pattern (indeterminancy, problematic, possible solutions, reasoning, testing,
etc.), notably in the sixth chapter of *Logic: The Theory of Inquiry* (LW
12:105–22).[13] But inquiry also involves certain attitudes or beliefs, such as
being critical or experimental or understanding the constructed character of
our beliefs and values. (The latter is no small accomplishment in a society
that thinks either that values mirror some reality, often understood to be
supersensible, or that since they fail to do so values are only relative to an
individual or culture.)

  Rorty demands something simple, readily identifiable—with "formal
properties." Dewey, however, had a complex understanding of intelligence
that included attitudes, beliefs, and activities. In brief, one could character-
ize intelligence as the use of causes as means to achieve desired consequences, where one is cognizant of a causal relationship and understands its
potential for satisfying some felt need. But the problem is that in order to
use causes meaningfully and pervasively one needs beliefs, such as the belief
that ideas are responses to difficulties or that directed change is possible.
One also needs attitudes such as open-mindedness, wholeheartedness, and
responsibility.[14] Finally, one needs to learn certain critical and experimental
skills, notably the skill of paying attention to conditions and consequences.
About as close as we can come to providing Rorty with a formal criterion is
this: Deweyan intelligence uses conditions and consequences that it has
identified to institute means and ends. In the rest of this chapter I will try to
make sense of this 'criterion' and show its significance.

Dewey's Natural Intelligence

  Dewey's concern to make practice intelligent rather than to make thinking useful begins conceptually with his biological or naturalistic understanding of experience. This model enabled him to identify successful ways of
achieving human growth, notably the use of inquiry in transforming problematic situations into more satisfying ones. What follows in this chapter
revolves around these key Deweyan notions of experience and intelligence,

with the latter being understood as a form of the former. Experience is the
inclusive reality; intelligence is that form of experience that enables us to act
indirectly to get what we want. But first the biological model.

Biology and Intelligence

In 1939, in a response to the contributions of his critics in the *Library
of Living Philosophers* volume, Dewey observed: "For many years I have
consistently—and rather persistently—maintained that the key to a philosophic theory of experience must proceed from initially linking it with the
processes and functions of life as the latter are disclosed in biological science." Experience, as he characteristically noted in the next sentence, was
"a matter . . . of interaction of living creatures with their environments"
(LW 14:15). The environments in which humans find themselves are not
simply biological; they are also social. But the key to understanding the latter aspect is the former. Humans, whatever else they are, are animals in a
natural setting. As such, they make inferences. This can be seen by examining and reflecting on a passage in *Democracy and Education* (1916). This
text (MW 9:152–53) is worth some attention because it clarifies the connection between the relatively undeveloped and clearly animal-like behavior of
a human infant and the more developed behavior of a fully intelligent
adult.[15]

I begin with Dewey's observation in *Democracy and Education* that
thinking "is the intentional endeavor to discover *specific* connections
between something which we do and the consequences which result, so that
the two become continuous." (The emphasis on *specific* is in the text; Dewey
regularly called for inquiry into specific rather than general conditions and
consequences.) When we see a situation in its continuity from prior conditions to eventual outcome, we understand it. We have made explicit the
intelligent element in our experience. This sort of thinking is retrospective.
But thinking can also be prospective. We can act with a purpose, or what
Dewey calls "an end in view," which is his distinctive way of referring to
"the condition of our having aims" (153). A fully intelligent person is one
who can trace out the connections both afterwards and before. He or she
can, as we say, think things through, noticing what led (or leads) to what.
Although it may not involve experimentation in the narrow sense of testing
a hypothesis in a laboratory, this is what Dewey understood to be the experimental method. It was most fully developed in the physical sciences, but it
was not—and should not be—limited to them. He was often misunderstood
on this point and therefore occasionally tried to correct the impression that
his approach was scientistic. For instance, in 1934 he observed that "exper-

imentation in the laboratory sense" was not to be "literally copied" or carried out wholesale "on any large scale in social affairs" ("Intelligence and Power," LW 9:108). Rather, in thinking experimentally one would be deliberately remaking situations in ways similar but not identical to those used by laboratory science.

After discussing thinking or intelligence as one might find it in an adult, Dewey turned (in the *Democracy and Education* text) to the case of an infant, providing this telling example: "As soon as an infant begins to *expect* he begins to use something which is now going on as a sign of something to follow; he is, in however simple a fashion, judging. For he takes one thing as *evidence* of something else, and so recognizes a relationship. Any future development, however elaborate it may be, is only an extending and a refining of this simple act of inference" (MW 9:153). Dewey thus traced inference back to the point in human development where the biological is clearly more evident than the cultural. Intelligence is not an extranatural process. It is a refinement of a biological activity. Moreover, Dewey not only situated thinking within biological activity generally; he also provided his readers with a specific type of situation, a referent for his theoretical observations. Note that even in this case of his reference to infants one could translate what he said into an operational directive: Look at an infant. Notice that he used something as a sign for something else, let's say the opening of a door as an indication that a parent is entering the room. Whatever the specific instance, Dewey could then note, as he in fact said, that the infant "takes one thing as *evidence* of something else, and so recognizes a relationship." Inferential activity is quite natural.

Dewey referred to the behavior of infants, but one could as easily talk about any organism that takes something as evidence for something else. Identifying this rudimentary instance of judging, Dewey thus situated thinking in experience and nature. Intelligence is something developed rather than imported. Dewey did not have to make intelligence practical, for he found thinking in practice. No matter how "elaborate" thinking "may be," it "is only an extending and a refining of" such simple acts "of inference."

Dewey then proceeded to talk about this more fully developed thinking, calling attention to the behavior of the wisest person: "All that the wisest man can do is to observe what is going on more widely and more minutely and then select more carefully from what is noted just those factors which point to something to happen" (MW 9:153). Thus there is continuity between the thinking of a simple organism and a careful investigator. Both, reacting to their environments, make inferences, but the more intelligent party observes "more widely and more minutely" and selects "more

carefully" the indicative aspects of the situation, "those factors which point
to something to happen." Factors do not stand alone; they are not unconnected atoms. Factors are aspects of a situation, and as such they "point to
something to happen." The thoughtful person is the one who can see these
connections, selecting the conditions that will lead to the desired outcomes.

Finally, Dewey called attention to action that is not very thoughtful. In
so doing he clarified his idea of intelligent behavior: "The opposites . . . to
thoughtful action are routine and capricious behavior." Routine behavior
"accepts what has been customary as a full measure of possibility and omits
to take into account the connections of the particular things done" (MW
9:153). One who persists in less thoughtful, routine behavior does not recognize the signs within the situation of new possibilities for action. This
behavior is similar, then, to the activity of a machine. We depend on
machines to be routine in their operation, and we sometimes value unvary-
ing human activity. But it is less thoughtful not to consider a variation that
would lead to more satisfying results. The more thoughtful person notices
possibilities not exhausted by the routine. One who exploits these possibilities is creative. The other sort of less thoughtful behavior Dewey termed
"capricious." The capricious person "makes the momentary act a measure
of value, and ignores the connections of our personal action with the energies of the environment" (MW 9:153). If the capricious person is the one
who acts on whim, he is one whose action has little connection with his surroundings. Capricious behavior, Dewey concluded, "says virtually, 'things
are to be just as I happen to like them at this instant,' as routine says in
effect 'let things continue just as I have found them in the past'" (MW
9:153). The one continues the past unchanged, the other the present
moment. Both, however, are less than fully intelligent, for they fail to consider the possibilities in the particular situation. A more intelligent person,
on the other hand, sees more and chooses more carefully. The more intelligent person is the one who makes informed choices.

The foregoing characteristic bit of Deweyan analysis is worth attention
not only for itself, but also because reflection on it underscores the concern
of this section—Dewey's biological model and the role of intelligence. If
Dewey was correct in thinking that experience is the interaction of an
organism with its environment, one can err in overstressing one or the other
of these aspects. The person mired in routine does not interrupt the continued functioning of the environment. Instead, he attempts to perpetuate it.
The capricious person, on the other hand, in ignoring the environment gives
too much play to the organism's whims. Dewey thought a balanced, unifying approach was needed. This he called intelligence, or thinking in its

fuller sense. As Abraham Kaplan wryly observes, in language that should not be taken literally: "Dewey's magic numbers are two and one: his thought may be characterized as a repeated movement from a dualism to a monism." Then he comments, in more straightforward language: "Over and over he formulates his problem as being posed by a dualism; he dealt with the problem by showing that the duality can be reduced to something unitary" (LW 10:xii). Here the "something unitary" is thinking in its honorific sense; the inadequate dualities are routine and caprice. That is the methodological point. The substantive one is that Dewey's taking for his biological model of experience the interaction of environment and organism enabled him to show not only that routine and capricious behavior are each partial in differing ways, but also just exactly why they are inadequate: Neither one gives proper weight to the interaction of environment and organism. Each one, in its opposite way, gives too much emphasis to one aspect or the other. Only the intelligent person maintains the balance.

Intelligence as Art

I will return to the *Democracy and Education* text in the next section, but first I want to continue with the contrast of intelligence with the less thoughtful behavior of routine and caprice. In *Experience and Nature*, in the next-to-last chapter, Dewey defined the limiting terms of art as "routine at one extreme and capricious impulse at the other." Routine and caprice are natural occurrences. What is unnatural is their occurrence in isolation from one another, "for nature is an intersection of spontaneity and necessity, the regular and the novel, the finished and the beginning" (LW 1:270–71). But when these naturally occurring phenomena are found together and refined, there is art: "Thus the theme has insensibly passed over into that of the relation of means and consequence, process and product, the instrumental and consummatory. Any activity that is simultaneously both, rather than in alternation and displacement, is art" (271). Later in the chapter he says explicitly, "Thinking is preeminently an art; knowledge and propositions which are the products of thinking, are works of art, as much so as statuary and symphonies" (283).

In art as in nature, there is "a union of the precarious, novel, irregular with the settled, assured and uniform." But in art the achievement of this union is deliberate: It is "the intentional direction of natural events to meanings capable of immediate possession and enjoyment" (269). Art that states meanings (LW 10:90) in order to lead to these possessions and enjoyments is science or "operative art"; art "that is charged with meanings capable of immediately enjoyed possession" (LW 1:269) is art as the term is usually understood—music, painting, dance, sculpture, literature, etc. In both forms of art there is intelligence, for both are "charged with meanings." Both make sense of events, as well as showing their significance: "Whenever a situation has this double function of meaning, namely signification and sense, mind, intellect is definitely present," as Dewey says earlier in *Experience and Nature* (LW 1:200).[16]

Intelligence, then, is a refinement of nature; it is not something apart from it. This point is crucial for Dewey. Where dualists find "practice *and* theory, art *and* science" (269), as well as body and mind, nature and experience, Dewey found continuities. This is why he thought the important distinction "is not between practice and theory, but between those modes of practice that are not intelligent, not inherently and immediately enjoyable, and those which are full of enjoyed meanings" (269). This is why he thought that it is a profound mistake to think that intelligence needs to be made practical rather than practice made intelligent. The former takes what has been, from his point of view, mentally separated into theory and practice and tries to relate them; the latter takes an existential whole—practice—and improves upon it. Intelligence is natural and artful.

There is another way to make this point, one that puts it in quite general terms. In *The Quest for Certainty* Dewey drew a distinction between experience as continuing interactions between organisms and environments and intelligence as *directed* interactions. Speaking of "intelligence within nature," he wrote, "This is part and parcel of nature's own continuing interactions." Interactions happen; they "produce changes." But such interactions are unintelligent; they are "not directed." These undirected interactions "are effects but not consequences, for consequences imply means deliberately employed. When an interaction intervenes which directs the course of change, the scene of natural interaction has a new quality and dimension. This added type of interaction *is* intelligence." Here we see that intelligence is both natural and artful. It is natural in that it is an interaction within nature. As Dewey wrote: "The intelligent activity of man is not something brought to bear upon nature from without." It occurs within nature. But it is not happenstance (LW 14:171). The intelligent actor deliberately selects that which he or she has observed as a cause of some desired effect in order to bring about the naturally occurring effect as a consequence. The effect is what occurs naturally; the consequence is the result of directed action. This directed activity is intelligence and is art, operative art.

But notice that this directed activity is also indirect. What is directly done is the institution of some change that functions as a condition for some consequence. The latter is, however, indirectly accomplished. Thus "intelligence signifies that direct action has become indirect." Rather than rushing to do something, the intelligent person thinks through the situation, identifying "obstacles and resources" and "projecting" what can be initiated in order to accomplish what is wanted. Therefore, in a sense thinking is "deferred action," but only in a sense. Actually, this so-called deferred action is present action in the sense that one is initiating a series of events that will result in the desired outcome (LW 4:178).

Intelligence, Directed Change, and Adjustment

As should be clear by now, Dewey was impressed with science, and in particular his biological model of inquiry. As a good naturalistic observer, he identified the conditions and consequences of our interactions as intelligent organisms with our environments. But, as one might expect, he was not simply an observer. His observations were made for a purpose: the development of an enhanced version of what he had discovered to be effective in nature.

As organisms we are constantly shaping ourselves to or modifying the environment with which we interact. It is unwise, Dewey thought, to be stuck in one mode or the other. Rather, one needs to develop the ability to do what a situation requires. In *The Quest for Certainty* he observed: "If a man finds himself in a situation which is practically annoying and troublesome, he has just two courses open to him. He can make a change in himself either by running away from trouble or by steeling himself to Stoic endurance; or he can set to work to do something so as to change the conditions of which unsatisfactoriness is a quality." Either one could be the smart thing to do in a particular situation. What one should do would depend on the situation. Dewey's preference was reconstruction. But he acknowledged that this may not always be possible: "When the latter course is impossible, nothing remains but the former"—flight or resignation. He also acknowledged that there may be a need for "some change of personal attitude" even when one finds it possible to remake the situation (LW 4:185–86).

Ironically, Dewey's balanced, secular approach has a religious analogue in the "Serenity Prayer" associated with one of his political allies but sharpest critics, Reinhold Niebuhr:

> God give me the serenity to accept things which cannot be
>   changed;
> Give me the courage to change things which must be changed;
> And the wisdom to distinguish one from the other.[17]

But although the prayer regards courage as the condition for change, Dewey insisted that what was primarily needed was an investigation of the conditions and consequences that are required for the desired change.

Life for Dewey was a continual process of adjustment. He believed that an individual, in interacting with others and with his or her physical surroundings as well as the past and future, both shapes and is shaped by these interactions. Experience is not static. The intelligent person is the one who deliberately reconstructs experience. All of us change. Such is the nature of existence. But the intelligent person is the one who increasingly transforms his or her mostly unwitting behavior into more thoughtful action, into directed action. Such a person is able to use the naturally occuring interactions to bring about those that he or she wants, thus acting artfully. But these artful interventions are reflexive. One does not simply operate on things; in interacting with aspects of one's environment one not only changes things, but is changed in the process.

Inquiry: The Activity of Intelligence

As we have seen, intelligence is directed activity, a type of activity that makes use of both direct and indirect action to accomplish one's purposes. Now we are in a position to describe more fully the activity of intelligence: interacting with the world in a way that Dewey, when he was being careful with his language, called "inquiry." For instance, in *The Quest for Certainty* he referred to inquiry as "a set of operations in which problematic situations are disposed of or settled" (4:183).[18] But inquiry was not, as the term might suggest, simply a mental process. It was not just an intellectual attempt to answer a question. Consistent with his holistic understanding of intelligence, Dewey regarded inquiry as a way to transform our experience. It occurred in time and made a difference existentially.

Untypically, Dewey offered a formal definition of *inquiry* in his last major book, *Logic: The Theory of Inquiry* (1938): "*Inquiry is the controlled or directed transformation of an indeterminate situation into one that is so determinate in its constituent distinctions and relations as to convert the elements of the original situation into a unified whole*" (emphasis in original; LW 12:108).[19] His idea was that one can deliberately change a situation that is unsettled or problematic into one that is ordered and satisfying. One does so by trying out a possible solution until one finds an appropriate resolution—hence "the experimental method." This transformation will involve ends in the sense of "ends-in-view," the recognition of existing or needed conditions and reasoning about likely consequences. Having sensed a difficulty, one formulates a possible desired outcome—the end-in-view—

then experiments. If there is no difficulty, there is no need for inquiry. One simply continues blissfully on one's way. But if there is a problem one identifies it as such, figures out the factors that are making the troublesome situation what it is (the conditions), projects likely solutions (dramatic rehearsal), and selects one of these possible solutions (the end-in-view with requisite operations), then implements it, paying attention to the actual outcomes (the consequences).

Note that the end-in-view is not identical to the actual outcome. The two may turn out to be the same, but they function differently. The end-in-view is a projection that serves as a means to accomplish the actual end. Sometimes one's projection is on the mark, sometimes not. At any rate, Dewey's ends-in-view are means, distinct from but continuous with the other means (or chosen conditions) and the actual ends (or consequences). This continuity of ends and means was an important concept for Dewey. He contended that ends-in-view and means are constitutive of (or instrumental to) the actual ends. Therefore, one must employ means that will in fact bring about the desired ends. One way to do this, and to guard against producing undesired ends, is to pay attention to the continuity of ends and means.

But there is an additional requirement. Not only must the means bring about the ends, but they must do so efficiently. In another late, not very readable book, *The Theory of Valuation*, published the year after the *Logic*, Dewey retold Charles Lamb's amusing story[20] to illustrate the desirability of the efficient relation of ends and means. I will give Dewey's account not only for this reason, but also to flesh out what he means by saying that inquiry is the deliberate transformation of experience:

> The story . . . is that roast pork was first enjoyed when a house in which pigs were confined was accidentally burned down. While searching in the ruins, the owners touched the pigs that had been roasted in the fire and scorched their fingers. Impulsively bringing their fingers to their mouths to cool them, they experienced a new taste. Enjoying the taste, they henceforth set themselves to building houses, inclosing pigs in them, and then burning the houses down. (LW 13:227)

Dewey's point in telling the story is to call attention to the absurdity of claiming that the choice of means is irrelevant to the desired end. One can get roast pork by building pig-enclosing houses and burning them down, but that, as we say, is not very smart. The more intelligent procedure is to use a spit or other similarly effective cooking process.

Burning down pig-enclosing houses to get roast pork is not, in and of itself, stupid. It is stupid only in relation to a more efficient method. The less efficient method was—to take the story as a history of the development of roasting pork—an advance over the happenstance of those who originally tasted the accidentally roasted pork. We should credit the intelligence involved in deliberately burning down pig-enclosing houses. The intentional house-burners did have an end-in-view—roasting pork. Moreover, they knew a set of operations that would produce it—burning down pig-enclosing houses. Since this means led to the desired outcome, there was some intelligence in their method. But of course it is even more efficient—and intelligent—to use a method less wasteful of time and materials.

We know what stupidity is. Stupidity is failing to notice the likely outcome of one's actions, and particularly when these consequences turn out to be harmful. Intelligence is the reverse. Intelligence is grasping the relation between aims, conditions, and consequences, then acting in a deliberate way on this knowledge (with an awareness of alternatives) to accomplish one's aims. But, as the roast pork story illustrates, there are degrees of intelligence. Roasting pigs in specially built houses is not so much stupid as it is less efficent—that is, less intelligent—than roasting them on a spit.

Similarly, there are differences in kinds of intelligence. Dewey distinguished between everyday reasoning, science, and philosophy (MW 10:42). Thus far I have been discussing intelligence generically without drawing the distinctions Dewey noted elsewhere. I now want to consider what happens, according to Dewey, when one becomes increasingly intelligent about intelligence.

Intelligence as an End-in-View: The Philosophic Move

Lamb's fanciful story of the accidental discovery of roast pork has analogues in history. Dewey contended that we had hit upon various goods accidentally or else deliberately but in some limited sphere. If we were smart we could achieve more goods deliberately in even wider spheres. We could do so intentionally rather than through happenstance, or we could do so by extending to the rest of life those successful activities that had been limited to some narrow sphere. Democracy was Dewey's favorite example of the former situation, science of the latter. I will begin with democracy and education, then move to science and philosophy. The differences between intelligence in ordinary life, intelligence as a disciplined mode of inquiry (that is, science—broadly conceived), and intelligence about intelligence (that is, philosophy) are not very clear. But there are clear differences between the paradigm cases of ordinary intelligence, science, and philosophy.

Democracy and Intelligence

I will have more to say about democracy in the next two chapters. For now I will limit myself to two points. The first has to do with the relationship between intelligence and democracy. For Dewey the connection was neither simple nor one-way. He thought that each enhanced the other. Fully operative intelligence was dependent upon the free exchange of opinions that one expects to find in a democracy, and democracy was to be advanced by intelligence. Nor was democracy a simple affair. Dewey did not think democracy was primarily a matter of particular decision-making procedures or even specific forms of government, but a "shared experience" involving common interests and interactions. In *Democracy and Education* he wrote: "A democracy is more than a form of government; it is primarily a mode of associated living, of conjoint communicated experience. The extension in space of the number of individuals who participate in an interest so that each has to refer his own action to that of others, and to consider the action of others to give point and direction to his own, is equivalent to the breaking down of those barriers of class, race and national territory which kept men from perceiving the full import of their activity."

For Dewey experience was, as he often reminded us, a matter of an interaction of an organism with its environment. These interactions are capable of adjustment. We sometimes submit to, sometimes modify, our situations. One situation in which we have traditionally found ourselves is that of being enclosed within a group, be it family, tribe, ethnic group, political group, or nation. Yet we sometimes find ourselves in proximity with others—through commerce or travel—with whom we have acquired common interests. Dewey continued: "These more numerous and more varied points of contact denote a greater diversity of stimuli to which an individual has to respond; they consequently put a premium on variation in his action. They secure a liberation of powers which remain suppressed as long as the incitations to action are partial, as they must be in a group which in its exclusiveness shuts out many interests" (MW 9:93). Democracy is the best form of shared experience because, through its open processes of consultation and change, individuals and groups can expand their common interests and common space. Democracy is thus the social manifestation of intelligence— that is, the deliberate reconstruction of experience by a group. It is the way in which collectives adjust themselves over time to the new situations in which they find themselves.

The second point about democracy has to do with our response to the realization that democracy had been, up to Dewey's time if not beyond, an accidental good. Dewey contended that democracy had come about in the United States through "the fortunate conjunction of circumstances" and thus, having experienced an accidental good, we should work for it deliberately. Not surprisingly, this accidental development did not entirely displace older, predemocratic practices and attitudes. Democracy developed within a nondemocratic context, and, Dewey thought, the newer beliefs and institutions came to exist in an uneasy relationship with older ones, even though the whole mix was regarded as democratic. Now (in the 1930s) these "old emotional and intellectual habits" were exerting themselves. Accordingly, he wrote that "the struggle for democracy has to be maintained on as many fronts as culture has aspects: political, economic, international, educational, scientific and artistic, religious." Then he concluded—and this is the point of my citing this passage from *Freedom and Culture* (1939): "The fact that we now have to accomplish of set purpose what in an earlier period was more or less a gift of grace renders the problem a moral one to be worked out on moral grounds" (LW 13:186). This was a moral problem precisely because it involved a deliberate choice of human goods. What had once been experienced more or less by accident could now be achieved by intelligence, the setting of aims based on knowledge of existing conditions, and tested by the actual consequences.

Democracy and Education

Clearly, democracy does not need to continue to be a happenstance affair. It can be deliberately remade. We learn from and within our experience in order to enhance our shared experience. This general experience-remaking has profound implications for our self-understanding, as well as our educational practices. The two are related. If we think that we can learn from and within our experience, we will not need to look to external authority for guidance. Nor must we encourage the younger members of our democratic society to rely on external authorities any longer than is required for their health and safety. We will be providing them with the means necessary to become fully functioning experience-reconstructors within our democratic society. We will be encouraging them to take responsibility for their own lives within the common life of society.

To illustrate the impact of this sort of thinking on schooling I will consider one brief text, and then I will underscore the point about our basic self-understanding as experience-dwellers. While the bearings of Dewey's view on schooling brought him into conflict with the traditionally religious, his metaphysical naturalism justified the antipathy of his religious opponents in the widest way possible. Whatever the merit of the religious right's general understanding of life and society, they are correct to think that Dewey's proposal is deeply at odds with their beliefs and practices.[21]

Early in the chapter "Thinking in Education" in *Democracy and Education* Dewey stressed that students should be encouraged to be "active learners" (to use our current phrase, which is, of course, due in part to Dewey's influence). Teachers should never assume that students have the necessary experiences stored up; rather, they should provide opportunities for experience within instructional situations. Nor should they regard the subject matter as "ready-made" for the student's stored-up experience (MW 9:160). Dewey closed the chapter by identifying three sorts of classroom approaches. The first and "least desirable treats each lesson as an independent whole." This approach not only fails to call attention to the connections between this lesson and others, but it also "does not put upon the student the responsibility of finding points of contact between it and other lessons in the same subject, or other subjects of study." A second and better approach is one that "systematically" makes use of the "earlier lessons to help understand the present one, and also to use the present [lesson] to throw additional light upon what has already been acquired." Even so, this method fails to connect the subject to that which is outside the course of study—either in other subjects or in out-of-school experiences. The third and "best type of teaching" makes the connection not only with what has gone before, but with other subjects and "the realities of everyday life" (MW 9:170). Education, then, was at its best for Dewey when it was interactive in two senses. Both students and teachers were to share the responsibility for learning, and the subject matter was to be related to other subjects and to the out-of-class experiences of the students. No longer were students to be passive recipients of knowledge from arbitrary authority figures. The teacher was to remain an authority, but was to be one who would enable students to see the connections and would provide them with the experiences necessary to learn for themselves what was being taught. Dewey thought that knowledge, ideally, is not transmitted, but made by the people involved, both students and teachers.

When one generalizes this educational model to all of life, the radical character of Dewey's program cannot be blinked. Dewey proposed that experience become "constructively self-regulative." No longer was the past to be maintained no matter what; no longer was change to be happenstance. "We *use* our past experiences to construct new and better ones in the future. The very fact of experience thus includes the process by which it directs

itself in its own betterment" (MW 12:134). If experience is what Dewey
thought it was, it could be made more intelligent. Thus experience, whether
personal or social, could become "constructively self-regulative." Just how
far-reaching this proposal is we will now consider.

Dewey's Science Lesson

Intelligence as a method finds its fullest development in science and
technology. Dewey's characteristic suggestion was that the method that had
worked so well in the science of the last three hundred years now be used in
the rest of life. But this must not be done in a scientistic manner. It was not
a matter of applying the scientific method to all areas of life; rather, he
urged that the method of intelligence, which was best exemplified in science,
now be used elsewhere. This distinction is important, because many have
taken Dewey to be an exponent of applied science, and therefore find his
treatment of art inexplicable.

To see just how far-reaching this proposal was I would like to turn to
Dewey's Gifford Lectures, published as *The Quest for Certainty*. The point
of the book was a familiar one to readers of Dewey. He contrasted the gains
in knowledge made by science with the persistence of outmoded beliefs
regarding conduct. Early in the book Dewey sharply contrasted the development of science in the last few centuries with the older alliance of religion
and philosophy: "According to the religious and philosophic tradition of
Europe, the valid status of all the highest values, the good, true and beauti-
ful, was bound up with their being properties of ultimate and supreme
Being, namely, God. All went well as long as what passed for natural science
gave no offence to this conception" (LW 4:34). But with the revolution in
science in the seventeenth century a new possibility emerged. We can now
develop standards within the course of experience to guide our conduct. We
can construct good.

To be sure, the early modern scientists did not realize the import of the
new experimental method (see the discussion of Galileo in LW 4:75–78).
But this method actually "marks a revolution in the whole spirit of life, in
the entire attitude taken toward whatever is found in existence" (LW 4:80).
There now exists "the possibility that actual experience in its concrete content and movement may furnish those ideals, meanings and values whose
lack and uncertainty in experience as actually lived by most persons has
supplied the motive force for recourse to some reality beyond experience: a
lack and uncertainty that account for the continued hold of traditional
philosophical and religious notions which are not consonant with the main
tenor of modern life. The pattern supplied by scientific knowing shows that

in this one field at least it is possible for experience, in becoming genuinely experimental, to develop its own regulative ideas and standards" (LW 4:86).

Dewey was careful—perhaps too careful—to say that "in this one field," by which I take him to mean natural science, "scientific knowing shows . . . it is possible for experience . . . *to develop its own regulative ideas and standards*" (emphasis added). But it is clear from the succeeding sentences—and the book as a whole—that he hoped the same success could be achieved "in larger, more humane and liberal fields" (LW 4:86)—namely, those having to do with human conduct. So he should have said that we know that science has developed its ways of proceeding successfully, and therefore it is possible that the same can be done in other areas of life. That is, we can at last begin to think about extending the experimental method into every part of life where there are problems to be solved. We no longer have to depend on external authorities. We can learn from our experience, developing the standards and values we need as we go along. Experience can become constructively self-regulative.

Indeed, in *Reconstruction in Philosophy* Dewey had not been reticent about drawing the implications for all of life. There he had said that "when experience ceased to be [merely] empirical and became experimental, something of radical importance occurred" (MW 12:133–34). This radically important development was that we could begin to govern our conduct within experience alone through the use of intelligence. He was quite explicit in advocating an "experimental intelligence, conceived after the pattern of science" (135): "Concrete suggestions arising from past experiences, developed and matured in the light of the needs and deficiencies of the present, employed as aims and methods of specific reconstruction, and tested by success or failure in accomplishing this task of readjustment, suffice" (134). This is a very good summary of Dewey's core project. Science shows us the way to reconstruct our lives—indeed, our culture. From its example we can know how to transform our experience from within experience.

But, once again, this was not a a matter of a simple transfer of science into other areas of experience. Late in Dewey's life, as he turned ninety, he tried once more to make it clear that what he was advocating was not the application of the scientific method to life's problems, but the development of "*new* methods as adapted to *human* issues and problems." Although science provides a model of what can be done, he wrote, "What is needed is not the carrying over of procedures that have approved themselves in physical science" ("Philosophy's Future in Our Scientific Age," LW 16:379, n. 2). I have cited this one last example from 1949 in order to blunt the charge of scientism that is often leveled against Dewey.

Philosophy and Social Intelligence

For John Dewey philosophy resembled the thinking that we do every day as well as under controlled conditions, including that done in a laboratory. There are differences between ordinary thinking, scientific experimentation, and philosophical reasoning, but what these three sorts of thinking have in common, as we have noticed, is an indirect way of solving problems or meeting needs. But needs are not just intellectual, and problems are not just mental puzzles. Dewey contended that thinking should be understood as a response to all sorts of difficulties, everyday difficulties as well as those we encounter when we are in a real jam.

Thinking in all three modes—everyday, scientific, and philosophic—is often referred to as *reason* or even *Reason*, denoting its special cognitive role in regulating our lives, particularly our desires and emotions. Dewey rejected this narrowly intellectual, external, and hierarchial understanding. He believed that thinking has a cognitive and regulative role to play, but it plays this role not by separating itself from and overcoming our desires. Its task is to resolve our doubts, satisfy our desires, or clear up our confusions. We think to solve problems, to meet our difficulties. Troubles are not conquered by reason; they are worked through intelligently. This we have seen. What is new is the generality of Dewey's reconstruction-of-experience model. Dewey thought that intelligence could be employed socially and culturally. He thought our culture was out of whack and intelligence could set it right. Therefore, he wrote often of specific social practices or institutions that needed to be improved by the sort of patient inquiry into conditions and consequences that we have been considering.

In his own lifetime—Dewey was born in 1859 and died in 1952—people had become quite exercised about challenges to the existence of God and traditional notions of creation and about the impact of science and technology on society. Many were unable to reconcile the theories that science was providing about the world with traditional religious and moral views. Evolution had no need for God. And without a divine lawgiver, many feared, there would be no moral order. Everything was up for grabs. People thought perhaps we should restrict what science could be used for. Perhaps science should be limited to dealing with the physical world. Then the traditional beliefs about the way human beings should relate to one another could be kept.

But Dewey would have none of this. In *The Quest for Certainty* (1929) he identified "the deepest problem of modern life" as one "of restoring integration and cooperation between man's beliefs about the world in which he lives and his beliefs about the values and purposes that should direct his conduct . . ." (LW 4:204; see also LW 12:84 and LW 14:8–9). He thought the way to reconcile our divided beliefs was not to limit science and preserve the inherited views and values, but to extend the intelligence found in science to the rest of our lives. It was a profound mistake to limit intelligent practice to only one part of our lives. The logic of the methods that had proven effective in dealing with the physical world could be adapted to deal with every part of our lives.

In carefully considering the society in which he found himself, Dewey identified beliefs that had been inherited from the prescientific era, such as the belief in "older" or "rugged individualism" (*Individualism Old and New* [1930], LW 5:84). He then traced out the conditions and consequences of these beliefs, contrasting them with more desirable attitudes that he found exhibited in scientific practice. For Dewey this was philosophy: not the tackling of some historic philosophical controversy for its own sake, but the employment of careful, creative thinking to meet the needs of society. Indeed this, in a way, was what philosophers had always done. Dewey argued that the seemingly irrelevant philosophical systems of the past had actually been responses to human needs. Perhaps previous philosophers had thought that they were describing ultimate reality, but actually their metaphysical speculations had addressed the concerns of their contemporaries. Consider the project of Socrates, Plato, and Aristotle and their successors. In *Reconstruction in Philosophy* (1920), after having made clear the challenges from matter-of-fact knowledge to the traditional moral and religious beliefs that had arisen in fifth-century Athens, Dewey sketched their project: "Develop a method of rational investigation and proof which should place the essential elements of traditional belief upon an unshakable basis; develop a method of thought and knowledge which while purifying tradition should preserve its moral and social values unimpaired; nay, by purifying them, add to their power and authority. To put it in a word, that which had rested upon custom was to be restored, resting no longer upon the habits of the past, but upon the very metaphysics of Being and the Universe" (MW 12:89).

Thus, in response to a cultural crisis, these great thinkers had developed not only a worldview that prized the invisible and eternal over the apparent and perishable, but also a methodology—critical inquiry. Dewey rejected the worldview, but valued the method, using it in the form of "the genetic method of approach" (MW 12:93) to undercut the substance of traditional philosophy. By tracing the origins and development of the classical beliefs about a timeless moral order, he effectively humanized those beliefs.

For one who accepted Dewey's historicizing account, the classical worldview no longer had the power it had once had. It could be seen for what it was— a human intellectual effort to cope with a social problem. The philosophers of classical times, astute as they were, did not realize the ad hoc character of their 'timeless' constructions.

Dewey's strategy in identifying philosophy as a response to the needs of society was similar to the one he employed in regard to democracy as an accidental good. Ancient Greek philosophy, without realizing it, had responded to a societal need. We, noticing this, can deliberately use critical inquiry to respond to our societal problems. We can do explicitly what they did less knowledgeably. Dewey referred to this explicit activity as "criticism" or "intelligence" in the last chapter of *Experience and Nature* (1925, revised 1929; LW 1:303).[22] This critical activity was genetic or contextual, as we have just seen, but also logical and transformative, as we would expect.

Dewey identified all three of these dimensions in a passage of a 1930 lecture, "Context and Thought." After observing that "the immediate subject-matter for philosophy is supplied by the body of beliefs, religious, political, scientific, that determines the culture of a people and age," he noted the implication for "the problem and method of philosophy." Often these beliefs are separated from their "context of origin, function and determining interests of attitudes" (LW 6:18). Indeed this separation may even contribute to their potency. It is the task of philosophy to expose these constructions and to examine their coherence. Having done so, one finds oneself in a new situation. But I am getting ahead of Dewey's thinking.

The first part of the paragraph following the one from which I just quoted is itself worthy of quotation, for it enables us to see Dewey's understanding of philosophical reflection as "reconstruction through criticism." Dewey wrote: "Here is the opportunity for that type of reflection which I should call philosophical. Philosophy is criticism; criticism of the influential beliefs that underlie culture; a criticism which traces the beliefs to their generating conditions as far as may be, which tracks them to their results, which considers the mutual compatibility of the elements of the total structure of beliefs. Such an examination terminates, whether so intended or not, in a projection of them into a new perspective which leads to new surveys of possibilities" (LW 6:19). Intelligence has now become focused and extensive. The philosopher (1) traces a belief in terms of both its history and its effects (or conditions and consequences), then (2) examines its coherence (or logic), and finally (3) realizes that this process has resulted in a new situation. For Dewey philosophy as reconstructive criticism was both historical (the first move) and conceptual (the second move), but finally reconstructive (the third move).

These three moves are present in the following text, the first perhaps more so than the other two. This passage is Dewey's conclusion to the first chapter of *Reconstruction in Philosophy*, "Changing Conceptions of Philosophy," from which came the discussion of the Greek philosophical project described earlier. With that discussion in mind and his "hypothesis . . . that philosophy originated not out of intellectual material, but out of social and emotional material" (MW 12:93), Dewey was then able to conclude: "Any one of you who arrives at such a view of past philosophy will of necessity be led to entertain a quite definite conception of the scope and aim of future philosophizing. He will inevitably be committed to the notion that what philosophy has been unconsciously, without knowing or intending it, and, so to speak, under cover, it must henceforth be openly and deliberately" (MW 12:94).

This is the strategic move I referred to earlier. It is not that past philosophers were stupid—he referred to their work in the preceding paragraph as the choices of "thoughtful men"—but they were unmindful of the culturally responsive nature of their work. It is only in this sense that they were unaware.

Dewey then continued, speaking not just of Greek philosophy, but of all previous philosophy: "When it is acknowledged that under disguise of dealing with ultimate reality, philosophy has been occupied with the precious values embedded in social traditions, that it has sprung from a clash of social ends and from a conflict of inherited institutions with incompatible contemporary tendencies, it will be seen that the task of future philosophy is to clarify men's ideas as to the social and moral strifes of their own day." Philosophy's aim is to be a tool for dealing with these conflicts of inherited values and contemporary developments. Therefore, what seems remote from life is actually fully engaged in it: "That which may be pretentiously unreal when it is formulated in metaphysical distinctions becomes intensely significant when connected with the drama of the struggle of social beliefs and ideals." This will involve a change in philosophy's self-understanding, but its loss of cosmic pretension will be repaid. As Dewey wrote, "Philosophy which surrenders its somewhat barren monopoly of dealings with Ultimate and Absolute Reality will find a compensation in enlightening the moral forces which move mankind and in contributing to the aspirations of men to attain to a more ordered and intelligent happiness" (MW 12:94).

Clearly, cultural criticism is present in this text. But there is also a reference to "incompatible contemporary tendencies," thus implying that coherence is a standard that should be used. Finally, as the last sentence shows, the result of this cultural and conceptual critique places one in a new position. A historicized and logical treatment of "Ultimate and Absolute Reality" frees one from its grip. Note also that Dewey's cultural criticism is not free-floating. It is an extension of the means-ends consideration discussed earlier. The reconstructive, philosophical critic notes the conflicts between "inherited institutions" and values on the one hand and "incompatible contemporary tendencies" on the other. The philosopher works within his or her society to resolve these conflicts. The cultural critic is using the method of intelligence to enable society to accept responsibility for its collective behavior, modifying the conditions as needed to bring about the desired results. To blindly continue in customary ways is unintelligent. The philosopher as social critic calls attention to the means-ends connections, enabling society to accept responsibility for its common life.

Philosophy's specific role, then, in making our practices intelligent is one of criticism. It works indirectly, criticizing our beliefs and methods of belief formation. Thus philosophical reflection is of two sorts. Philosophers criticize both our practices and the ways in which we establish them. Philosophers are, then, in Dewey's view, cultural critics and logicians, understanding the latter not as mere proof-checkers, but as cultivators of the methods of intelligence. But this critique, because it is a critique of influential beliefs and practices, is not just an intellectual exercise. It is, or can be, one part of the effort of society to transform itself. For Dewey philosophy—like intelligence generally—was an evaluative and logical activity which enables us to exercise control over our practices and institutions. We do not have to be submissive in all of our activities. We can sometimes modify our situations so that we can increase our enjoyments. This is intelligence. But when we are systematically and self-consciously intelligent, refining our more pervasive beliefs, habits, and institutions and our methods of securing the goods of life, we are engaging in philosophy. This is not an idle, contemplative philosophy; it is a culturally transformative one.

Experience and Its Possibilities

Thus far I have concentrated on the *reconstructing* of experience, and I will continue to do so. This is the focus of this book. But something needs to be said about Dewey's metaphysical naturalism. I will have more to say about this in the last three chapters, but I should call attention to it here. Ontologically, it is presumed by the notion that intelligence is found in our practices and then developed through democracy, education, science, and philosophy. Indeed, I noted earlier that for Dewey experience was the biologically suggested model of the interaction of an organism with its environment, but I have not really paid attention to his understanding of experience itself. To see this most clearly we need to look at what he said about experience in relation to art.

Aesthetic-Artistic Experience

In *Art as Experience* (1934) Dewey declared that "esthetic experience is experience in its integrity." Later in the same paragraph, he wrote: "To esthetic experience, then, the philosopher must go to understand what experience is" (LW 10:278). An aesthetic experience is "*an* experience," that is, the sort of experience in which "the material experienced runs its course to fulfillment. Then and then only is it integrated within and demarcated in the general stream of experience from other experiences" (LW 10:42). Later in the same chapter, "Having an Experience," he wrote: "I have tried to show in these chapters that the esthetic is no intruder in experience from without, whether by way of idle luxury or transcendent ideality, but that it is the clarified and intensified development of traits that belong to every normally complete experience" (LW 10:52–53).

These citations show that Dewey thought there are some experiences that are characterized by completeness, intensity, and definition. These qualities are most clearly seen in esthetic experience, but they are not confined to that. Indeed, the point is that we can have these "consummatory" experiences at many times and places in our lives. They are not confined to special realms and moments, nor do they originate in other worlds. They come within life as we live it. The important point is that the "interaction of the live creature and environing conditions" (LW 10:42) is "heightened and intensified" (LW 10:298) to such a degree that it can be appropriately termed "integral" or "consummatory" (see LW 12:47 and 62). This is the sort of experience that Dewey thought we value—and is possible here and now without divine intervention or special states of consciousness.

In order for one to reconstruct experience, to make practice more intelligent than it would otherwise be, experience or practice must be transformable. This is possible because our interactions are not only satisfying; they are also unsatisfying. Life is a mixed affair. But by being intelligent we can reshape situations so that they become consummatory rather than slack or incomplete. If life contained no satisfactions that could be extended or reproduced or if we lacked the ability to modify situations, Dewey's experience-remaking model would be unrealistic. As it is, his reconstructive model of intelligence is situated in his biological understanding of

experience-existence. We are organisms that are engaged in constant interactions with our environments. Some of these interactions are more desirable, some less so or even distinctly undesirable. Through intelligized
behavior we can adjust our situations as necessary, thus enlarging the desirable in our lives.

One of the ways in which interpreters divide Dewey up is to distinguish
between his metaphysics of experience and his instrumentalist theory of
knowledge. But for Dewey there was a single phenomenon—experience—
that could be understood metaphysically, aesthetically, politically, or epis-
temically. Earlier I discussed his treatment of thinking (in the honorific
sense) as an alternative to capricious and routine behavior. The latter,
undesirable, polarities show up again in his discussion of aesthetic experience in the "Having an Experience" chapter of *Art as Experience*, being
placed here in a wider context: "The enemies of the esthetic are neither the
practical nor the intellectual. They are the humdrum; slackness of loose
ends; submission to convention in practice and intellectual procedure. Rigid
abstinence, coerced submission, tightness on one side and dissipation, inco-
herence and aimless indulgence on the other are deviations in opposite
directions from the unity of experience" (LW 12:47).

The contrasts in the earlier discussion cannot be fitted easily into this
one, yet in a rough sort of way we can see that routine and caprice are part
of a larger contrast in this passage and are to be distinguished from "the
unity of experience." Whether Dewey was focusing on methods of experience or experience itself, he tended to employ similar analytic categories.
This is because he distinguished no radical separations between being,
doing, and knowing. At the end of the first chapter of *Experience and
Nature* he affirmed that "common experience is capable of developing within itself methods which will secure direction for itself and will create inherent standards of judgment and value" (LW 1:41). Or, as he had said a few
years earlier in *Reconstruction in Philosophy*, "The very fact of experience
thus includes the process by which it directs itself in its own betterment"
(MW 12:134). It is precisely because our transactions are both precarious
and stable, capricious and routine, satisfying and unsatisfying that we are
capable of enhancing them in ways that are more satisfying. "Nothing in
Dewey's thought," declares Alexander, "makes sense unless the basic doctrine that *experience grows*, and in growing takes on *meaning*, is remembered."[23] This natural growth of experience permits us to enhance, to develop from "the very fact of experience" deliberate processes, such as science,
"to expand and enrich experience" (MW 12:134).

If we focus on the fact of experience and attempt to understand it in a
very wide sort of way, we have begun to do ontology; but if we cultivate the

natural processes of experience, we are doing Deweyan epistemology. The former is not your father's metaphysics and the latter is not his epistemology, for the former is a functional, open-to-revision description of what there is and the latter is an attempt to develop an existentially transformative method—or, better—skill. I just quoted Alexander on the significance of growth in experience for Dewey, but I left out his qualifying phrase, "especially his theory of aesthetic meaning," which he had inserted between "Dewey's thought" and "makes sense." I omitted it then and call attention to the omission now because I want to make the point that the Deweyan doctrine should not be qualified in this way.

The consummations of experience with their meanings and the possibility of deliberate cultivation of experience are both misunderstood if one does not grasp the Deweyan doctrine of the natural occurence of growth of experience. This is a major reason why Rorty's neopragmatism rankles paleo-pragmatists. Rorty dispenses with talk of experience and the method of its deliberate transformation. I too have shied away from a full discussion of the metaphysics of experience, because I have not wanted to get drawn into discussions that would detract from the main point. Dewey thought that our practices are such that they can be modified to be more satisfying. These practices are experience; and, suitably modified, they are also intelligent action. The latter is aesthetic or consummatory experience and is artistic in Dewey's wide sense that takes science and intelligence generally as art. There is a Deweyan distinction to be made between the metaphysics of experience and his instrumentalism, but ultimately he is talking about the same thing—experience and its possibilities. One of these possibilities is intelligence. For, as we have seen, it is an "added type of interaction" (LW 4:171); it is enhanced experience that enables one to live in a more satisfactory way.

Intelligence as Experiential or Cultural Criticism

This understanding of intelligence has profound implications for Dewey's social philosophy. Where some radicals would have rejected outright the beliefs, values, and language they had encountered in the culture, Dewey was committed to working from and through the existing situation, attempting to transform it. To say that he was an idealist in a realist's body would make the dualist's mistake against which he was constantly alert. Rather, he participated fully in the society as it was, grasping the possibilities for improvement that were inherent in the existing reality. It is not that there was a fixed reality and a set ideal, calling the former into question. The situation was more dynamic than that. Ideal and reality were constantly changing as they influenced one another.

We are now at the heart of Dewey's project. For Dewey thinking was not an end in itself, but a means of transforming problematic situations into more satisfying ones. Since the test of thinking was its contribution to lived experience, he thought one must never stray too far from the latter. To do so was to commit the philosopher's fallacy—"neglect of context." In *Context and Thought* (1931) Dewey declared, "Neglect of context is the greatest single disaster which philosophic thinking can incur" (LW 6:11). Philosophers tend to take as real their own intellectual constructions, regarding the products of an analysis as unconnected elements or abstractions as timeless realities. Speaking directly of "the permanent" in the first chapter of *Experience and Nature*, Dewey acknowledged that it meets various needs, but "the demand and response which meets it are empirically always found in a special context; they arise because of a particular need and in order to effect specifiable consequences. Philosophy, thinking at large, allows itself to be diverted into absurd search for an intellectual philosopher's stone of absolutely wholesale generalization, thus isolating that which is permanent in a function and for a purpose, and converting it into the intrinsically eternal, conceived either (as Aristotle conceived it) as that which is the same at all times, or as that which is indifferent to time, out of time" (LW 1:32–33).

To counter this tendency Dewey proposed that the ad hoc nature of thinking be recognized. He thought one should always be aware of the origins of one's thinking in actual experience and the effects of one's thinking on experience. This he recognized in calling his philosophy "instrumentalism." His intention is reported in a letter to a former student that was included as an appendix to *Knowing and the Known*, cowritten with Arthur F. Bentley (1949). Having just discussed the usefulness for a physicist of treating water as H_2O, Dewey noted that it was "pertinent at this point . . . to refer to that aspect of my theory of knowledge to which I gave the name 'instrumentalism.' For it was intended to deal with the problem just mentioned on the basis of the idea or hypothesis that scientific subjectmatter grows out of and returns into the subjectmatter of the everyday kind" (LW 16:291). Hickman usefully designates this "growing out of" and "return to" everyday experience the "excursus" and "recursus" of productive inquiry.[24] Instrumentalism, then, is the awareness that one's ideas are mental products drawn from life, and also the commitment on the part of the inquirer to return them to everyday experience. He or she uses hypotheses, theories, or ideals to inform the problematic situation, making it more satisfying. Instrumentalism is the opposite of the decontextualized thinking that Dewey deplored.

Dewey's instrumentalism played itself out in cultural criticism, since he regarded culture as the relevant context for what we do and his thinking was directed toward the improvement of cultural activities.[25] *Cultural* is definitely not to be taken in the Matthew Arnold sense. For Dewey *culture* was "that immense diversity of human affairs, interests, concerns, values which compartmentalists pigeonhole under 'religion' 'morals' 'aesthetics' 'politics' 'economics' etc., etc." (LW 1:363). This anthropological understanding of *culture* is what Dewey late in life considered using in place of *experience.*[26] But whichever term he used, the referent was the same—the various interactions of organisms and their environments, including the "immense diversity of human affairs." One experiential or cultural activity is intelligence—experience or culture criticizing itself.

Realizing Life's Potential

The point is to live well. Dewey thought we can do this best by developing the intelligent elements within our personal and collective experience in such a way that our practices and institutions become more fulfilling. We can modify who we are and what we do in such a way that we increase our satisfactions and create the conditions for future satisfactions. Being intelligent is not an end it itself; living well is the point. But intelligence is the best way to enhance our practices and institutions so that we might live well.

What is radical about Dewey's proposal is not that he urged us to be intelligent. Few deny the value of thinking clearly and well. Dewey's radicalism consisted, in part, of his understanding of the sufficiency of intelligence as a transforming activity. He believed that nothing is needed beyond the universe in which we find ourselves and the ability and disposition to remake our practices and institutions intelligently. Intelligence, broadly conceived as a critical and creative technology for bettering our lives, is sufficient, he claimed. Traditionalists of all sorts cannot accept this. They will always want to qualify Dewey's proposal by calling attention to what else is needed—God, family, nation, or custom. Dewey's reply was that perhaps we need one or more of these values. But if we do we must justify such through reflection. And, more than likely, we will need to remake these values to meet our current needs. Nothing is absolute—not even this claim. Everything, including our methods of knowing and choosing, is open to criticism and modification.[27]

Some nontraditionalists are also uneasy with Dewey's proposal. Intelligence is well and good, but they want more specifics, more content. Just exactly what does being intelligent mean? Where is the program of action? Surely we cannot expect everyone to measure up to a scientist's or philosopher's intellectual standards. We need to develop a program that the smart and not-so-smart can buy into. Only by outlining a course of action and laying it out in a set of rules or a political program can we hope to deal with the very real problems that confront us. We cannot educate enough experience-reconstructors to solve our problems. Besides, it is obvious that intelligent, well-educated people disagree. Any proposal that fails to go beyond education and problem-solving techniques is not enough. We need a plan—and, even better, an organization to implement it.

Dewey's reply was that of course we need plans and organizations, but these are situational—not for all time. What endures is the need for intelligence. Fortunately, intelligence is for the having. Within almost every situation there are better and worse possibilities. By reflecting on these and the conditions needed to realize the more desirable (or effective) ones, we can choose ends (and means) that remake our lives. We can learn to live better than we do now.

To illustrate and deepen Dewey's understanding of intelligent action, I will now discuss his cultural instrumentalism. This will involve me in the exposition of various Deweyan texts, examination of others' critiques, and consideration of some of Dewey's social and political involvements. Therefore, in the next two chapters I will use a mix of approaches that will enable me to fill out what has been sketched in this chapter. Those two chapters must be read together, for they deal with closely related matters. Chapter 3 concentrates on Dewey's instrumentalism, and chapter 4 concentrates on the social-cultural setting needed for the effective realization of this cultural instrumentalism. But this distinction is too simply drawn; the next two chapters cover much the same ground.

3

❖

TRANSFORMING SOCIETY
DEWEY'S CULTURAL
INSTRUMENTALISM

Better it is for philosophy to err in active participation in the living
struggles and issues of its own age and times than to maintain an
immune monastic impeccability, without relevancy or bearing in the
generating ideas of its contemporary present.
—John Dewey, "Intelligence and Morals" (MW 4:44).

DEWEY'S EFFORT to intelligize practice, his use of the term *instrumen-*
talism to distinguish his version of pragmatism, his repeated calls for
a method of social inquiry consonant with the scientific method, and,
above all, his willingness as a thinker to address specific social and political
problems in a variety of public settings—all contributed to the perception
that Dewey, if he was anything, was a politically minded philosopher.

In the first part of the twentieth century Dewey was America's public
philosopher, an academic who understood and helped shape his society.
Alfred North Whitehead declared, "John Dewey is the typical effective
American thinker; and he is the chief intellectual force providing that environment with coherent purpose."[1] But some of his critics, notably
Randolph Bourne, insisted that Dewey had failed to cultivate the required
vision to guide the choice of means. As Bourne declared, "You must have
your vision and you must have your technique. The practical effect of
Dewey's philosophy has evidently been to develop the sense of the latter at
the expense of the former."[2] Moreover, Bourne argued, a concentration on
technique at the expense of larger values resulted in a failure in the immediate situation: "A philosophy of adjustment will not even make for adjustment. If you try merely to 'meet' situations as they come, you will not even

meet them" (344). Therefore, Dewey's instrumentalism failed in terms of both ends and means, because his ends were shortsighted or nonexistent. Building on Bourne's critique, Lewis Mumford observed, "Without vision, the pragmatists perish."[3] Dewey, in particular, was dismissed as one who had "faith in the current go of things" (131), a faith Mumford thought was ineffective. Ironically, his critique reinforces Dewey's image as one who *would be* effective, a pragmatist in the shallow, opportunistic sense.

Dewey, of course, did not accept the charge of blind instrumentalism. He thought his attention was sufficiently directed to ends as well as means. In the next chapter I will attempt to come to terms with his larger vision. There I will have more to say about the sort of democratic society he envisioned. In this chapter I want to gain a better understanding of his cultural instrumentalism. My strategy will be to focus initially on some of the cruder characterizations of Dewey's thought, working toward a precise identification of its shortcomings.

MISREADING DEWEY

I will have many occasions to correct misreadings of Dewey in the course of this study, but for now I want to illustrate the tendency to read Dewey in a reductionistic, dichotomous, uncontextual way with two readily understandable misreadings. I will reserve for later those that clearly arise from basic disagreements and are more difficult to sort out.[4] From Dewey's point of view one of the most prevalent ways in which critics mistreat him is failing to take as whole that which he thought was unified. Late in life, in 1950, he complained to Sidney Hook in a letter (with Dewey's characteristically casual spelling): "As I see it now, tho not at the time, ive spent most of years trying to get things together; my critics understand me only after they split me up again."[5] Tiles correctly points out, "Dewey always starts with the inclusive and the connected, and considers the process of differentiation. His opponents assume the task is to assemble wholes out of isolated elements." And later: "For Dewey's opponents what is *given* in experience is particulars and the function of thought is to build complexes while remaining true to the given parts. Tiles thought that for Dewey what is given, 'the original datum, is always a qualitative whole' (L 5, p. 250)."[6] The misreadings in the two cases, one long, one short, that I will now consider are not difficult to understand. They, like the more involved ones, however, share the dichotomizing feature that begs the question against Dewey.

Questioning Dewey's Intelligence: Case 1

Intelligence was Dewey's constant concern. Indeed, one of the complaints about him is that he failed to provide hard answers, operational solutions; instead he provided only pious sermons on the saving properties of science, intelligence, and education. James Miller, in a review of Westbrook's book, has made the following charge: "Dewey's political thought, like his philosophy generally, is disappointingly soft at its center. Too many crucial claims unravel under close scrutiny; too many difficult choices are evaded. As liberals and social democrats have learned the hard way, free inquiry cannot, by itself, produce a community united by shared insight; even with the wisest of teachers, schools cannot, by themselves, solve the problems of society; the methods of modern science are no guarantee of freedom and equality, and neither is pious rhetoric."[7]

Science, schools, shared insight, and free inquiry are the forms of the socialized intelligence that Dewey advocated. Of course Miller has misrepresented Dewey's understanding of intelligence, reducing it to the forms listed (and understood in their conventional senses) and ignoring what Dewey has to say about the use of force and the inappropriateness of even seeking guarantees. But Miller's claim is given some plausibility by a casual reading of such statements of Dewey's as the following observation from *The Public and Its Problems:* "The prime condition of a democratically organized public is a kind of knowledge and insight which does not yet exist. In its absence, it would be the height of absurdity to try to tell what it would be like if it existed. But some of the conditions which must be fulfilled if it is to exist can be indicated. We can borrow that much from the spirit and method of science even if we are ignorant of it as a specialized apparatus. An obvious requirement is freedom of social inquiry and of distribution of its conclusions" (LW 2:339).

Here we have many of the elements of Miller's caricature—"knowledge and insight," "spirit and method of science," "freedom of social inquiry and distribution of its conclusions"—and only a vague specification of "the prime condition of a democratically organized public." Indeed, to attempt such a precise specification would be "the height of absurdity." A closer and contextual reading shows, however, that this statement by Dewey is not as innocuous or void as it may first appear. Miller thinks that Dewey's claims "unravel under close scrutiny," but I contend that reading Dewey correctly requires one to get inside his language and work outward. Then one can appreciate his hard, careful thinking.

More than Intellect

Dewey did not say that "a kind of knowledge and insight" is the only condition of "a democratically organized public"; he said that such is "the prime condition." Dewey fully recognized that mental activity is not sufficient to change existent conditions. This is one part of his pragmatic critique of "intellectualism." Thinking is not apart from action; it is a part of it. To make this point I refer to two essays, initially published in *The New Republic*, in which Dewey discussed the use of force. In the later one, "Intelligence and Power," written in 1934, he declared: "Intelligence has no power *per se*," and "Intelligence becomes a *power* only when it is brought into the operation of other forces than itself" (LW 9:109). To be sure, as he argued in "Force, Violence and Law" (1916), force should be "efficiently" and "economically" used, for the "objection to violence is not that it involves the use of force, but that it is a waste of force, that it uses force idly or destructively." His point was not that we must choose between thinking as a mental activity and violence as "force running wild," but that we must use force intelligently (MW 10:212).

Dewey concluded "Intelligence and Power" with a reference to education: "'Education' even in its widest sense cannot do everything. But what is accomplished without education, again in its broadest sense, will be badly done and much of it will have to be done over." Then he made the "intelligizing practice" point on which I am insisting: "The crucial problem is how intelligence may gain increasing power through incorporation with wants and interests that are actually operating" (LW 9:111). One does not choose between thinking and action, even forceful action, but ideally between intelligence and violence. The former is intelligent behavior; the latter is destructive in a way counter to one's purposes. Dewey once used the example of a "dynamite charge" blowing up "human beings instead of rocks" as an instance of energy becoming violence by defeating or frustrating "purpose instead of executing or realizing it" (MW 10:246). Such action is stupid, whereas, all other things being equal, blowing up rocks instead of human beings is intelligent.

It was in part because Dewey sought to inform action with thinking that he supported Woodrow Wilson's war aims, thus incurring the rhetorically effective opposition of his former admirer, Randolph Bourne, one of many pacificists who felt betrayed by Dewey's action.[8] In the 1916 essay just cited, Dewey was attempting to articulate a middle way between Tolstoy's view that "all force is violence and all violence evil" and the militarist approach with its "glorification of force" (MW 10:212). Then, in 1917, when war was declared, Dewey felt that "to talk about being neutral"

was "to talk foolishness." Rather, what was needed was a "unity of mind
and effort" (MW 10:158). Dewey was willing to risk being wrong about the
war in order to be engaged in an effort to make its prosecution as intelligent
as possible. He thought that one could exercise intelligence as matters
unfolded. Bourne, however, thought that war entailed unacceptable consequences. It was foolish of Dewey, having chosen to support the war, to
protest dismissal of teachers for disloyalty. He should have expected that
the "war-technique" would entail "mob-fanaticisms."[9] Once one chose war,
one chose all that went along with it, including many practices that were
abhorrent to Dewey, such as suppression of individual liberty in the interest
of the war effort. Dewey later acknowledged that his "idealistic aims" had
been defeated. But that defeat was due to "the failure to use force adequately and intelligently" ("The Discrediting of Idealism" [1919], MW 11:181).
He regretted that the United States had not been more skeptical of the
Allies' goals, demanding assurances that the war was in fact being fought
for democratic ends. Once more he regretted the failure of intelligence, not
the attempt to use force intelligently.

More than Schooling

To return to the text from *The Public and Its Problems*, when Dewey
referred to a "distribution of the conclusions" of "social inquiry" he was not
speaking of schooling in the way one might suppose. He was thinking of
education "in its broadest sense"; he was referring to an artful communication of the findings of a reconstructed social science through a variety of
media. No bland appeal for more insight and education in the conventional
sense, his discussion in the succeeding pages turns out to be a suggestive,
hard-edged critique of social science, the media, and society itself (LW
2:339–50).

First Dewey noted that "social inquiry" was more than the absence of
"legal restrictions." Nor was it the scholasticized "academic specializations"
that passed for social knowledge. Nor was it "publicity" (by which he meant
"advertising"), "propaganda," and sensationalized reporting (340). Then
Dewey sharply criticized a society that limits science to physical matter. In
such a society knowledge is "divided against itself," for the human disciplines are separated from the physical sciences. This allows technology to
play "its part in generating enslavement of men, women and children in
factories in which they are animated machines to tend inanimate machines.
It has maintained sordid slums, flurried and discontented careers, grinding
poverty and luxurious wealth, brutal exploitation of nature and man in
times of peace and high explosives and noxious gases in times of of war.

Man, a child in understanding of himself, has placed in his hands physical tools of incalculable power. He plays with them like a child, and whether they work harm or good is largely a matter of accident. The instrumentality becomes a master and works fatally as if possessed of a will of its own—not because it has a will but because man has not" (344). Because society refuses to see situations whole, tracing out the various connections, it permits unjust conditions to develop and continue. Invoking the metaphor of modern man as a child, Dewey called attention to the devastating effects of the thoughtless use of technology.

The remedy, Dewey thought, was in part to develop "a genuine social science," one that spoke to "contemporary events" (348). But this connected social science should not be presented "academically," for "a newspaper which was only a daily edition of a quarterly journal of sociology or political science would undoubtedly possess a limited circulation and a narrow influence" (349). Instead this reconstructed social science should be presented artfully. What was needed was for artists—poets, dramatists, novelists—to distribute the news of a genuine social science (349–50). Clearly, Dewey was not content with school and society as he found them, nor with business as usual. He advocated both a reconstructed social science and a reconstructed mass media.

More than Pious Rhetoric

Dewey's discussion of social science and the media in *The Public and Its Problems* was a response to Walter Lippman's analysis in *Public Opinion*. Lippmann had concluded that neither the press nor political science as then constituted (1922) was adequate for the formation of the requisite public opinion in a contemporary democracy.[10] Acknowledging the force of Lippmann's charges, Dewey was not content to let the matter rest where Lippmann did. He wanted to show that a reconstructed social science and mass media could do what was needed in a contemporary democracy. Therefore, Dewey was not writing a systematic social and political philosophy; he was responding to a specific analysis with a similarly pointed critique of his own. He was not writing for the ages; he was after Lippmann—in a temporal and dialectical sense, but not in a personal one. He respected Lippmann's analysis, taking it seriously enough to probe and test it.

Rather than being soft at the center as Miller charged, Dewey was a critic of capitalism who recognized the necessity of force, albeit as a power that was to be used intelligently. He did not uncritically advocate the extension of physical science into society. Science was to be reconstructed in such a way that it included a social science relevant to human concerns and was to be presented in an artful way, enabling society to remake itself. Finally, when Lippmann mounted a telling intellectual attack on the possibility of an informed public opinion, Dewey responded with a vigorous intellectual defense of the opportunity for a reconstructed public opinion.

A Moving Target: Case 2

Dewey was not soft at the center; he was soft at the edges. He refused to spell out in detail the needed reconstruction of society, insisting that this was not possible for him as a philosopher to do. This was a task for the people involved. To ask Dewey for a complete model of the new society and its institutions was to ask for the sort of certainty that he said was not possible. Dewey thought that citizens (with the help of social scientists and others) could size up their situation, locating difficulties and the conditions that made for them, figure out more attractive possibilities, and implement the requisite changes. He also altered his thinking about important matters. It would be surprising for an advocate of criticism to have resisted change, just as it would have been inconsistent for one who thought criticism should be dispersed throughout society to have attempted to limit his fellow citizens' innovative efforts.

Charles Frankel, who should have known better, missed an important shift in Dewey's thinking regarding the place of schooling in society, thus distorting Dewey's views. Here is his summary of three "recurrent doctrines in Dewey's thought":

1. Scientific method should be employed to solve social problems.
2. The validity of democracy lies in the analogy between its procedures and those of scientific method, and from its openness to the application of scientific method.
3. The primary practical instrument for transforming and improving society is the school.[11]

The first point, as we have seen and will notice again, must be qualified. Dewey did not argue for a direct application to social problems of the scientific method as employed in the physical sciences. The second point, accordingly, must be modified. There is an analogy between science and democracy, but democracy was validated for Dewey by more than this analogy. (The relationship between science—or, better, intelligence—and democracy will be considered in this and the next chapter, particularly the latter.)

Frankel's third point, which is the one I most want to consider, is too simply stated. Dewey placed great value in the schools as mechanisms of social formation. Indeed, he once thought that they could be instruments of social transformation. In 1897 he declared, "I believe it is the business of every one interested in education to insist upon the school as the primary and most effective interest of social progress and reform." ("My Pedagogic Creed," EW 5:94). But he changed his mind. In "Education and Social Change" (1937), one of several articles he wrote for *Social Frontier, a Journal of Educational Criticism and Reconstruction*, Dewey could not have been more clear: "It is unrealistic, in my opinion, to suppose that the schools can be a *main* agency in producing the intellectual and moral changes, the changes in attitudes and disposition of thought and purpose, which are necessary for the creation of a new social order." This is so because of "the constant operation of powerful forces outside the school which shape mind and character." A school is "but one educational agency out of many, and at the best is in some respects a minor educational force. Nevertheless, while the school is not a sufficient conditon, it is a necessary condition of forming the understanding and the dispositions that are required to maintain a genuinely changed social order" (LW 11:414; see also LW 13:296).

Dewey was not always as careful as he was here to speak of education in a wider sense than just schooling and to acknowledge schooling's limitations. Because he continued to think that schools had an important role to play, he often urged educators to do their part, and he did not always qualify his exhortations, particularly when he was addressing educators. But it was in the broader sense, which, of course, would include schools, that he thought education—or, better, the intelligizing of practice—could be a means of social transformation. Therefore, it is a misrepresentation to claim that the mature Dewey thought that "the primary practical instrument for transforming and improving society is the school."

Dewey's thinking and writing can be elusive, for he did not regularly declare himself completely and fully at any given time. He was not a systematic writer, so one must often bring together a variety of related statements to get the whole picture. He also used common language in distinctive ways, which some regarded as "word-twisting."[12] But one can trace out his usage and pin down his meaning. Dewey also left many matters deliberately open because the matter itself was undefined or unfinished. Finally, his thinking was always developing, for he continually changed his mind. One should expect no less from an experimentalist. But these characteristics do not present insuperable problems for interpretation. One must pay attention to when Dewey was writing and what else he has had to say on this or a related matter. One needs to read him contextually.

Toward a Nuanced Reading of Dewey's Social Thought

Dewey himself acknowledged that his social and political thinking was not as practically effective as it needed to be. Yet we must be careful neither to downplay the emphasis he gave to education in social transformation nor reduce his proposal to a sheerly educational one. To dismiss his thinking in either of these ways would be to miss the extent to which his cultural instrumentalism can be effective and has contributed to the development of the political technology that he thought was required. Nevertheless, it seems odd that a pragmatist, particularly an instrumentalist such as Dewey, would forego specifying the means of reconstruction. One would think that a philosopher of technology committed to social change would be able to spell out, if not a blueprint, then certainly some of the possible means of social change.

The reason Dewey did not do this is more complicated than those suggested thus far. Dewey was reluctant to do the work of the people involved, and he did think that new political forms had to wait on new developments.[13] But in seemingly countless articles in a variety of periodicals Dewey did make specific programmatic suggestions. After reviewing some of the charges of Frankel, H. S. Thayer, and Morton White, as well as some of Dewey's proposals, James Campbell concluded: "It should be clear from this brief survey that, in spite of the opinions of many commentators to the contrary, Dewey did suggest courses of action with regard to matters of both broad and narrow scope. Moreover, were this survey expanded to include the rest of Dewey's many other suggested courses of action, a rather thorough program for social reconstruction would emerge."[14] So it cannot be that Dewey was reluctant to spell out a program either because he deferred to the citizenry or because his pragmatism would not permit it. Indeed, his instrumentalism, as I have suggested, seemed to require operational development.

I will begin the consideration of Dewey's cultural instrumentalism and its political limitations by dealing with a prominent objection to his approach, his alleged failure to take evil and power seriously. This, of course, is one form of the ineffectiveness complaint. If human nature is recalcitrant to the point that education is useless or inadequate, Dewey's insistence on intelligence and education is wrongheaded. This objection is conceptually more basic than other forms of the ineffectiveness charge, because it points to human nature itself. Some of those who complain that

Dewey's proposals are vague or incomplete could agree that humans are educable and insist that Dewey just had not hit on the right social change strategy. But if human nature, like a rubber band, always reverts to form, there is no sense in trying to shape it in new ways. One needs, instead, to confront evil with power and not mere education. Only power is able to best the irrational forces one encounters in the real world of interest politics. The rubber band must be held in the position in which one wants it to remain.

The Dewey-Niebuhr "Debate"

Among the many well-known critiques of Dewey's social and political thought are those of Reinhold Niebuhr, C. Wright Mills, and Charles Frankel. All three questioned the effectiveness of Dewey's approach. They also doubted the usefulness of physical science techniques to cope with social problems. Finally, they charged Dewey with being limited by his middle-class liberalism. Fortunately I do not need to deal with all three here. Mills's criticism was in some ways a secular analogue to the criticism of Reinhold Niebuhr (whose views I will consider). But, as Campbell deftly shows, Mills did not offer "a full picture of Dewey's work," and the later Mills turned out to have much in common with Dewey.[15] Frankel also distorted Dewey's social and political philosophy, as I showed above.

Perhaps the sharpest and most persistent critic of Dewey's social and political thinking was Reinhold Niebuhr. Ironically, as many have pointed out, Niebuhr shared much with Dewey politically and philosophically, yet often used him as a convenient target. This was a tangled affair that has been ably discussed, and I am dependent on others' accounts of the history of the Niebuhr-Dewey relationship.[16] This exchange is worth reviewing here because Niebuhr remains a hero to some intellectuals, as evidenced by Diggins's *The Promise of Pragmatism*. Also, a consideration of Dewey's thought in relation to an attack that was not very well thought out, but persistent and continually well received, helps us to understand Dewey in the context of his times and beyond.

Niebuhr's Attack

Reinhold Niebuhr was by all accounts a charismatic preacher, social critic, activist, and teacher. "Prophetic" was the adjective often used. He could not have been more dissimilar in style from the deliberate Dewey, hesitant in speech, whom George Dykhuizen, his biographer, has described as "mild and unaffected."[17] Niebuhr came to Union Theological Seminary in New York in 1928 to teach Christian Ethics. He arrived after an initial pastorate in Detroit, where he achieved prominence for, in his own words, "'de-bunk[ing]' the moral pretensions of Henry Ford."[18] At Union he was just across Broadway from Columbia Teacher's College and across 120th Street from the rest of Columbia University, where Dewey was soon to retire from teaching, but not from other activities. As professor emeritus Dewey continued to draw his salary, maintain an office, and see graduate students, many of whom were also attracted to Niebuhr. Dewey's main attention in the 1930s was focused on writing, public lectures, and increasingly radical political activism, but geographical proximity and these activities, particularly the political ones, brought Niebuhr and Dewey into association with one another. John Bennett, Niebuhr's younger colleague, a fellow Christian ethicist, and later president of Union Theological Seminary, recalled that "while Niebuhr was using Dewey as a target in some of his writings, he would be on a committee with him engaged in founding a new political party or trying to get some poor fellow out of jail."[19]

In addition to backgrounds and professional commitments, the differences between Dewey and Niebuhr had to do with temperaments, as well as theories. While neither was the optimist or pessimist that each (or his partisans) thought the other to be, Dewey was generally more hopeful and Niebuhr more despairing of the human condition. Westbrook used two criteria, suggested by Niebuhr in the last paragraph of the introduction to *Moral Man and Immoral Society*, to draw the contrast. Niebuhr had written that the task of the book was to consider human nature and its consequences for society and politics. But ultimately the task was "to find political methods which will offer the most promise of achieving an ethical social goal for society. Such methods must always be judged by two criteria: 1. Do they do justice to the moral resources and possibilities in human nature and provide for the exploitation of every latent moral capacity in man? 2. Do they take account of the limitations of human nature, particularly those which manifest themselves in man's collective behavior?"[20] After quoting this passage, Westbrook observed that Dewey tended to emphasize the moral resources and possibilities and downplay the limitations of human nature. Niebuhr tended the other way, calling attention to human limitations and questioning human possibilities. Where Dewey was worried about despair, Niebuhr was worried about arrogance.[21] This is a correct, balanced assessment; but it does not give the flavor of the conflict. To sense that we need to look at some particulars.

The more quotable examples are to be found in the writings of Niebuhr, for he was more personal and persistent in his attacks on Dewey than Dewey was in his criticisms of Niebuhr. For example, several years after

Niebuhr's initial provocation in *Moral Man and Immoral Society* (1932) and Dewey's responses in the mid-thirties, Niebuhr accused Dewey of *naïveté*, insisting, "Not a suspicion dawns upon Professor Dewey that no possible 'organized inquiry' can be as transcendent over the historical conflicts of interest as it ought to be to achieve the disinterested intelligence which he attributes to it."[22] Dewey did not advocate a "disinterested intelligence"; as a pragmatist he frankly acknowledged the interest of the inquirer. Nor did he ignore class interests; Dewey was prominent on the national scene in the 1930s as a democratic socialist. For instance, as president of the People's Lobby he wrote regularly in the organization's *Bulletin*, as Anne Sharpe noted in her textual commentary, "about unemployment relief and the need for redistribution of the national income through taxation" (LW 9:474). In one such contribution he wrote: "We cannot achieve a decent standard of living for more than a fraction of the American people, by any other method than that to which the British Labor Party and the Social Democratic Parties of Europe are committed—the socialization of all natural resources and natural monopolies, of ground rent, and of basic industries" (LW 9:290). Moreover, as we shall see, Dewey noted Nieburian inconsistencies and inaccurate representations. But, perhaps because of age, his interest in avoiding conflict with political allies, or a realization of the futility of such efforts, he did not continue to respond to Niebuhr's attacks. Niebuhr, however, maintained his criticism into the 1940s and beyond.

It is important, as Daniel F. Rice has noted, to keep in mind that Niebuhr was thirty-two years younger than Dewey and of a different generation (xii). But, where Rice pointed to the differences in the intellectual developments that influenced each, I call attention to a more specific difference in their situations that helps to explain Niebuhr's attacks. Dewey represented for Niebuhr the liberalism that Niebuhr had once embraced, but had come to reject. Dewey took no notice of Niebuhr before the mid-1930s, but perhaps the younger man felt keenly Dewey's secular attacks on tradition, including religious institutions and dogmas, and his continual effort to reconstruct the political liberalism that Niebuhr was increasingly willing to reject. Niebuhr's attitude toward liberalism was ambivalent. In 1923 he wrote: "There doesn't seem to be very much malice in the world. There is simply not enough intelligence to conduct the intricate affairs of a complex civilization."[23] And his younger brother, H. Richard, who was his academic better, accused him of continuing to be a liberal because he regarded religion as a human power, whereas true religion relied on the power to which it was directed—God.[24] But most people saw Reinhold as a critic of liberalism and John Dewey as its chief exponent.

This was certainly the unambiguous message of Niebuhr's provocative *Moral Man and Immoral Society*. In the introduction he quickly took aim at Dewey, quoting a lengthy passage from *Philosophy and Civilization*, then accusing him of unclarity and middle-class bias. Reducing Dewey's notion of social intelligence to a reason that masks its indebtedness to his class's economic interest, Niebuhr insisted that the educator's "moral and rational suasion" was impotent in the face of the persistent class conflict that was due to "our predatory self-interest." The problems of society were not due to ignorance and thus could not be corrected by education. Only power could adequately confront power (xiv–xv). Niebuhr's Marxism is readily apparent, but his Christianity is not so patent. As we will see, however, the accusatory term "predatory self-interest" is a proxy for the original sin in which he believed.

This wedding of Marxism and Christianity was a conscious strategy on Niebuhr's part. Two years later, in 1934, he wrote about the essays published as *Reflections on the End of an Era:* "The basic conviction which runs through them is that the liberal culture of modernity is quite unable to give guidance and direction to a confused generation which faces the disintegration of a social system and the task of building a new one. In my opinion adequate spiritual guidance can come only through a more radical political orientation and more conservative religious convictions than are comprehended in the culture of our era."[25] Eventually Niebuhr backed off the Marxist rhetoric, increasingly finding sufficient resources in the Christian tradition. Bennett observed that Niebuhr "was never an uncritical liberal believer in progress or an uncritical Marxist, but it took him years to see through the illusions of both. Marxism helped him to recognize the illusions of liberal progressivism, and classical Christian theology helped him to see through the illusions of Marxism."[26] But in the 1930s the mix of Christianity and Marxism was an effective weapon in the battle against Dewey's liberalism, enabling Niebuhr to position himself both to the left of Dewey politically and to the right of him religiously. Dewey, who arguably had the more integrated and self-consistent position, was portrayed as an heir of the Enlightenment who lacked a realistic view of the human situation.

Dewey's Limited Response

Although Niebuhr continued to attack Dewey for two decades, the latter limited his reply to two articles in 1933 and 1934 and a veiled discussion in *A Common Faith*. Dewey was concerned, as the title of the first article, "Unity and Progress," signaled, that there be "unified thought and action on the radical front" (LW 9:75). This first article was a response to

Niebuhr's "After Capitalism—What?", which had appeared in the journal *World Tomorrow* in March 1933 the week before Dewey's article. Niebuhr had not mentioned Dewey by name, but he did not have to do so. His reference to "middle-class liberals," given his identification of Dewey as such the previous year in *Moral Man and Immoral Society*, was enough to target his opponent. Dewey chose to reply diplomatically. He did not outright accuse Niebuhr of inconsistency, but he did suggest that "some such outcome seems to follow naturally from his inverted mode of approach" (73). The inversion Dewey discerned was in predicating "political policies for the present upon a conception of what the future is practically sure to be" instead of "finding out what are the urgent needs of the present and then try[ing] to shape policies to meet those needs" (72). The latter, of course, was Dewey's recommended strategy. He then mildly protested that the liberalism attacked by Niebuhr was not what he advocated: "I am concerned only to point out the irrelevancy of his description and condemnation to the kind of procedure which I am proposing" (74).

The 1934 response, "Intelligence and Power," is one to which I have already referred and to which I shall return a bit later in this chapter. It is a crucial text in gaining a balanced view of Dewey's understanding of intelligence. Dewey began by acknowledging that proponents of intelligence could "readily be made to appear ridiculous." He then noted that the alternatives—"habit, custom and tradition"—have not only been more dominant in human history than intelligence, but they have also, he slyly added, "reinforced the power of vested interests" (LW 9:107). It is because intelligence has been overwhelmed in the past and the results have not been favorable that the method of "intelligence and the experimental method is worth a trial." If there had been any doubt to this point about the identity of the critic to whom he was responding, it was removed by a footnote quoting *Moral Man and Immoral Society*. In an allusion to Niebuhr's call to believe "resolutely" the "illusions" that are "the truest visions of religion," Dewey replied, speaking of intelligence: "Illusion for illusion, this particular one may be better than those upon which humanity has usually relied" (108).

There is another reason as well to try the experimental method in social affairs—its success in the physical world. This was a point that Dewey often made, and it would surely have irritated Niebuhr, for it was a part of the "cultural lag" thesis that Niebuhr repeatedly criticized. Dewey first observed that social intelligence had been "misunderstood by critics," explaining: "For it is not held that the particular techniques of the physical sciences are to be literally copied—though of course they are to be utilized wherever applicable—nor that experimentation in the laboratory sense can be carried out on any large scale in social affairs. It is held that the attitude of mind exemplified in the conquest of nature by the experimental sciences, and the method involved in it, may and should be carried into social affairs." What gave this contention "force" was the unattractiveness of the alternative, "dogmatism," which was "reinforced by the weight of unquestioned custom and tradition, the disguised or open play of class interests, [and] dependence upon brute force and violence" (108).

Dewey then noted Niebuhr's objection that the physical and social sciences were dissimilar in what they had or have to overcome. The physical sciences were opposed, wrote Dewey quoting Niebuhr, by "traditionalism based on ignorance," but the social sciences faced a tradition "based upon the economic interest of the dominant social classes." Although ignorance was the problem in the earlier situation, Niebuhr had contended, it was not the problem in the 1930s. Therefore, social intelligence was not the answer. Rather, power must be used against power. Dewey readily conceded that the current traditionalism was supported by socioeconomic power, but, returning Niebuhr's *naïveté* insult, wrote, "It is a naïve view of history that supposes that dominant class interests were not the chief force that maintained the tradition against which the new method and conclusions in physical science had to make their way" (108). In other words, there was a similarity between the earlier and later periods. In both cases tradition was supported by powerful interests. It was only by the rise of newer, comparatively stronger interests that the scientific method became effective in the physical world. And it would be only by an alignment of social intelligence and powerful interests that the experimental method could become effective in the twentieth century in dealing with social affairs. "Here we come to the nub of the matter," he continued. "Intelligence has no power *per se*." Intelligence must be employed by interested, powerful individuals and groups. He then declared: "The real problem is whether there are strong interests now active which can best succeed by adopting the method of experimental intelligence into their struggles, or whether they too should rely upon the use of methods that have brought the world to its present estate, only using them the other way around" (109).

Niebuhr tried to make Dewey into a proponent of a narrow rationalism who would cope with a problem that was reducible to ignorance alone. He then argued that the problems of the 1930s were not primarily due to ignorance, but to the dominance of socioeconomic powers. Hence Dewey's analogy with the scientific revolution was inapplicable. The problem was not one of cultural lag—the social sciences catching up with the physical—but of oppression by powerful class interests. Hence Dewey's proposed social intelligence could not be effective; it was the wrong solution for the time. Dewey replied by reestablishing the analogy—stating that the twentieth century was not that dissimilar from the seventeenth. In both situations strong interests and tradition were aligned. Moreover, the method he advocated was not a self-contained intellectualism, but an intelligized practice, one that worked with and through human interest. Accordingly, in both centuries intelligence had been and must be "incorporated with wants and interests that [were and] are actually operating" (111).

In the same year (1934) as the second essay, Dewey's *A Common Faith* was published. It is useful to examine what Dewey himself said about evil in this, his only book devoted to religion, for it will illustrate his proposed method, as well as the content that Niebuhr found objectionable. It can even be read as an attack on Niebuhr. Although Niebuhr was unnamed, his characteristic positions and even language ("the sinfulness of man, the corruption of his heart, his self-love and love of power") were targeted.

In the third chapter, arguing against the need for an appeal to the supernatural and for the "use of natural means and methods," Dewey considered the causes of evil. He first noted the existence of powerful interests that hinder "the growth and application of the method of natural intelligence." Given this resistance, the advocates of "intelligence" were required to "fight" even more strenuously than they would otherwise have to. "But one of the greatest obstacles in conducting this combat," he continued, "is the tendency to dispose of social evils in terms of general moral causes." This tendency parallels the one that once prevailed in premodern science: "The sinfulness of man, the corruption of his heart, his self-love and love of power, when referred to as causes are precisely of the same nature as was the appeal to abstract powers (which in fact only reduplicated under a general name a multitude of particular effects) that once prevailed in physical 'science,' and that operated as a chief obstacle to the generation and growth of the latter. Demons were once appealed to in order to explain bodily disease and no such thing as a strictly natural death was supposed to happen. The importation of general moral causes to explain present *social* phenomena is on the same intellectual level." This appeal to "general moral causes" is "reinforced by the prestige of traditional religions" and "backed by the emotional force of beliefs in the supernatural." Thus "growth of that social intelligence by means of which direction of social change could be taken out of the region of accident" is stifled. "Accident in [the] broad sense" of nonhuman control "and the idea of the supernatural are twins. Interest in the supernatural therefore reinforces other vested interests to prolong the social reign of accident" (LW 9:51–52).

From Dewey's perspective he was identifying the existing conditions—reliance on the supernatural, acceptance of accident (that is, nonhuman control) in human affairs, and the alliance of both with vested interests—that prevented "the growth of social intelligence." Moreover, the appeal to "general moral causes" to account for "social evils" by religious apologists paralleled the appeal to "abstract powers" at the beginning of the modern era. Therefore, there was an analogy between the physical sciences in the seventeenth century and the social sciences in the twentieth century. Progress in both came (or comes) with attention to specific conditions and consequences and not to unseen, untestable general causes.

Dewey then charged some "contemporary theologians" with being "interested in social change and . . . at the same time depreciat[ing] human intelligence and effort in behalf of the supernatural." Such theologians—he does not name Niebuhr, but the description seems to fit—"are riding two horses that are going in opposite directions." More consistent, Dewey thought, would be either a rejection of a concern for "mere individual salvation of individual souls" and *laissez faire* "in politics and economics" or affirmation of the "old-fashioned ideas of doing something to make the will of God prevail in the world . . . and of assuming the responsibility of doing the job ourselves." But does the description fit Niebuhr? The answer turns, from Dewey's point of view, on the link between belief in the doctrine of original sin and belief in the need for supernatural intervention. To affirm the one was to affirm the other (see LW 9:48-51). Niebuhr thought otherwise. He affirmed his belief in original sin, but did not consider himself a supernaturalist. At this time, according to his intellectual biographer, Richard Fox, "Niebuhr tried to seize the middle ground between the supernaturalist [Karl] Barth and the naturalist Dewey" (164). But even though Niebuhr may have rejected the supernaturalist label, he was not willing to confine God to history alone, as was Dewey, nor was his understanding of God as thoroughly secular as Dewey's. Moreover, Niebuhr was unable, as we will now see, to make intelligible his affirmation of both original sin and human responsibility.

Niebuhr's Affirmation of Absurdity

Niebuhr did not effectively criticize Dewey's social intelligence proposal, as is generally conceded, because he never really engaged it. Dewey rightly complained in both 1933 and 1934 that what he proposed was not what Niebuhr had attacked.[27] But enough has been said of this polemical misrepresentation to establish that Niebuhr was attacking a straw man.

I will now turn to what has not been explicit in Niebuhr thus far, his rhetorical reliance on the doctrine of original sin. I will then show that he did not himself follow the logic of his own belief. Nevertheless, his rhetorical invocation of pervasive, irradicable evil was thought by many to make for a more realistic "pragmatism" than Dewey's "softer" liberalism.

In his review of Dewey's *Liberalism and Social Action* Niebuhr concurred with what Dewey had to say about historic liberalism's emphasis on liberty. The problem was with Dewey's affirmation of liberalism's other emphasis, a reliance on intelligence in social change, for this reliance "betray[ed] a constitutional weakness in the liberal approach to politics."[28] Niebuhr did not spell out what he meant by "constitutional weakness" in this review. Rather, he used his limited space in this secular journal—*The Nation*—to charge that liberalism's intelligence was beholden to the dominant social and economic interests.

To see what Niebuhr understood by "constitutional weakness" one can turn to his religious writings. In *The Children of Light and the Children of Darkness* he asserted that "the doctrine [of original sin] makes an important contribution to any adequate social and political theory"; for "it emphasizes a fact which every page of human history attests. Through it one may understand that . . . there is no level of human moral or social achievement in which there is not some corruption of inordinate self-love."[29] The problem with Dewey and all modernists, then, was that they failed to see that human beings individually and collectively assert themselves in such a way that they corrupt their achievements. This was the "constitutional weakness" of humanity. But this inevitable tendency to sin did not excuse humanity from responsibility: "The Christian doctrine of sin in its classical form offends both rationalists and moralists by maintaining the seemingly absurd position that man sins inevitably and by a fateful necessity but that he is nevertheless to be held responsible for actions which are prompted by an ineluctable fate."[30]

Niebuhr then considered several options, but his final view was that the human situation is one of inevitable sin *and* being held responsible for it. The chapter ended with a declaration that "there is no resource in logical rules to help us understand complex phenomena" and with a discussion of Hegelian and Kierkegaardian dialectic (263).[31] It may well be that the human situation is too complex to be sorted out logically, but then Niebuhr was left with only a weakly defensible middle position between Barth's supernaturalism and Dewey's naturalism. Only those who were satisfied with paradoxical explanations could be satisfied.

But, as it turned out, there was a double paradox. Not only did the doctrine of human depravity not excuse humanity from responsibility; it also did not negate the need for human reason. Despite his criticisms of the pretensions of the latter, Niebuhr did not mean that societies should not try to govern themselves or that intelligence was worthless. Indeed, the subtitle of *The Children of Light* is *A Vindication of Democracy and a Critique of Its Traditional Defense*. Of interest here is Niebuhr's response to Morton White, who had sent him a copy of his critique "Original Sin, Natural Law and Politics." Niebuhr insisted in a July 4, 1956, letter to White that White had misunderstood his "criticism of Dewey," saying if "I criticized him for using intelligence in solving historical problems, what would I do with all the political science and the historical inquiries with which I have spent my life?"[32] Clearly, Niebuhr did not think that his affirmation of the doctrine of original sin precluded the use of intelligence. Human beings were still responsible for their own actions, and intelligence was an important tool. In *Faith and History* he declared, "Scientific knowledge of what human nature is and how it reacts to various given social situations will always be of service in refashioning human conduct."[33]

Despite Niebuhr's prophetic thunderings about secular arrogance, then, the issue between Niebuhr and Dewey came down not to whether one should be intelligent or not, but to a debate over the the scope of intelligence in human affairs. Dewey thought that one could rely on an appropriately expansive intelligence—that is, one that affirmed interest and recognized power; Niebuhr thought there were limits that Dewey did not recognize. As Niebuhr said in the letter to White, "My criticism of Dewey is that he follows the Comptean thesis that it is comparatively easy to transfer the objectivity of the natural sciences to historical inquiries, if only these sciences can be freed of the heavy hand of 'church and state'" (Rice, pp. 204–205). But, as we have seen, this charge of scientism was one Dewey could escape.

Fox, examining Niebuhr's temperate review of Dewey's *A Common Faith*, in which Niebuhr suggested that Dewey's faith was closer to his own prophetic faith than Dewey realized, concluded that "Niebuhr's analysis actually revealed, despite his intention," just "how close his own prophetic faith was to Dewey" and "how far away it was from Barth." Niebuhr's "starting point, like Dewey's, was man's drive for meaning and his quest to realize ideals in history. His religion and Dewey's were, as Richard [Niebuhr] had earlier shown, religions of human power. Niebuhr might put more stress on the pitfalls that men encountered—social structures, human pride—but Dewey was scarcely unmindful of them. Niebuhr could not have stomached the thought" that "his faith was shot through with the very liberalism that he flailed at and caricatured. Like Dewey he was a pragmatist, a relativist, and a pluralist at heart. He hated absolutism of any kind. Life was an adventure in which people could create their own world if they had the courage and intelligence to do so" (165). Fox, in my view, overemphasizes the similarities and ignores crucial differences. Niebuhr and Dewey were both pragmatic and pluralistic, but Niebuhr was comfortable in a reconstructed Augustinian Christianity and Dewey had ceased being Christian at all. Also, Niebuhr was rhetorically freer—some would say irresponsibly so—than the more plainspoken Dewey.

One of the difficulties in understanding Dewey is to learn to appreciate his pervasive concern for the ordinary, the mundane. He thought that the way forward was by developing the possibilities of everyday life. He contended that it was regressive to continue to rely on doctrines, such as original sin, that had arisen in a premodern past and were no longer useful in making sense of the present. Contemporary human beings, he argued, were divided in their loyalties. In matters of commerce and practical matters, they looked to science and technology, but in matters of morality they relied on beliefs they were unwilling to criticize. In the closing paragraph of *Reconstruction in Philosophy* he wrote: "We are weak today in ideal matters because intelligence is divorced from aspiration. The bare force of circumstance compels us onwards in the daily detail of our beliefs and acts, but our deeper thoughts and desires turn backwards. When philosophy shall have cooperated with the course of events and made clear and coherent the meaning of daily detail, science and emotion will interpenetrate, practice and imagination will embrace" (MW 12:201). Dewey thought one began with "the daily detail," making its meaning "clear and coherent." Niebuhr, from Dewey's point of view, was a dualist, separating the mundane (or secular) and the sacred. But Niebuhr was more complicated than this. What made him interesting and appealing was his ability to speak in both sacred and secular terms. Unfortunately, as we have seen, this mixture was often a volatile one, combining elements that could not be harmonized. But it was this very volatility that made him more attractive than the more ordinary, if consistent, Dewey. Next to the prophetic Niebuhr Dewey appeared quite mundane.

DEWEY AND THE MEANS FOR SOCIAL RECONSTRUCTION

It is to Dewey's mundane method of social and political reconstruction that we now turn. Unless we can grasp the possibilities that Dewey sensed in the ordinary interactions of life, we will not be able to grasp his distinctive approach. Where others saw the need for a reliance on the irrational and an embracing of the instruments of power, even violence, Dewey aspired to a more intelligent—yes, educational—approach.

Dewey's Cultural Instrumentalism

Once again we are at the heart of the issue. Some thought that Dewey had replaced politics and its inevitable concern for the distribution of power with a nonpolitical—and, they thought ineffective—concern for education. But Dewey thought that, in reality, he had developed his social and political philosophy instrumentally. He was reconstructing politics by making explicit the instrumental character of education, intelligence, and democracy. Such talk disappointed his critics, for it struck them as preparatory, vague, or inadequate. But Dewey thought education, intelligence, and democracy were crucial to social and political reconstruction; they were of the utmost importance in remaking society. To expand Dewey's answer to the question of the appropriate means for social transformation, I will begin with the instrumentalist point, a consideration of which will open up the rest of Dewey's answer—namely, the part about education, intelligence, and democracy.

Dewey once remarked that *The Public and Its Problems* (1927) was his most "instrumental" book.[34] Dewey's remark is significant for Hu Shih, who was China's ambassador to the United States, because the question posed in Hu's paper, "The Political Philosophy of Instrumentalism," was "Has Dewey worked out a political philosophy that can be regarded as consistent with his logical theory of instrumentalism?" (205). Hu's conclusion was that Dewey had proposed such a theory, but had shelved it (218). It is true that there was a shift in Dewey's political views, but it was not the case that Dewey abandoned his instrumentalism, logical or political.

Hu identified several Deweyan emphases or even distinct political theories. The first was that of the national state as "conductor"—that is, "an instrumentality for promoting and protecting other and more voluntary forms of association" (MW 12:196; Hu, 209). The second could be found in *The Public and Its Problems* (1927). There the state was understood as an organized public, functioning through its designated representatives to protect the public's interests. But Hu regarded this as still "too 'neutral' and too indefinite to be truly instrumental" (211). But, since Dewey regarded *The Public and Its Problems* as his "most instrumental book," either the two men did not understand *instrumental* in the same way or they disagreed about its application or both.

Hu's understanding of *instrumental* is made clear in the next section of his essay. He began with this announcement: "After rereading practically all

the political writings of Dewey, I have come to the conclusion that he began
to work out a truly instrumentalist political philosophy early in 1916, but,
for some unknown reason, has apparently never taken up nor continued to
develop this instrumentalist line of political thought during the last quarter
of a century" (212). In the 1916 essays Dewey had developed a threefold
distinction between force as energy, coercion, and violence. *Energy* he
defined as "effective means of operation"; it "means nothing but the sum of
conditions available for bringing [a] desirable end into existence" (MW
10:246). To go to the other extreme, he defined *violence* as force "run
amuck" (246); it is idle or destructive (MW 10:212). *Coercion* however,
had similarities to each of the extremes, falling in the middle. Functioning
as a constraint, it, like energy, accomplished some purpose. But as a constraint it, like violence, seemed to the one being constrained as idle or
destructive. Dewey's example was that of traffic regulations: "To turn to the
right as an incident of locomotion is a case of power [or energy]: of means
deployed in behalf of an end. To run amuck in the street is a case of violence. To use energy to make a man observe the rule of the road is a case of
coercive force. Immediately, or with respect to his activities, it is a case of
violence; indirectly, when it is exercised to assure the means which are
needed for the successful realization of ends, it is a case of constructive use
of power." Law, then, was coercion. It was the organization of force, which,
if left unorganized, would "result in violence" (10:246).

The state, as Hu pointed out, "may be conceived as an instrumentality
for the effective realization of definite human ends." The resulting political
theory, he thought, was Dewey's "most daring and most original attempt to
develop a political philosophy on the foundation of logical instrumentalism"
(217). But such a theory tended "toward undue expansion of governmental
power and unwarranted governmental interference." Hu then observed:
"Probably this danger of seeming to justify too great governmental interference led Dewey to shelve a theory which is undoubtedly far more consonant
with his instrumental logic than his other political theories" (218). It is true
that in the late 1930s Dewey came to prefer a more voluntary, cooperative
form of socialism than the version he preferred earlier in the decade that
looked to governmental solutions. But it is not the case that this development meant that his political thought was less instrumental. After docu-
menting the change, I will make good on my claim that Dewey's altered
political perspective was nevertheless still an instrumental one.

In a 1939 letter to Hu, Dewey acknowledged that he had become "more
socialistic" earlier in the decade: "You are quite right in suggesting that my
political philosophy has changed in emphasis at least at various times,

according to what was uppermost at the time. The economic collapse, the reaction from the capitalist orgies of the twenties, made me more socialistic than I had been."[35] But, as the decade progressed, there had been another shift. It is this "last change" that was reflected in "I Believe," a statement also written in 1939. There Dewey noted that there had been a change of emphasis in his views from a previous statement of his beliefs in 1931. As a result of the political events of the decade, notably the rise of fascism and the "decline of democracy," he had come to place more emphasis on the role of individuals and less on that of the state. But this did not mean a lessening of his faith in "associated life." He wrote: "In re-thinking this issue in the light of the rise of totalitarian states, I am led to emphasize the idea that only the voluntary initiative and voluntary cooperation of individuals can produce social institutions that will protect the liberties neccessary for achieving development of genuine individuality" (LW 14:91–92). He now envisioned, but did not spell out, a less statist form of socialism, one that stressed the role of voluntary and cooperative institutions.[36]

But did this change represent a "shelving" of Dewey's political instrumentalism? The answer turns on the meaning and application of the notion of instrumentalism. For Hu a truly instrumentalist political theory required an expansive and interventionist state; for Dewey it did not. Hu thought only an activist state could be the means necessary to bring about the ends desired: "The state is a tool for us to use, to experiment with, to master and control, to love and cherish—but not something to be afraid of" (219). But Dewey had come to realize that the state was not the main constitutive means for the realization of the desired human ends. The state, given appropriate "democratic control," could be the "powerful instrumentality" that Hu envisioned; but Dewey was concerned, because of the "present conditions," that "the instrumentality [could] become itself an end." Therefore, he emphasized "voluntary initiative and cooperations," insisting that they were the "prerequisites of a state or government that can be the instrumentality required" (Dewey to Hu, October 27, 1939).

Instrumentalism, as usually conceived, is taken to be a focusing on means or technique. One pays attention to the way in which some end is achieved. Dewey often made this point, insisting on the role of ideas and theories as means. Intellectual products did not have to be idle or irrelevant; they could be means. Indeed intelligence, properly understood, was the employment of mental products as means to the realization of one's ends. For instance, in *Art as Experience* Dewey declared, "Knowledge is instrumental to the enrichment of immediate experience through the control over action that it exercises" (LW 10:294). It was this concern for ideas as instruments that prompted the criticisms of Niebuhr, Mills, and others. They thought Dewey was relying exclusively on nonphysical means, on mere ideas or education alone. Therefore, he had to insist, as he did in "Intelligence and Power": "Intelligence becomes a *power* only when it is brought into the operation of other forces than itself" (LW 9:109). Then, in a manner reminiscent of the 1916 articles discussed by Hu, he continued: "But power is a blanket term and covers a multitude of different things. Everything that is done is done by some power—that is a truism. But violence and war are powers, finance is a power, newspapers, publicity agents and propaganda are powers, churches and the beliefs they have inculcated are powers, as well as a multitude of other things. Persuasion and conference are also powers, although it is easy to overestimate the degree of their power in the existing economic and international system. In short, we have not said anything so long as we have merely said power. What first is needed is discrimination, knowledge of the distribution of power" (LW 9:111). Intelligence is this discrimination. It is the *effective* use of force or power.

Dewey's instrumentalism was not reducible to a concentration on means or instruments. Closer to the mark was his insistence on the means-ends continuum. A Deweyan instrumentalism, despite the nominal focus on instruments, actually paid attention to means and ends. As Dewey insisted, "Means and ends are two names for the same reality" (MW 14:28). What distinguished them was perspective or judgment. The end was but the last act in a contemplated series; the means were the acts leading to this temporally final one. But this last event could well be a means in some other contemplated series of events. Even more, as will be developed more fully later, an end-in-view, one's intended end or objective, served as a means to the actual end or result. Therefore, one of the means to the actual result was itself an "end" of sorts, that which Dewey called an "end-in-view."

The developments in the 1930s had led Dewey to question the value of a centralized, coercive state that was not sufficiently continuous with the open society he envisoned. But this was not a new understanding of instrumentalism, for it reflected his long-standing view that the best means were those that were continuous with both the end sought (the end-in-view) and one's commitment to democratic participation. What changed was his conception of the value of an activist state as a means to a democratic society. In his October 27, 1939, letter to Hu Dewey made explicit the nature of his political instrumentalism: "Probably the best balanced of my writings is The Public and its Problems, and also the most 'instrumental', at least by implication, for it brings out more the principle of relativity. . . . But unfortunately [I] did not make that fact explicitly conscious to myself and so not to readers." The phrase "principle of relativity" is actually Hu's phrase, which he used to express the Deweyan principle that an inquiry should address "specified spatio-temporal conditions."[37] We are to understand that Dewey had come to realize that what he had written twelve years earlier in *The Public and Its Problems* was his "most" instrumental work in the sense that it was directed to the problems of the time. He had not made this problem-orientation sufficiently clear. Therefore, many readers took his book (and many still take it today) to be a work in political theory, not realizing that the theoretical early part was directed toward a problem-solving end.

In his response to Hu Dewey then wrote, "I had meant . . . to emphasize—what was implicit but not explicit in my earlier statements—the absolute importance of democratic action in determining the policies of the government—for only by means of 'government by the people' can government *for* the people be made secure" (LW 2:430). Therefore, he had not made as explicit in 1927 as he was to come to realize in 1939 "the absolute importance of democratic action in determining the policies of the government." Dewey had a sense that democratic ends required democratic means, but he did not fully appreciate this until sometime in the 1930s.

"Genuine Instrumentality" and Democratic Means

To understand Dewey's insight about the necessity of democratic means we need to consider his notion of "genuine instrumentality" and relate it to his discussion of the need for democratic means in the latter part of *The Public and Its Problems*. A valuable discussion of "genuine instrumentality" is found in a consideration of art in *Experience and Nature*. After noting that "the prevailing conception of instrumentality" fastened only on the temporal succession of events, observing that the prior event was a means to the latter, Dewey turned to his own understanding. Means are causes and therefore temporally prior, and ends are effects and thus temporally posterior. But, he argued, what distinguished them as means and ends is "an added qualification": Means become so by "being freely used, because of perceived connection with chosen consequences" (LW 1:275).

Dewey's instrumentalism required a concentration not just on means, but also on ends. Moreover, this attention to causes and effects should be sufficiently well informed and imaginative that one could trace out a variety of causal relationships and choose the best route to the desired end. And the best route would be one in which means and ends were compatible with one another. This compatibility would be attained when the means were constitutive of the end. Dewey offered several examples: "Paints and skill in manipulative arrangement are means of a picture as end, because the picture is *their* assemblage and organization. Tones and susceptibility of the ear when properly interacting are the means of music, because they constitute, make, are, music. . . . A good political constitution, honest police-system, and competent judiciary, are means of the prosperous life of the community because they are integrated portions of that life." Then, in summing up his own understanding, he recapitulated the point about the limitation of temporal succession as the defining feature and made his positive point: "The connection of means-consequences is never one of bare succession in time, such that the element that is means is past and gone when the end is instituted. An active process is strung out temporally, but there is a deposit at each stage and point entering cumulatively and constitutively into the outcome. A genuine instrumentality *for* is always an organ *of* an end. It confers continued efficacy upon the object in which it is embodied" (LW 1:275–76).[38]

Dewey's instrumentalism, then, was not an exclusive concern with means. It was an advocacy of a constitutive instrumentality in which the means were integral to the end sought. Moreover, it required—indeed, it constituted—intelligence as he understood it. To be intelligent was to be able to choose among alternative causal connections the one that best achieved the desired end. This choice, he contended, would be the one in which the means were constitutive of the end.

The relevant example of "genuine instrumentality" in *The Public and Its Problems* is found at the beginning of the next-to-last chapter, "The Search for the Great Community." After making his characteristic distinction between "democracy as a social idea and political democracy," Dewey rejected "the old saying that the cure for ills of democracy is more democracy," if what was meant by this was "more [political] machinery of the same kind as that which already exists, or by refining and perfecting that machinery" (LW 2:325). But if what was meant was that there would be an expansion of "democracy as a social idea" such that the public could more meaningfully participate in its own governance, then "in this sense the cure for the ailments of democracy is more democracy." He then declared, "The prime difficulty . . . is that of discovering the means by which a scattered, mobile and manifold public may so recognize itself as to define and express its interests" (327). But neither in this nor in subsequent books did Dewey specify precisely and completely the forms that the resultant political democracy would take. All he could do, or so he thought in 1927, was specify some of the conditions that were necessary.

I quote again the passage that I quoted earlier in this chapter: "The prime condition of a democratically organized public is a kind of knowledge and insight which does not yet exist. In its absence, it would be the height of absurdity to try to tell what it would be like if it existed. But some of the conditions which must be fulfilled if it is to exist can be indicated. We can borrow that much from the spirit and method of science even if we are ignorant of it as a specialized apparatus. An obvious requirement is freedom of social inquiry and of distribution of its conclusions" (339). In 1927 Dewey knew that the democratic practice of free social inquiry was essential to the creation of the Great Community. What he apparently did not fully realize and make explicit at that time was the extent to which this and other democratic practices were some of the constitutive means of the democracy he desired. Therefore, Dewey was vulnerable to the criticism that he failed to specify the political means required to organize a public that was, in his own terms, in an "inchoate and amorphous estate" (LW 2:313). By limiting himself to the task of "search[ing] for conditions under which the Great Society may become the Great Community" (LW 2:327), Dewey not only failed to counter Lippmann's claim that democracy was beyond the competence of most people, but he also failed to meet his own criteria for the reciprocity of means and ends. Unable to specify precisely the means, he was, according to his own doctrine of "genuine instrumentality," unable to specify the end. Where his philosophy permitted no gap, there appeared to be one.

But, at least by late 1939, he had a better grip on the solution. In the same month as the letter to Hu Shih and on the same day (October 13) as he mailed "Creative Democracy—The Task Before Us" to Horace Kallen for the latter to read at the eightieth birthday celebration on October 20, Dewey's message, "Democratic Ends Need Democratic Methods for Their Realization," was read to the first public meeting of the Committee for Cultural Freedom. The title was adapted from a line in the speech and conveyed succinctly his message. Some of the methods he identified were the "methods of consultation, persuasion, negotiation, cooperative intelligence" and were to be practiced in "politics, industry, education—our culture generally." Moreover, democracy could "be served only by the slow day by day adoption and contagious diffusion in every phase of our common life of methods that are identical with the ends to be reached" (LW 14:367–68).

Democracy, then, for Dewey is political machinery—frequent elections, universal suffrage, majority rule, protection of minorities—but it is more than this as well. It is also, and more fundamentally, the day-to-day practices of "consultation, persuasion, negotiation, cooperative intelligence." But these activities not only define democracy; they are also both end and means. Democracy as an end comes about by engaging in "consultation, persuasion, negotiation, cooperative intelligence." These democratic activities are the "genuine instrumentalities" of democracy. They are both means and end.

The trouble with this way of putting the matter is that it emphasizes the discursive, slighting Dewey's recognition of the continuing role of power in our lives. This recognition in the foregoing statement, if present at all, is buried in the word *intelligence*. An unsuspecting reader would most probably take Dewey's listing of democratic means in such a way as to limit democracy to talking and thinking. This interpretation receives support from Dewey's explicit rejection of "military force" in both the October 13 speech cited above (LW 14:367) and the parallel passage in *Freedom and Culture* (LW 13:187) written at the same time (see "Textual Commentary," LW 13:415). Democratic means would seem to be limited to talking and thinking, exclusive of physical and institutional force. But they are not.

At the end of this chapter I will return to the problem of a lack of political technology, a lack Dewey acknowledged. But first I will consider a recent historical treatment of Dewey's limited success in overcoming this gap between his cultural instrumentalism and a realized political technology.

Westbrook's Assessment of Dewey's Political Instrumentalism

Westbrook's *John Dewey and American Democracy* is a well-received, full, informed history of Dewey as a publicly engaged democratic thinker. Although sympathetic with Dewey's political vision, Westbrook is critical of his lack of a political technology. In Westbrook's view, in only two instances—his efforts in the outlawry-of-war movement and his participation in radical politics in the 1930s—did Dewey develop a political means consistent with his desired moral end; otherwise either his means were insufficient to achieve the democratic end or, in what amounts to the same thing, the means employed were themselves undemocratic. I will examine Westbrook's critique by discussing his treatment of three cases: Dewey's political advice to the Chinese, his intervention in the Polish question, and his participation in the outlawry-of-war movement. But before I consider these cases, I need to fill in some background regarding Westbrook and what he brings to his study of Dewey.[39]

Westbrook was clearly motivated by a concern to establish that Dewey was not a maker of the dominant version of liberalism in this century, but rather a radical, minority voice. Liberalism had been captured by the realists and elitists who thought that most people were neither intelligent enough nor good enough to be trusted with self-governance. Dewey was not, however, "the father of 'democratic elitism,'" as Westbrook had initially been led to believe as a Stanford University graduate student in the 1970s. Rather, he was "the most significant American liberal theorist who had refused to back away from a commitment to an expansive democratic ideal."[40] In the preface to his book on Dewey he identifies Dewey as "the most important advocate of participatory democracy" among twentieth-century liberal intellectuals and writes that he understands this form of democracy as pivoting on "the belief that democracy as an ethical ideal calls upon men and women to build communities in which the necessary opportunities and resources are available for every individual to realize fully his or her particular capacities and powers through participation in political, social, and cultural life" (xv). But, as I have noted, in this book Westbrook is not uncritical of Dewey.

Westbrook reports that over time he came to believe that Dewey "was never able to constitute participatory democracy as a compelling working end."[41] Nor did he "provide any evidence that the means were at hand" to reconstruct "a democratic public sphere." Westbrook reluctantly concedes that Walter Lippmann, the true father of "democratic elitism," had gotten "the better of Dewey in their debate in the 1920's" on the role of citizens in public life (29:505). Dewey never adequately answered the challenge of Lippmann, because Dewey was not able to identify the means by which the public could effectively organize itself to meet its needs.[42]

Westbrook regrets that his narrating of "Dewey's weaknesses" has become ammunition for the foes of direct democracy, such as William Galston,[43] for Westbrook shares Dewey's faith. In a review of Jim Campbell's *The Community Reconstructs* he declares: "Now, even more than in the 1930's, we require a politics that not only will address our mind-numbing social problems but one that will in the process rebuild and expand the institutions of a fully participatory, democratic public life—a politics that has not been practiced on a mass scale in this country since the organizing drives of the CIO during the Depression and the Civil Rights movement of the early 1960s."[44] Westbrook, the historian, can find little evidence of participatory democracy in our national life. Nor does he think, as we have seen, that Dewey was able to supply a working model. This is his principal criticism of Dewey as a political theorist.

There are several examples of this critique in Westbrook's book, for he amply documents Dewey's failings and finds only occasional, qualified successes in this regard. As promised, I will discuss three. The first two are regarded as outright failures; the third is a qualified success at best.

On Dewey's Giving Political Advice to the Chinese

One instance of Dewey's political ineptitude cited by Westbrook was Dewey's giving advice to the Chinese during a two-year stay in China arranged by Hu Shih and others. In addition to lecturing in Beijing and

Nanjing, Dewey visited more than half of China's provinces. After describing Dewey's stay and lectures, Westbrook offers this judgment: "Dewey was not the man to talk politics with the Chinese in the early twenties." He then outlines the problem Dewey faced: "Securing the society he urged them to create required both politics and education or, to be more exact, a strategy that would simutaneously make and empower democratic citizens—a political movement that would prefigure the democratic society it sought in its own institutions and 'movement culture,' and would struggle for the power to extend those institutions and that culture." Westbrook identifies the failure: "But while he repeatedly called in the abstract for the steeling of idealism with force, Dewey had yet to conceive of an exercise of force, a politics, which would be at once effective and democratic."

Continuing, Westbrook refers to Dewey's political shifts during and after World War I in order to illustrate and extend his thesis about the limitations of Dewey's political thinking: "When confronted with particular political problems during the war and its immediate aftermath, he had fluctuated wildly between sentimental moral exhortation and hard-boiled defense of the counterproductive violence of war without carefully considering the combinations of idealism and force which might lie between these extremes." Then Westbrook returns to the Chinese and their situation: "To the Chinese, Dewey proposed radically democratic ends without proposing means commensurate with those ends, and—though it is unlikely, given the situation in China, that creative political thinking by a visiting American philosopher would have made much difference—he did little to help resolve the strategic dilemmas of his disciples. Although the Deweyans dominated Chinese educational theory from 1919 until 1927, they were subsequently swept aside with ease by revolutionaries who thought first of power and whose movement culture was far from democratic."[45] Westbrook charges Dewey with failing to provide "means commensurate with the proposed ends." In effect, he accuses Dewey of not exemplifying his own theory of "genuine instrumentality." Moreover, he believes the consensual tools of conversation and deliberation would not lead to the desired end, for they depended on a societal consensus that did not exist. Therefore, Dewey's proposals were ineffective. Indeed, his followers lost out to the "revolutionaries who thought first of power and whose movement culture was far from democratic." This, of course, is the realist critique of Niebuhr and Mills: Dewey's reliance on education and intelligence could not succeed against power politics as it is played in the real world.

On Dewey's Intervention in "The Polish Question"

When Dewey did attempt to play power politics, such as in his intervention in what has become known as the Polish question, he was forced to abandon his reliance on democratic means. *The Polish question* refers to a 1918 study financed by Albert Barnes and carried out by Dewey and some of his graduate students. Attempting to understand the difficulty of integrating an immigrant community into a democratic society, Dewey and his students set out to understand the Polish community in Philadelphia, but became involved in an effort to influence the Wilson administration's efforts to deal with the Polish community nationally. Dewey wrote confidential reports to the War Department and even met with Woodrow Wilson's political advisor, Col. Edward M. House ("Note on 'Confidential Report of Conditions among the Poles in the United States,'" MW 11:398–408).

After a few months of investigation, Dewey had determined that an impending meeting of Poles in Detroit should be postponed. This gathering was designed to support a bill in Congress that would recognize what Dewey had concluded was the undemocratic faction in Polish politics; moreover, the upcoming convention was itself undemocratic in its organization. But Dewey was unsuccesful in trying to prevent the Detroit meeting. The convention was held, and the Wilson administration recognized the faction that Dewey judged to be undemocratic.

I want to call attention to Westbrook's charge that "Dewey, in the name of democratic self-determination, called for the state to intervene undemocratically in the undemocratic politics of the Polish-American community." Not limiting himself to "calls for procedural reform of Polish politics and freedom of the Polish press," Dewey, "no less than the Polish reactionaries he was battling, was anxious to secure a rigged convention." Then, in a nice turn of phrase, Westbrook concludes: "Just as he supported a war to end war, Dewey here called for manipulation to end manipulation" (220–21). For Westbrook Dewey was in these two episodes either ineffective, as seen in his giving advice in China, or, as in his intervention in Polish-American affairs, undemocratic. Dewey's 1939 principle—democratic ends require democratic means—is, on Westbrook's analysis of these two affairs, untenable in the first and untried in the second. But Westbrook's analysis is not universal; he finds hope in another of Dewey's involvements.

On Dewey's Efforts to Outlaw War

Dewey's hopes that democratic developments would result from American involvement in World War I were severely disappointed. He acknowleged in 1919 that the "defeat of idealistic aims has been, without exaggeration, enormous." America had entered the war prematurely, failing to secure the necessary Allied commitment to democratic ends. Force had not been used "adequately and intelligently" (MW 11:181). Westbrook takes this admission as a partial acknowledgement of "the logic of Bourne's pragmatic critique" of Dewey's support of Wilson's war effort (240). A full recognition of the argument advanced by Bourne—but not that it was Bourne's argument—that war by its very nature requires undemocratic techniques came, according to Westbrook, with Dewey's participation in the effort to outlaw war in the 1920s.

The movement, initiated by S. O. Levinson, a Chicago lawyer, resulted in the Kellogg-Briand Pact of 1928. In the Pact of Paris, as it was also known, France, the United States, Great Britain, Japan, and several other nations condemned war and renounced it, Westbrook reports, "as an instrument of national policy and agreed to settle conflicts among themselves by peaceful means" (272). Dewey, however, was disappointed in the result because the method of adoption was not what he had recommended. The Paris Pact had become just another treaty brought about by diplomatic maneuvering and was not, as he had insisted was necessary, the result of "irresistible public demand" (LW 6:190).

Dewey's analysis is characteristic, revealing much about his approach to social transformation. In a 1923 essay in the *New Republic*, "If War Were Outlawed," he noted that in time of war "moral conviction and sentiment have no channels of operation." Citizens who were opposed to war were caught "in a tragic moral predicament": If they supported the war that their country, whose protection and benefits they enjoyed, had decided must be waged, they denied their consciences. As long as war was recognized as a legitimate means of effecting national policy, there was no middle ground; either one supported his nation and denied his own conscience or he followed his moral convictions and stood against the country that sustained him (MW 15:111). Certainly Dewey and others had been in this bind in World War I. Dewey had reluctantly chosen to support the war and had been much disappointed with many of the war's results. The way out, a third option beyond supporting one's country in war or failing to support one's country because one was a pacifist, was to outlaw war. If nations rejected war as a way to pursue their ends, changed international agreements to reflect this rejection, and agreed to resolve their differences through negotiation and, if necessary, submitting international disuputes to a world court, the social misfit would not be the pacifist, but the nation that went to war.

Although some proponents of outlawing war were willing to resort to military sanctions to enforce an international agreement outlawing war, Dewey clearly saw the inconsistency. He proposed instead that public opinion be mobilized in such a way that a nation would be prevented from going to war by its own people. He argued that the end sought—outlawing war—could be effected by the very means of outlawing war, provided that these means included the full participation of the people. Two points are crucial for understanding Dewey's thinking: one, the necessity of mobilizing popular support, and two, the functioning of this support as the necessary (and constitutive) means to the end sought. Regarding the necessity of popular participation, Dewey declared: "Other schemes for peace, excepting the purely educational and moral ones, have relied upon the initiative of rulers, politicians or statesmen, as has been the case, for example, in the constitution of the League of Nations." But this one "is a movement for peace which starts from the peoples themselves, which expresses their will, and demands that the legislators and politicians and the diplomats give effect to the popular will for peace. It has the advantages of the popular education movement, but unlike the other educational movements for peace it has a definite, simple, practical legislative goal" (MW 15:100).

The genius of this approach, from Joseph Ratner's and Westbrook's point of view, is that means and ends are, in Ratner's words, "conceived together as integral parts of one whole and progressive historical process"; they are "qualitatively continuous with one another and functionally interactive with one another." This is so because the means (popular ratification of the plan) would create a World Court that would issue decisions (the end sought) that would reinforce the means (popular support). Therefore, means and ends would be reciprocal. Ratner concludes, "The Outlawry Plan fulfills the basic requirements of Dewey's philosophy of instrumentalism; it admirably and completely exemplifies his conception of *the method of intelligence* in social affairs."[46] Westbrook agrees, writing, "Dewey's writing on outlawry did for the first time envision a politics consistent with his ethics, a politics that dialectically related democratic means and ends and might well be applied to more modest projects than the democratization of the world" (270).

Therefore, a politics consistent with Dewey's ethics would consist of the usual sorts of methods of political organization, education and action. Nothing remarkable would be required. No doubt there would be committees, public statements and debate, elections, legislative action, and diplomatic agreements. The point Dewey emphasized was that the initiative should belong to the public, and the agreement—unlike in the case of the

Paris Pact—would come at the end of extensive campaigns of public education in the various countries. If this had occurred, Ratner and Westbrook
insist, Dewey's political instrumentalism would have been realized; a means
consistent with the ends would have been found.

Dewey's View of Politics as Social Intelligence

Westbrook's way of putting the matter is misleading. It is not the case
that Dewey "envision[ed] for the first time a politics consistent with his
ethics." Dewey had been insisting all along on the importance of education
construed both broadly and narrowly. The political means that Westbrook
thinks Dewey discovered in the outlawry-of-war proposal were as much
educational as they were political. Westbrook writes, "As Dewey conceived
it, the means for securing the outlawry plan—the creation of active, well-
informed, vigilant, democratic publics in the nations of the world—was
subsequently to serve as the means for making it effective" (270). Writing
in 1933, Dewey himself summarized the outlawry proposal, noting that the
proposed change in international law was "to be effected or attended by
national plebiscites to insure the education and registration of public opinion" (LW 8:14). Westbrook's comment on Dewey's summary calls attention to the formation and subsequent action of these "democratic publics":
"The most important difference in Dewey's version of outlawry lay in its
concern with the means by which war would be outlawed. For Dewey, it
was absolutely essential that this be the act of democratic publics. Insofar
as such publics did not exist, they had to be created if outlawry was to
work" (269).

But what was novel about Dewey's outlawry proposal did not lie in the
recommended means—at least not for Dewey. The understanding of politics
as a form of education and the insistence on consulting the people affected
by a public policy were not new ideas for Dewey. Indeed, they are to be
found in the very book—*The Public and Its Problems*—that Westbrook
judged to be an inadequate response to Lippmann's challenge. As
Westbrook wrote: "Dewey could not dispute Lippmann's contention that
the public had become a phantom, and although he offered a powerful ethical argument in *The Public and Its Problems* for reconstructing a democratic public sphere, his inability to provide any evidence that the means were
at hand to do so only enhanced the effectiveness of Lippmann's contention
that it was time to forego participatory democracy. If ideals were not to be
fantasies, Dewey said, they had to be constituted as 'working ends,' but he
was never able to constitute participatory democracy as a compelling working end."[47] This passage clearly shows that Westbrook does not think that

Dewey matched his ethical notion of democracy with an adequate means "for reconstructing a democratic public sphere." Yet, as we saw in the previous section, Westbrook thinks that in his outlawry- of-war proposal Dewey did "envision . . . for the first time a politics consistent with his ethics." But Westbrook is mistaken, for, as I will now show, the solution achieved in the outlawry-of-war proposal is found—*in principle*—in *The Public and Its Problems*. In other words, the solution is there, but not the issue of outlawing war.

Dewey's Sociopolitical Technology

The proposal of using politics as a form of education and the related nonelitist understanding of democracy are found together in the last chapter of *The Public and Its Problems*. Challenging Lippmann's thesis that democracy must rely on experts and insiders because the omnicompetent citizen was an illusion, Dewey proposed an alternative. He suggested it as early as 1922 in his review of Lippmann's *Public Opinion* and then filled it out in his 1927 book-length reply to Lippmann's two books, the second of which was *The Phantom Public* (1925). I will begin with the review and then turn to the fuller treatment in *The Public and Its Problems*.

Dewey thought that much of the analysis of his fellow contributor to *The New Republic* was correct, but he could not accept the limited role assigned to the public. He closed his review of the 1922 book with these words of praise and disagreement: "Mr. Lippmann has thrown into clearer relief than any other writer the fundamental difficulty of democracy [an uninformed public]. But the difficulty is so fundamental that it can be met, it seems to me, only by a solution more fundamental than he has dared to give. When necessity drives, invention and accomplishment may amazingly respond. Democracy demands a more thoroughgoing education than the education of officials, administrators and directors of industry. Because this fundamental general education is at once so necessary and so difficult of achievement, the enterprise of democracy is so challenging. To sidetrack it to the task of enlightenment of administrators and executives is to miss something of its range and its challenge" (MW 13:344). Dewey only alluded to his alternative in the phrase *fundamental general education*, but clearly the elements of his nonelitist approach to democracy were present in this 1922 review.

Dewey's development of these elements came five years later. Before concluding the *The Public and Its Problems* with his famous call for the restoration of face-to-face communities, Dewey took up the problem of "the relation of experts to a democratic public" (LW 2:362). He shrewdly noted that the argument for reliance on experts by an incompetent public "proves too much," writing: "If the masses are as intellectually irredeemable as its premise implies, they at all events have both too many desires and too much power to permit rule by experts to obtain. The very ignorance, bias, frivolity, jealousy, instability, which are alleged to incapacitate them from a share in political affairs, unfit them still more for passive submission to rule by intellectuals" (363). But a more serious objection is that an elite ruling class is too remote from the people they serve to be effective: "In the degree in which they become a specialized class, they are shut off from knowledge of the needs which they are supposed to serve" (364). This is in fact the strength of democracy's political forms as they have developed thus far: "Popular voting, majority rule and so on . . . to some extent . . . involve a consultation and discussion which uncover social needs and troubles."

Dewey next cited de Tocqueville's observation that "popular government is educative as other modes of political regulation are not. It forces a recognition that there are common interests, even though the recognition of *what* they are is confused; and the need it enforces of discussion and publicity brings about some clarification of what they are." He then employed one of his favorite examples: "The man who wears the shoe knows best that it pinches and where it pinches, even if the expert shoemaker is the best judge of how the trouble is to be remedied." Hence political leaders need to consult continually with the electorate. Dewey then pointed out the deeper meaning of majority rule: It is more than a political mechanism; it is a educational process as well. "Majority rule, just as majority rule, is as foolish as its critics charge it with being. But it never is *merely* majority rule. As a practical politician, Samuel J. Tilden, said a long time ago: 'The means by which a majority comes to be a majority is the more important thing': antecedent debates, modification of views to meet the opinions of minorities, the relative satisfaction given the latter by the fact that it has had a chance and that next time it may be successful in becoming a majority" (364–65). Here we have both elements of the theory that Westbrook praised in his evaluation of Dewey's proposal on the outlawing of war: politics as education and consultation with the people affected. Moreover, they are put forth in the very book that Westbrook says failed to address Lippmann's challenge. Where Westbrook had found no means of organizing an inchoate public, Dewey had in fact sketched an alternative process to Lippmann's elitism.

Admittedly, Dewey's alternative was abstractly presented. It was enhanced by the addition of the example of the outlawry proposal. But this is not Westbrook's claim. He contends that prior to the outlawry proposal

Dewey had not matched his ethics with a political means. Westbrook would be on firmer ground if he were to argue that until the outlawry proposal Dewey had not found an issue that illustrated his democratic instrumentalism. But even this would misunderstand Dewey's theory, for it would unnecessarily narrow and politicize it. Dewey was arguing that democratic political forms must be understood as a part of a larger democratic ethos. They may further democracy in the wider sense, but they do not exhaust it.

Dewey's Cultural Strategy

It is perhaps this focus on political democracy that causes Westbrook to underplay one of the significant accomplishments of Dewey's Chinese followers, the development of a national written language based on the spoken language. Hu Shih is credited with this replacement of the stilted classical literary forms with those of the vernacular.[48] Dewey, writing from China in 1920, described this change as "an attempt to make the spoken language the standard language for print," then noted, "Literary Chinese is as far away from the vernacular as Latin is from English, perhaps further." The reformers saw this as a needed step in universal education, because under the existing system school children had to master, in effect, a second language, the literary or classical one, in order to become educated. The reformers began to use the spoken language as a medium of public discussion in a variety of publications, thus displacing the classical language. The literary classicists resisted, arguing that the unity of China resided in "the moral traditions" embodied in the "literary classics," and "to neglect them is to destroy China" (MW 12:24–25).

Not surprisingly, Dewey reported, "the fight merged into one between conservatives and liberals in general, between the representatives of the old traditions and the representatives of western ideas and democratic institutions." But the immediate point of conflict continued to be linguistic. Dewey noted one recent, extended discussion in a Beijing newspaper "by voluntary correspondents about a single particle that is used freely in colloquial speech—a discussion already running into ten thousands of words." Dewey, nevertheless, understood the significance of the conflict, concluding: "Those who know what the change from a learned language to the vernacular meant for the transition from medieval to modern Europe will not despise this linguistic sign of social change. It is more important by far than the adoption of a new constitution" (MW 12:25). But Dewey's valuation of the linguistic change must be read in connection with his comment the next year. After surveying the New Culture movement he declared: "Chinese educated youth cannot permanently forswear their interest in direct political action. Their attention needs to be devoted more than it has been to detailed, practical economic questions, to currency reform, public finance and problems of taxation, to foreign loans and the Consortium" (MW 13:119).[49] Dewey may have valued cultural development over political action, but he understood the necessity of both.

Westbrook, however, limits himself initially to a neutral characterization of "the New Culture Movement" as one "which was seeking to democratize Chinese culture and foster a vernacular literary renaissance" (243). Later Westbrook correctly depicts Hu Shih and other Chinese Deweyans as being "cool to the political radicalism of the May Fourth movement," emphasizing instead the needed "cultural reconstruction." He then cites the observation of Barry Keenan, in *The Dewey Experiment in China: Educational Reform and Political Power in the Early Republic*, that the Chinese Deweyans' "strategy . . . was extremely shortsighted in that 'it assumed that educational and cultural improvements could both avoid repression and begin the process leading gradually to desirable political consequences.'" Failing to note Dewey's own reservations about this strategy and his awareness of the generality of the conflict generated by it, Westbrook charges Dewey with a similar "shortsightedness": "In this sense, the program of Hu Shih and other Chinese Deweyans suffered from the same strategic weaknesses as Dewey's own hopes to make the school the unsteepled church of democracy. Both assumed that cultural reconstruction could be separated from politics and thereby circumvent the democratic reformer's problem of powerlessness, ignoring the fact that any effort to establish a democratic culture was itself a political act and would entail a struggle for power" (251). Whatever the merits of the claims about Dewey's Chinese followers, the charge of Deweyan strategic shortcomings with regard to China is not accurate. Dewey recognized that China needed both a new culture and a new politics, and the two were not unrelated.

Westbrook has a narrower and shorter-term focus than Dewey. He emphasizes political effectiveness, where Dewey had argued that such effectiveness was dependent in the long run on cultural changes. Because Dewey and his followers lost political campaigns, Westbrook thinks they were ineffective. Dewey, however, measured success ultimately by cultural transformation. It was not enough to win an election. Dewey wanted the people involved to be changed, to be educated, in the process. Surely the transformation of the Chinese vernacular into the standard written language is no mean accomplishment. But, as Dewey recognized, attention to cultural changes was not enough to liberate China. Political change was needed also.

Dewey's wider vision can be seen in his discussion of "embodied intelligence" in *The Public and Its Problems*. Dewey concluded the discussion of the role of experts in democratic society by calling attention to the need for a general improvement in the level of intelligence. He contended that the "knowledge and judgment" of a less "well endowed person in an advanced civilization" made him superior in intelligence to a "superior" one in a "savage culture." One does not have to agree in order to see the point of Dewey's analogous but less charged remark: "Many a man who has tinkered with radios can judge of things which Faraday did not dream of" (LW 2:366). The point is that Dewey was concerned to raise the general level of intelligence to the point where people would take for granted what was needed for the general welfare. Political action was important. But if one too narrowly focused on the immediate victory, he might not be doing what was necessary for the long run.

In his 1939 rejoinder in the Schilpp volume Dewey did not comment on the observation of his former student, George Geiger, that "the ideas of Dewey are now unconsciously taken for granted,"[50] but he would have been gratified if he had thought it were so. More recently, in a review of Westbrook's book Richard Rorty contended: "There have always been cynical politicians whose words resemble Dewey's and whose deeds resemble Richard M. Nixon's. But surely the mainstream of American political rhetoric, and of American intellectual life, since World War II has (thanks in part to Dewey himself) taken for granted that participatory democracy, in precisely the sense that Westbrook defines it, is our goal. Lots of the rhetoric has been disingenuous, yet you could no more get elected to office after *opposing* participatory democracy than you could after burning the flag."[51] Rorty is well aware of the differences between Dewey's vision of America and what existed in his time or exists now. And Rorty is careful to limit the taking-for-grantedness of participatory democracy to "the mainstream of American political rhetoric, and of American intellectual life." But even if he is not correct (as I think he is not) about what has come to be taken for granted, nevertheless Dewey would have been pleased if it were now commonplace in our society that "every individual" could "realize fully," in Westbrook's words in the preface to his book, "his or her particular capacities and powers through participation in political, social and cultural life" (xv). Moreover, if this were a commonplace efforts to limit such participation would not be up for discussion.

Dewey did not choose between political effectiveness and education. Characteristically, he combined them, insisting that political victories must result from cultural transformation. He thought that an adequate politics required educational activities. Indeed, political means were themselves educational. The very process of the proposed national campaigns to outlaw war would be the development needed to secure the educated publics who would continue to hold the politicians accountable to the standard of not using war to resolve international conflicts. Dewey was not pleased with the Kellogg-Briand Treaty precisely because it short-circuited this political and educational process. It did not come as a culmination of the required process.

Once again we see Dewey trying to hold together what others think are separate. Intellect and practice he combined as intelligized practice. Intelligence and power he combined as educative politics. Where others saw dichotomies, Dewey formulated a third option, particularly when the original choices led to undesirable outcomes. The danger of a politics understood as simply a contest over power is that either the losers will not share the benefits or the contesting parties will stalemate, denying each party the benefits that cooperation could bring to both. Education understood too narrowly as a replication in the young of existing societal values or a training of one's mental abilities is ineffective as an instrument of social transformation. Only an education-politics can become such an instrument.

Dewey's Limited Success

Concluding a personal statement published in 1930, "From Absolutism to Experimentalism," Dewey wrote, "I do not expect to see in my day a genuine, as distinct from a forced and artificial, integration of thought." Then he cautioned against an egocentric impatience, urging philosophers "to help get rid of the useless lumber that blocks our highways of thought, and strive to make straight and open the paths that lead to the future." Changing biblical allusions, he closed by observing, "Forty years spent in wandering in a wilderness like that of the present is not a sad fate—unless one attempts to make himself believe that the wilderness is after all itself the promised land" (LW 5:159–60). Although he was speaking of the philosophic situation in which he found himself, his assessment has a more general application. Dewey was under no illusion that social and political practice had been sufficiently intelligized in his time. Nor, he thought, had he himself developed a political technology sufficient to the task.

In an essay in the Schilpp volume, "Dewey's Interpretations of the History of Philosophy," John Herman Randall, Jr., cited a series of passages from *Liberalism and Social Action* in which Dewey called for the use of a social intelligence to change the institutions that had been inherited from a premodern age. Randall then suggested that if Dewey's analysis was right and his program adequate, "the most insistent problem today is precisely this one of political education" in the broad sense of intelligent, directed institutional change. He then chided Dewey for having failed to inquire into the requisite political skills: "Instead of many fine generalities about the 'method of coöperative intelligence,' Dewey might well direct attention to this crucial problem of extending our political skill. For political skill can itself be taken as a technological problem to which inquiry can hope to bring an answer. . . . Thus by rights Dewey's philosophy should culminate in the earnest consideration of the social techniques for reorganizing beliefs and behavior—techniques very different from those dealing with natural materials. It should issue in a social engineering, in an applied science of political education—and not merely in the hope that someday we may develop one" (90–91). The logic of Dewey's intelligized practice and his insistence on the use of the sort of thinking one finds in science to transform prescientific institutions required an attention to the methods of social change.

Dewey readily accepted the criticism. In a footnote he wrote: "I wish to take this opportunity to express my full agreement with what Dr. Randall says in his paper about the importance of developing the skills that, if they were produced, would constitute political technology. The fact—which he points out—that I have myself done little or nothing in this direction does not detract from my recognition that in the concrete the invention of such a technology is the heart of the problem of intelligent action in political matters" (note 57, p. 592; LW 14:75). Dewey could have replied to his younger Columbia University colleague that it was enough for him as cultural critic to have pointed out the need for integration of thought and action and that it was the work of someone other than a philosopher to develop a political technology. As we have seen, he had often declined in the past to get into the specifics, the political machinery, of institutional change. He had often contented himself with the conceptual reconstruction that needed to be done prior to actual political change, leaving to others or a later time the invention of the needed political means. This time, although not accepting the challenge himself (for he was eighty years old), he readily agreed that "in the concrete the invention of such a technology is the heart of the problem of intelligent action in political matters" (note 57, p. 592; LW 14:75).

Intelligent political action requires a political technology, a specification of the means to the ends desired. In late 1939, if not before, Dewey knew that democratic ends required democratic means, and he could describe both—to a point. But he admitted in his response to Randall that he could not specify "in the concrete" the political means to effect the democratic ends. Therefore, there was a hiatus in his thinking, but it was not a necessary one. Far from it, for his project of intelligizing practice permitted none. Moreover, he had many useful things to say about how one would intelligize practice, and in the next chapter we will see some of the means he himself employed. The problem was not how one would go about developing a political technology. The problem was that this itself was a subject for inquiry. It was not that it could not be done or that such would have been inconsistent with or beyond his philosophy. Rather, it had not been done by him or others, at least not to the point that it could be formulated as a technology.

But we must not make too much of this admission. All along Dewey had been insisting on the need to understand democracy as something more than the existing political machinery. He often pointed to the need for such an enlarged understanding in order to counter the tendency of some, if not most, to reduce it to the actions of voters, politicians, and government officials. His admission is the corollary of that long-standing practice. What was new was his way of putting the matter and a shift of emphasis. Always before he would say, in effect, "I am going to concentrate on the non-political aspects of democracy as a way of life," without denying the need for improved political techniques. But in the response to Randall he said that the problem of an effective politics was also important.

To be sure, Dewey had himself paid attention to politics, significantly so in the 1930s. In public statements and articles and in service on various committees he had engaged in political action. But he had not reflected on this political practice in the same way that he had on education. The situation was this: His cultural instrumentalism required that practice, including political practice, be intelligized. He had himself engaged in political practice. But he had not made explicit the political technology employed in the same way that he and others had developed an educational one. Accordingly, his cultural instrumentalism was incomplete. It lacked the political edge that it needed to be the truly intelligized practice that he proposed. What he admitted to Randall was what he had long foreseen and had been moving toward—"the invention of such a technology"—but had never himself developed "in the concrete."

This, however, is not the last word. Dewey had himself been engaged in some of the activities that constitute such a technology. His political activities—speeches, articles, public statements, and chairmanships—were also forms of social inquiry. He conducted himself politically in a manner that exhibited the form of social inquiry that he had long advocated. It is therefore important to examine the manner of his political activities in order to see the way in which he anticipated the social intelligence that he hoped would come to exist more generally. To this I will turn in the next chapter. In so doing I will not only be able to show how Dewey's political activity was a form of his cultural instrumentalism, but I will also be able to link conceptually his instrumentalist method to the content of his vision of democracy.

4

❖

A TRANSFORMING SOCIETY

DEMOCRATIC

MEANS AND ENDS

Democracy is belief in the ability of human experience to generate the aims and methods by which further experience will grow in ordered richness. . . . Democracy . . . is the sole way of living which believes wholeheartedy in the process of experience as end and as means.
—John Dewey, "Creative Democracy—The Task Before Us" (LW 14:229–30)

ROBERT WESTBROOK'S CRITIQUE, as we saw in the last chapter, was that Dewey never adequately answered Walter Lippmann's challenge because he failed to specify the means by which the public could govern itself. In Dewey's response to John Herman Randall, Jr., as we have also seen, he acknowledged both the importance of developing a political technology and that he had "done little or nothing in this direction" (LW 14:75). But this convergence of Westbrook's critique and Dewey's self-critique is not as complete as the verbal agreement about the need for a political technology indicates.

Westbrook, while acknowledging that Dewey recognized the need for elected representatives, thinks that "the logic of Dewey's political theory and ethics pointed to a government that would include, indeed maximize, agencies of direct democracy—that is, agencies through which the public would choose to govern itself."[1] Clearly, Westbrook thinks that Dewey's thinking is inclined toward the "agencies of direct democracy." He knows that Dewey's view is not reducible to a form of participatory democracy, but

Westbrook's own interest in this sort of political action tends to bend Dewey in this direction.[2] One aim of this chapter is to consider "the logic of Dewey's political theory and ethics" and what sort of means it requires. Creating a political technology for a direct democracy is a more difficult task than developing one for a representative one, for the former requires more invention than the latter. Therefore, to the extent that I can show that Dewey's practice contributed to the increase of participation within a representative political system and that the logic of his political theory and ethics does not require direct democracy overall—to this extent I can make Dewey's thinking less utopian.

Accordingly, my strategy will be first to look at some instances of Dewey's political involvements, considering the values to which he appealed in these interventions. We will find that these values squared with his writings about democratic ends; they also did not require the advocacy of direct democracy. Dewey's proposal made use of seemingly conventional means to a considerable extent, but was, of course, not limited to these means. His use of such methods as group fact-finding and deliberation, while not remarkable in themselves, was often quite extraordinary in context. Where others would have thought social intelligence impossible or unwise, Dewey patiently sought to build consensus through mundane educational and political activities. Therefore, the invention of a political technology is not as urgent as Dewey's response to Randall suggested. What is usually needed is a matching of available political means and ends, not the introduction of new techniques. To make the problem of political effectiveness one of inventing new political technologies is to miss the genius of Dewey's approach. Rather than requiring new techniques, Dewey suggested that we assess current conditions and consquences. Sometimes we will need novel approaches. Usually we can effectively realize our democratic ends with available democratic means. Dewey's instrumentalism is a steady insistence on the matching of appropriate means and worthy ends, not a continual search for novel techniques.

In this chapter I will be working on two fronts. I will be continuing the discussion of the nature and effectiveness of Dewey's instrumentalism, but I will also be defending the integrity of Dewey's project. This defense is not an apology for everything Dewey did and said; it is primarily an explanation of the coherence of Dewey's recommended intelligizing of democratic practice. This explanation of his project's integrity must take account of the alleged difficulty in Dewey's thinking that is often presented in the guise of another supposed discontinuity between his method and his values. James Campbell, in an otherwise sympathetic treatment, accepts "the frequently heard criticism that Pragmatic social thought, and Dewey's work in particular, operated to advance a set of social values like democracy and equality that were not generated by Pragmatism itself. The claim here is true: Dewey's support for values like democracy and equality was not the result of his philosophical method."[3] At stake is the integrity of Dewey's proposal. If his method of intelligizing practice does not produce or require his core values, then a fault line occurs. While Campbell would not exploit this gap, others would and have. Therefore, overcoming this gap, if there is such, is no small matter. By tracing out the continuity between Dewey's understanding of experience, his proposal to intelligize practice, the methods employed in doing this, and the values involved in the democratic way of life, I will show that his philosophy hangs together. There is no fundamental split.

DEWEY AS A POLITICAL INQUIRER

Successful inquiry, for Dewey, resulted in a new situation, one informed by intelligence. That we are engaged in activities involving doing, feeling, and thinking was not in question; how we go about these activities was. In the final chapter of *Experience and Nature* Dewey observed that "the line to be drawn is not between action and thought, or action and appreciation, but between blind, slavish, meaningless action and action that is free, significant, directed and responsible" (LW 1:324). Dewey was concerned that practice, including political practice, be intelligized. He thought such an intelligized political practice was not constituted merely by winning an election, passing a piece of legislation, or enacting a treaty, but by the development of means and ends through a process of considering the conditions and consequences of a situation that would lead to continued development, particularly of the individuals involved. Such a "growth situation"—a phrase that combines two characteristically Deweyan terms into what I take to be a Deweyan concept—is a situation that is marked by, to use one of Dewey's phrases, "ordered richness" (LW 14:229)—that is, a situation in which the individuals involved are able to lead rich, expanding lives. Later in the chapter I will examine this concept of "ordered richness." Now I want to look at some examples of Dewey's attempts to achieve this sort of situation. The two examples are Dewey's involvement in "the Polish question" and his chairmanship of the Teachers Union Grievance Committee (and his subsequent involvement in this union and the one that replaced it).

Reconsideration of Dewey's Involvement in the Polish Question

As we saw in the last chapter, Westbrook accused Dewey of manipulative behavior in his efforts to persuade the American government to use its influence to delay the scheduled Polish Congress in Detroit and to revise a bill that would recognize a conservative faction, the Paris Committee, "as the official government-in-exile of Poland and give the committee the authority to decide which nonnaturalized Poles in the United States would or would not be designated as enemy aliens."[4] Westbrook contended that "Dewey was not simply calling for policies to guarantee a freer circulation of information on Polish affairs but was recommending that the American government take an active, indeed a controlling, role in Polish-American politics." Therefore, Dewey "was . . . seeking a policy that would counter the manipulative politics of the conservatives with a policy of manipulation by liberal Wilsonians" (219). A reconsideration of this affair will not only illustrate Dewey's method of social inquiry, but will also bring out the limitations of Westbrook's understanding of Deweyan democracy. Dewey was being consistent with his grasp of democratic social intelligence by intervening in the situation in the way in which he did.

The alleged wrong move by Dewey took the form of secretly intervening with the White House, attempting to balance the influence of the conservative faction that had Col. Edward M. House's ear, and sending confidential memoranda to the U.S. Military Intelligence Bureau, prepared at the Bureau's request. Therefore, Westbrook charged, Dewey sought "to circumvent the politics of the Polish community itself," a politics that Westbrook acknowledged was "dominated by conservatives." According to Westbrook, Dewey aimed "to persuade [President Woodrow] Wilson to use his authority to impose a set of procedures and policies on" the Polish-American community that "would guarantee the KON [the Committee of National Defense, the liberal and social democratic faction favored by Dewey] a voice in Polish-American policy and secure the commitment of American Poles to Wilsonianism." Therefore, "Dewey, in the name of democratic self-determination, called for the state to intervene undemocratically in the undemocratic politics of the Polish-American community" (220).

This is a good issue to examine, because it presents the democrat's dilemma from Westbrook's point of view. Either one is open and noncoercive or one participates in a process that is closed and coercive in order to be effective. As it turned out, Dewey chose the latter course and still failed. But the issue remains: Can a democrat intervene in a secretive manner in a process in which the control lies primarily not with the people involved? For an advocate of direct democracy the answer is clearly that one can not. But Dewey was not such a democrat. He recognized the authority of the President of the United States and his influence in this matter, and he chose, after careful study of the situation, to appeal to this influential person. Westbrook conceded that had Dewey's "recommendations been limited to calls for procedural reform of Polish politics and the freedom of the Polish press this episode might not have been particularly ironic." But Dewey made the mistake, in Westbrook's view, of "identifying democracy with the adoption by Poles of substantive policies that had [in Dewey's words] 'the antecedent sanction of the State and War Department'" (220).

Therfore, Westbrook was making two charges: the less serious one for Westbrook was that regarding the non-public, participation-limiting manner of Dewey's intervention; the more serious one was that Dewey supported Wilson's war policy and confused the latter with democracy. Admittedly, this policy was undemocratic, as Dewey himself came to recognize (see "The Discrediting of Idealism," MW 11:180–85). But with regard to the Polish intervention that is beside the point. In that situation Wilson's war policy was a given; in order to advocate the broader participation that he sought, Dewey needed to be able to appeal to this policy, because it was shared by the two Polish factions and the United States government. The issue here is Westbrook's lesser charge that Dewey secretively attempted to get Wilson to use his power in behalf of greater participation. Once again, however, there were certain givens. It was Wilson's choice to make, and his subordinates— Col. House and the Military Intelligence Bureau—set the form of the intervention. Also, there was limited time. If Dewey was to intervene at all in the time available, he would have to do so privately.

If there had been more time than the six weeks or less that Dewey in fact had, then he should have chosen a more public route, as his democratic ideal does favor open procedures. But this was not the situation. The issue here was this: What means were available to a democratic participant in a time of war with limited time and a decision to be made by the President? I fail to see how the democratic ideal requires in every situation the sort of openness and nonuse of power that Westbrook's criticism suggests. One works with the means available to bring about the end desired. The problem with Dewey's approach was not that it was manipulative or undemocratic in an absolute sense. Rather, Dewey lacked the time (and perhaps the organizing skill) to develop an effective public. But, more to the point, given these deficiencies he lacked a sufficiently compelling analysis of the situation to bring about what he regarded as a successful transformation. Therefore, his inquiry failed on Deweyan terms in this respect. Dewey sought a more democratically inclusive situation. He tried to bring this about through study, analysis, and persuasion, but his effort was not effective.

Let's say there had been more time and that Dewey could have educated large numbers of people, who, in turn, could have influenced President Wilson to act in the way Dewey recommended. This would appear to have been more "democratic." Dewey was trying to transform a situation through education, but his method does not require that everyone affected be educated. Of course he would have preferred that everyone involved come to see the situation in an informed way, but his method does not require this. It requires only that the crucial persons be educated, that the practice in question be intelligently informed sufficient to the end-in-view. To require more than this is unrealistic. Note that Dewey was willing for Wilson to use his influence to coerce the recalcitrant Polish faction into adopting more inclusive, accountable behavior. The choice in this situation did not have to do with the manner of Wilson's intervention; it had to do with which side he would favor. Dewey did not insist on the impossible; he was not unrealistic.

Those who think that Dewey was undemocratic need to think about this last hypothetical example. If "the people" had been consulted and Wilson had felt sufficiently pressured to acquiesce, would this have been a democratic process? If so, then there is no requirement that every key player be uncoerced. Democratic process was not an absolute for Dewey. There was no fixed standard to which it had to conform.

Nor was education an absolute for Dewey. One engaged in education because it was a beneficial activity. It was a way to transform situations so that they stayed transformed and transformative. Coercion alone has adverse consequences, but coercion tempered with education has the potential of reducing counterproductive side effects. The intelligent course of action is the one that hits upon the right combination of education and coercion to bring about the desired change with the smallest number of negative consequences. Dewey did not come up with the right combination in his intervention in the Polish issue, but we can see his method at work: He appealed to commonality (the Wilsonian war policy). He identified what he thought was an effective end-in-view (get Wilson to use his influence to bring about more inclusive processes in the Polish community). Finally, he used an educational approach to transform the crucial person and the situation. It did not work in this instance, but we can begin to see the elements of a political technology consistent with Dewey's democratic ends. To see it clearly, we need to look at one more political involvement and get a firmer grasp of his democratic ideal. But first I would like to make an additional comment about Westbrook and "the logic of Dewey's political theory and ethics." Then I will turn to some of Dewey's union activities in the 1930s.

Westbrook's mistake was in deducing from a conception of democracy what Dewey should have done in a particular situation. Dewey's approach was the reverse; he was working from within a situation, figuring out possibilities that would make the situation more democratic than it was and trying to bring about the possibility that showed the most promise of working, yet was consistent with his democratic ideal. Dewey's democratic ideal, as we shall see, was not absolute; it was a tool to be used to bring about what appeared to be preferable to the current situation. It was an attractive, realizable possibility, not a fixed goal.

Dewey and the Local 5 Conflict

Dewey had been a charter member of the New York Teachers Union when it had been started in 1916 and had served for three years as its first vice president.[5] But in 1927 he characterized himself as a "somewhat nominal" dues-paying member rather than an "active working" one (LW 3:275). His role, however, was not as slight as his self-characterization indicated, for the address in which it occurs, "Why I Am a Member of the Teachers Union," was still being "used in American Federation of Teachers recruitment brochures" in 1984, according to the textual commentary of Patricia Baysinger (LW 3:441). He had also, since his retirement in 1929, become increasingly active politically. For these and other reasons, he was a good choice to chair the committee that attempted to resolve the conflict brought on by the challenge of two radical factions in the Teachers Union, Local 5, of the American Federation of Teachers.

An Overview of the Conflict and the Issue Involved

The two factions, the Progressives and the Rank and File, opposed one another as well as the union's leadership—Henry Linville and Abraham Lefkowitz. In 1932 Lefkowitz, the union's legislative representative, moved to expel the leaders of these two factions for disruptive behavior and repeated misrepresentations of the leadership's actions. At a meeting of the general membership in October, a five-person grievance committee was elected. This committee then elected Dewey as its chair. Over the next several months the committee met extensively, hearing more than a hundred witnesses on both sides, as well as the six members against whom specific charges had been made. Dewey wrote the report submitted to the general membership in advance of the latter's meeting on April 29, 1933. The report recommended that a delegate assembly be created and that a provision for suspending members from meetings be adopted. A separate report, which was not submitted until the meeting was held, dealt with the specific charges. At the meeting the recommendation to suspend one of the six failed to gain the necessary two-thirds majority vote. The cases against the other five were then dropped (LW 9:320–21, 342–43, and 476–78).

The crucial requirement of a two-thirds majority vote was actually a self-inflicted mistake on Linville's part. As president, the only one the union had had, Linville chaired the meeting. According to Robert W. Iversen's account, "he had calmly announced that a two-thirds vote would be required on any disciplinary action recommended." This, however, was a more stringent requirment than the union's constitution specified. The constitution stipulated that a two-thirds majority vote was required for expulsion, but that the vote of only a majority of those voting was required for a suspension. Linville had expected Dewey's committee to recommend expulsion, and so he was caught by his own ruling when the committee recommended the less extreme penalty. Lefkowitz, Linville's ally, sought to correct the error by appealing Linville's ruling, but the mistake was compounded by the failure of their rank-and-file allies to be similarly alert. Iversen explains what happened: "At this critical point in the proceedings, the administration forces, which were in the majority, should have seen that a vote against Linville's ruling would have been a vote *for* him, because Lefkowitz was obviously voicing the Linville position. Instead, the meeting upheld Linville's ruling of the two-thirds requirement."[6] Therefore, Dewey's moderating committee report was less effective than it could have been. The radicals, thanks to the mistakes of the chair and his supporters, were able to avoid being disciplined. Dewey's effort to find sufficient common ground for the union to proceed was compromised.

In subsequent years, after much turmoil, the leadership unsuccessfully "petitioned the American Federation of Teachers to revoke the original charter and to draw up a new one that would enable the union to protect itself against obstructionists" (Dykhuizen, 257). The leadership, with a large minority of the members, then withdrew from Local 5 to form the independent Teachers Guild. In 1941, following the expulsion of Local 5 from the AFT, the "Guild was admitted to membership as Local #2."[7] Therefore, in the short run Dewey and the liberal leadership lost, but not over the long run. Eventually the radicals were outmaneuvered. The liberals were also helped by international events. The anti-Communists gained strength with the signing of the nonaggression pact between the Soviet Union and Germany in 1939 and the assassination of Leon Trotsky in 1940 (Iversen, 116–17).

But one's assessment of the success of the liberals in a democratic political effort depends to a large degree on one's understanding of democracy. Advocates of direct democracy who deplore any recourse to power politics will grant the success of the liberals, but attribute it to undemocratic means. For instance, Hogan and Karier see a straight line between the recommendations of the Grievance Committee in 1933 and the development of the anti-Communist movement in the next two decades, including the activities of Senator Joseph McCarthy. They conclude that "Dewey's legacy in shaping the role of the professional reached well into the Cold War" (2:402). It is not necessary for my purposes to enter fully into this issue. I will only call attention to a significant document that they fail to cite, one that shows Dewey to be an advocate of academic freedom even during the Cold War. In 1949 Dewey wrote *The New York Times* to state and explain his opposition to a proposal to prohibit known Communists from teaching in institutions of higher education. His major reservation was the possibility that a limited campaign to exclude known Communists could get caught up in a larger "blind and emotional action." His fear had in fact been realized "in the action of the Committee on UnAmerican Activities, or at least of its chairman (LW 17:137).[8] For Hogan and Karier Dewey's mediating position was undemocratic, a precursor of the position that was to reveal itself as cold war anti-Communism in the next few decades. The issue of democratic political effectiveness, then revolves to some degree around one's understanding of democracy.

The grievance committee's recommendations clearly reveal Dewey's willingness to embrace representative democracy and coercive measures. But neither is at the center of his understanding. To grasp this we need to consider the report in greater detail. I will do so by looking first at the forms of democracy Dewey employed and recommended and then at what he regarded as the condition necessary for democracy.

Democratic Forms

The grievance committee determined that "the real cause" of the conflict came not from the specific demands put forward by the minority groups, but by a disagreement over the basic purpose of the union. As Dewey wrote in the report: "The leaders of the minority groups conceive that the proper purpose of the Union is to join the class war in order to promote the cause of workers against employers" (LW 9:332). This alternative conception was not dismissed out of hand by the committee, but, they contended, such a radical departure from the present policy required "a patient process of education." In a democratic organization "such changes must come as a matter of growth and development, . . . rather than through a fight resulting in victory for one side and conquest of the other" (344).

Consistent with the committee's call for democratic process was the analytic and deliberative form of their report. The committee felt compelled to identify the real cause and Communist orientation, if not affiliation, of the minority group leaders for three reasons: One, "the cause of the trouble in the Union cannot be understood apart from the desire of some individuals at any cost to use the Union as an instrument in militant war to overthrow the existing economic system." Two, open discussion of this issue was not "red-baiting," the exploiting of "the prejudice against Communists," but adherence to the "principle of democracy" that "demands that within our ranks we speak openly of all that vitally concerns the Union." Three, it would be a "silly policy" to shut "one's eyes to the facts," namely, the use of "tactics employed by the Communists" (341–42). Although the facts were painful to talk about and difficult to establish to everyone's satisfaction, the committee felt that democracy required an open, candid discussion of the issues and fundamental causes of the conflict. The report, in its length, the explicit account of the committee's process, and the citation of evidence and fully displayed reasoning, modeled and encouraged open deliberation. Indeed, in exhibiting the social intelligence that Dewey continually recommended, the report illustrated the sort of democracy that he advocated. The report was a democratic means to a democratic end.

But this democratic orientation did not keep the committee from recommending a delegate assembly. They had determined that the size of the union was such that a smaller but appropriately representative group was needed to assume some of the powers of the existing business meetings of the general membership. General membership meetings would henceforth be deliberative but not policy-making sessions (342–43). Nor did this orientation keep them from recommending that the membership meeting's chair or the executive committee have the power to suspend members for improper conduct for a period of time. Both changes were thought needed to enable democratic discussion.

The Condition Necessary for Democracy

The committee determined that the minority groups' leadership had crossed the line from acceptable opposition to a fundamental disagreement with the purpose, policies, and procedures of the existing organization. This alienation was of such magnitude that these leaders should be suspended from the union. The reason for this was that democracy cannot rest on a "cynical contempt for the average membership or on a general suspicion concerning the motives of fellow members whose opinions differ." Moreover, in characteristic Deweyan language, the report continued: "Democracy does not consist merely of the machinery for registering the opinions of the membership, as in frequent elections, proportional representation, free discussion, etc. These mechanics of democracy can function only when there is a clear understanding of the community of interest that the membership has, and likewise a deep, sympathetic understanding of one another's weaknesses, shortcomings, and proneness to error" (344). This "community of interest" was lacking. Accordingly, the members who had been charged should be suspended.

Dewey amplified his reasoning two years later in *Liberalism and Social Action*. After arguing against the "suppression of democracy" as a means to "the adequate establishment of genuine democracy," he declared: "The one exception—and that apparent rather than real—to dependence upon organized intelligence as the method for directing social change is found when society through an authorized majority has entered upon the path of social experimentation leading to great social change, and a minority refuses by force to permit the method of intelligent action to go into effect. Then force may be intelligently employed to subdue and disarm the recalcitrant minority" (LW 11:61). Here he contended that it was not antideliberative and thus antidemocratic to suppress a "recalcitrant minority." Indeed, it was in the interest of social intelligence to do so upon occasion.

Democracy and the Local 5 Case

Hogan and Karier take the passage quoted earlier from the committee's report about the necessity of a "community of interest" to mean that Dewey thought there must be "a prior organized community where differences were not divisive and where changes of policy could occur by educational rather than political means" (2:399). They thus misconstrue Dewey's insistence on shared purpose as an initial requirement rather than as a continuing condition for democracy. They also mistakenly oppose educational to political means. For Dewey the problem in the Local 5 conflict was that the dissidents were using political means that were not only devoid of educational possibilities, but made education impossible. By failing to be open about their true aims and by misrepresenting the leadership's actions in their advocacy of specific proposals, the minority leaders were not using the very activites that could have effected the fundamental change that they sought, and they were employing tactics that obstructed constructive change. Dewey did not think they should have avoided politics; rather, they should have gone about their politics in an educational—that is, socially intelligent—manner.

Flatly wrong is Hogan and Karier's explanation of Dewey's views. They write: "The emphasis on prior commitment to organic unity, along with a de-emphasis on the political procedures of democracy, reflected Dewey's own fear of conflict and quest for unity" (2:399). Admittedly, Dewey was an irenic person who promoted commonality. But his behavior in this and other episodes was not fearful. When the committee presented its report Dewey confronted his former student, Isadore Begun, the spokesman for the

Rank and File faction, expressing "contempt for the 'baby act' that Begun and the opposition had put on" (Iversen, 44). Moreover, Dewey and the committee chose to place the conflict in the context of the Communist infiltration of labor unions. They did not have to do so. They could have limited their report, avoiding this painful issue. Dewey, it should be recalled, was himself a victim of "red-baiting" in a confrontation with Matthew Woll in the winter of 1928–29 (see the Textual Commentary, LW 5:522–24). Dewey and the grievance committee dealt with the conflict in an open, thorough manner, exposing conflicts rather than suppressing them. Dewey was neither fearful of nor obsessed with unity. Indeed, the latter charge misunderstands Dewey's "quest for unity." He was insistent that unity must come about through conflict rather than by avoiding it. This can be seen in his behavior in this affair. It is also reflected in his approach to philosophy. Not only was he a persistent polemicist, but he also intellectually appreciated the role of conflict, as can be seen in this autobiographical statement: "With respect to more technically philosophical matters, the Hegelian emphasis upon continuity and the function of conflict persisted on empirical grounds after my earlier confidence in dialectic had given way to scepticism."[9]

It was not so much that Dewey deemphasized "political procedures" as that he sought to balance the mechanics of democracy with what he thought were the attitudes and processes necessary for the machinery to work. He wanted to place political democracy within the context of social democracy, but he did not try to supplant political activities with educational ones. Characteristically, he tried to reconstruct politics, making this activity, as we have seen, an educative one having existentially transformative effects.

For Dewey democracy was specific forms, including open deliberation, representative assemblies, and frequent elections. But these forms depended upon a basic purpose shared by the members, for without this sense of common purpose the forms would not work. Moreover, the apparently undemocratic practice of suppression could be used against members who by their behavior had shown that they did not share the organization's values. Such suppression was only apparently undemocratic, because it was done only after careful and democratic deliberation and in the interest of the group's continued functioning as a democratic organzation. The condition of Local 5 in the winter of 1932–33 was such that Dewey and the grievance committee were willing to suspend some of the members after a full inquiry into the charges, a consideration of the larger context, and a statement of the requirements of democracy. Once again, as in Dewey's handling of the Polish question, we see an appeal to commonality and a willingness to use what some regard as undemocratic means. But in the Local 5 case we also clearly see the use of means—open and full deliberation—that are constitutive of the end-in-view, a self-transforming, cohesive organization. Therefore, we have an example of Deweyan social intelligence and its functioning within a democratic organization. In the next section I will make this concept of democracy explicit.

ORDERED RICHNESS

Randolph Bourne, it will be recalled, accused Dewey of emphasizing technique at the expense of vision. This critique has become a standard charge against Dewey's instrumentalism. As Alan Ryan put it in a recent review of John Patrick Diggins' *The Promise of Pragmatism*: "One of Dewey's friendlier critics . . . wanted to know *what* to think, but all Dewey would tell him was *how* to think."[10] This is a reference to Diggins' mention (273) of George Raymond Geiger's critique of Dewey in the Schilpp volume. Geiger, who had been a student of Dewey's at Columbia, had asked, "Instrumentalism, yes; but instrumentalism for what?" According to Geiger, either there were no ultimate values or there were and Dewey did not acknowledge them. If the latter, the candidate values seemed to be either "reflective inquiry itself" or "the processes of social reform."[11]

In his response to Geiger Dewey readily acknowledged that inquiry was ultimate in a temporal sense; inquiry as "the method of intelligent action" terminated a series of valuations occasioned by a problematic situation; it brought it to a close. But inquiry, while temporally final, was not an absolute (Schilpp, 594; LW 14:77). Dewey thus affirmed that the method of inquiry was valuable and denied there were fixed ends, including adherence to the method of inquiry itself. His critics, however, thought he was simply blind to his own fixation on intelligence, which, as a technique, was not a proper end. He lacked, as Bourne had insisted, "poetic vision." Such a criticism, of course, assumes the very dichotomy between ends and means that Dewey denied. It ignores Dewey's insistence that ends could function as means and that ends were implicit in the means selected and should be made explicit as ends-in-view.

The problem for Dewey was how to make his values manifest, including the continued reliance on deliberation, without making these values absolute. He solved the problem by pointing to the possibilities of experience that could be realized through the method of inquiry. This method was therefore of enduring value. But Dewey did not regard it as an absolute. It was qualitatively different from the absolutes of the philosophies he criticized, for it was developed through experience and modifiable through further experience. Specifically, Dewey resolved the problem by employing ends as means, thus acknowledging that ends were action-guiding, but denying that they were either fixed or apart from the process of deliberation and action. Ends, like the means of his critics, were temporal and thus modifiable as the occasion required. Such ends were too ordinary to satisfy his critics.

One such temporal, mundane end or ideal was the open-ended one of "ordered richness." I will introduce it as a way of understanding Dewey's democratic vision and then show how it functioned as an ideal for Dewey. This discussion will not answer the critics who demand more of an ideal than Dewey was willing to concede, but it will at least show how Dewey employed an ideal that was fully a part of ongoing experience to contribute to that process.

Democracy as Growth in Ordered Richness

An often-discussed speech of Dewey's is the one read by Horace Kallen at the celebration of Dewey's eightieth birthday on October 20, 1939—"Creative Democracy—The Task Before Us." Commentators have called attention to Dewey's call for democracy as a personal way of life. Indeed, Richard Bernstein once used this speech as a point of departure to summarize Dewey's philosophy and issue a new call for a "creative" and "radical" democracy.[12] I will analyze the latter part of this address to show the connections between Dewey's thinking on democracy, intelligence, and experience. We will find that democracy as both a means and an end was sufficiently vivid to Dewey to be action-guiding, but not so fixed as to be an absolute end. If the preceding discussion of the Teachers Union conflict provided a case study of Dewey as a democratic thinker in action, this speech will function as a case study of Dewey as a democratic thinker *simpliciter*. I will avoid taking the latter Dewey as just an abstract thinker, however, by tying this discussion back into the former one. A grasp of his proposal to intelligize practice requires that we not divorce Dewey as philosopher-speaker from Dewey as chair of a union grievance committee.

Democracy as a Way of Life

Dewey did not want to go through another large public celebration similar to the one that had marked his seventieth birthday. He acknowledged in his March 30, 1939, letter to Horace Kallen that he would "have difficulty in justifying rationally" his reluctance to do so. He was vulnerable, however, to the suggestion that this public event would provide an opportunity to advance the cause of democracy. But what finally persuaded him was the suggestion that he write something to be read by Kallen. This he did.[13]

In the first few paragraphs Dewey contrasted the period of "social and political inventiveness" that marked the formation of the United States with the more recent period in which people acted as if "democracy were something that perpetuated itself automatically" (LW 14:225). Therefore, he was pleased that many were now speaking of "democracy as a way of life," for this had the possibility of signifying not that democracy was a matter of institutions external to the individual, but that democratic institutions were "expressions, projections and extensions of habitually dominant personal attitudes" (226). He then elaborated this point, specifying a threefold faith in human nature, intelligent judgment and action, and cooperative activity and calling attention to the ways these found expression not only in international affairs, but in daily life. To the possible charge that he had reduced democracy to "a set of moral commonplaces" he replied that "democracy is a reality only as it is indeed a commonplace of living" (226–28).

Some examples of these moral commonplaces, examples that could have been depicted in Normal Rockwell paintings, were the ones he cited as "the heart and final guarantee of democracy": "free gatherings of neighbors on the street corner to discuss back and forth what is read in uncensored news of the day" and "gatherings of friends in the living rooms of houses and apartments to converse freely with one another" (227). Dewey was well aware that full and free communication could be blocked in a variety of ways, ranging from racial and class barriers to the corporate control of the media to the manipulation of the news by governmental officials. But he thought that the seemingly mundane activity of everyday conversation could bear much of the weight of democracy, provided that this talking was characterized by free, informed exchange and that it was situated in mutual regard for one another. Democracy, whatever its political forms, must be marked by free, informed exchange, for, as he observed in *The Public and Its Problems*, "The essential need, in other words, is the improvement of the methods and conditions of debate, discussion and persuasion. That is *the* problem of the public" (LW 2:365). But, as we saw in our discussion of the Teachers Union conflict, he thought a sufficiently common purpose was required also.

To the assembled group of educators, religious and labor leaders, and political activists Dewey's "set of moral commonplaces" would have had great significance, because many who were there had been engaged in the social and political struggles of the preceding several decades with him or were well informed about these activities. Sharpe listed the sponsoring organizations for the birthday celebration in a footnote to her textual commentary. While they are not exhaustive of Dewey's wide-ranging activities, they do reflect his many involvements and indicate who would have been in attendance: "the Progressive Education Association, the American Civil Liberties Union, American Philosophical Association, Conference on Methods in Philosophy and the Sciences, Department of Philosophy at Columbia University, John Dewey Labor Fellowship, New School for Social Research, New York Teachers Guild, and Society for Ethical Culture in the City of New York" (14:463). For these social and political liberals Dewey's "moral commonplaces" were understood against a backdrop of decades of liberal political and educational activity. For us these "moral commonplaces" can take on meaning as we read them against the events of the Teachers Union struggle.

Dewey's insistence that democracy worked itself out in the free exchange of ideas in a framework of mutual respect found expression in his committee's attempt to resolve the Teachers Union conflict not by denying it or exacerbating it, but by trying to find a way to get everyone involved to work together in a civil way. In the very difficult situation of 1932–33 he attempted to apply the belief that found expression in the following words he used in the 1939 address: "To take as far as possible every conflict which arises—and they are bound to arise—out of the atmosphere and medium of force, of violence as a means of settlement into that of discussion and of intelligence . . ." (228). When the preceding words are brought together with Dewey's practice in the Teachers Union conflict, they are made more meaningful. We can grasp what Dewey meant by referring them to the sorts of situations of which the grievance committee work was but one example. In fact, Dewey made no mention of any specific event in which he had been involved. He sought to give his words meaning by referring to typical or current events.

Democracy and Deweyan Philosophy

But there was an additional way that ideas and practice came together in this address, for Dewey closed by relating his "democratic faith" to his "philosophic position." Here we find Dewey's "poetic vision," such as it was. In terms of his "philosophic position," he said that "democracy is belief in the ability of human experience to generate the aims and methods by which further experience will grow in ordered richness" (229). Dewey believed that from within the transactions of individuals and groups in their interactions with one another and their environments both "aims and methods" could be "generated" that would lead to "further experience" that would develop in "ordered richness."

The method we see that Dewey employed is the method of intelligence—that is, inquiry. The aims are as varied as the individuals interacting. In this sense Dewey was a pluralist. But he thought that common to everyone involved in a democratic system was the cultivation of the ordering framework that enabled each to lead a full, rich life. This ordering framework was not just political; it was also social. Nor was it the same in every society. But there needed to be for any given group or society, as we saw in the Teachers Union conflict, a way to organize the disparate interests that would allow the members sufficient cohesiveness to be a group. Dewey understood full well the need for commonality—shared beliefs, values, and procedures. But the aim of a common framework was not an end in itself; it was a means to the flourishing of the individual members. "The task of democracy," wrote Dewey, "is forever that of creation of a freer and more human experience in which all share and to which all contribute" (230).

Dewey's aim was the promotion of neither the individual alone nor the community alone, but the developing social individual in a community that advanced the well-being of its individual members. "Democracy as a moral ideal," he declared in the *Ethics* "is thus an endeavor to unite two ideas which have historically often worked antagonistically: liberation of individuals on one hand and promotion of a common good on the other" (LW 7:349). In more poetic language than he employed in the 1939 address, he closed *Individualism, Old and New* with these lines, with which he attempted to strike the balance: "To gain an integrated individuality, each of us needs to cultivate his own garden. But there is no fence about this garden: it is no sharply marked-off enclosure. Our garden is the world, in the angle at which it touches our own manner of being. By accepting the corporate and industrial world in which we live, and by thus fulfilling the pre-condition for interaction with it, we, who are also parts of the moving present, create ourselves as we create an unknown future" (LW 5:123). The admoniton to accept "the corporate and industrial world in which we live" is jarring to romantic individualists who see a sharp contrast between individuality and contemporary society. Dewey, however, was attempting to work through existing conditions to a better—that is, richer and more fulfilling—existence. He was constantly trying to integrate individuality and community, existing conditions and their possibilities, theory and practice, ideal and actual. The phrase "ordered richness" can be taken as a designation for this overriding aim to integrate and liberate experience.

In *Context and Thought* (1931) Dewey defended "certain kinds of bias," arguing that a "standpoint which is nowhere in particular and from which things are not seen at a special angle is an absurdity." The standpoint he preferred was one that gave "a rich and ordered landscape" rather than one that provided a confused and meager scene (LW 6:14–15). If we recall his understanding of inquiry as that which transformed an indeterminate situation into a "unified whole" and his belief that education was a growth in integrative, liberating experience, we can begin to appreciate the aptness of the phrase "ordered richness" for Dewey's overriding aim.

Ordered Richness as an Ideal

For Dewey ideals were imaginary general aims. They existed as projected possibilities; they were not fantasies. More general, he thought, than immediate ends-in-view, they nevertheless organize experience, enabling a person or group to integrate and liberate their activities. "Ordered richness" was such a projection. Although never formally identified by Dewey as a comprehensive ideal, it can serve as a referent for his aspirations. That to which "ordered richness" referred was not fully realizable, yet "ordered richness" was constructed by Dewey from the stuff of his experience to serve as an inclusive end. I will first fill out this picture of the Deweyan ideal, then show how "ordered richness" guided Dewey's pragmatism, preserving it from mere opportunism.

Deweyan Ideals as Generalized Ends-in-View

Dewey thought that we resolve problematic situations by projecting a plan that takes into account the conditions or causes of the present difficulty, the desired resolution, and the likely consequences of our action. Sometimes he referred to the plan as an end-in-view; sometimes the desired objective was the end-in-view.[14] Since Dewey thought ends could serve as means, the confusion is understandable. He sometimes regarded the objective or aim as part of the process that would realize the objective, referring to both the objective alone and the process as a whole as ends-in-view. Or, as he put it in *Theory of Valuation*: "The *end-in-view* is that particular activity which operates as a coordinating factor of all other subactivities involved" (LW 13:234). Strictly speaking, then, the end-in-view is the objective insofar as it organizes the "subactivities" into the process that brings about the sought objective. As such, it is a specific end sought in a specific situation. The end actually realized, the product of this process, if successful, is a value or consummation of this process (Gouinlock, 133–34). Over time a consummation in one situation may become an end-in-view in a later situation and, if successfully realized, a value. Hence, ends-in-view and values can be confused with one another.

As we have just seen, situations are not unconnected. Our sought objectives in specific situations can be sufficiently similar to one another to be assimilated into "a generalized end-in-view" or "ideal" (LW 13:226). These ideals may also be spoken of as values. This can be seen in the following passage from *Theory of Valuation*, the citation of which also serves to summarize the preceding discussion:

> Generalized ideas of ends and values undoubtedly exist. They exist not only as expressions of habit and as uncritical and probably invalid ideas but also in the same way as valid general ideas arise in any subject. Similar situations recur; desires and interests are carried over from one situation to another and progressively consolidated. A schedule of general ends results, the involved values being "abstract" in the sense of not being directly connected with any particular existing case but not in the sense of independence of all empirically existent cases. . . . These general ideas are used as intellectual instrumentalities in judgment of particular cases as the latter arise; they are, in effect, tools that direct and facilitate examination of things in the concrete while they are also developed and tested by the results of their application in these cases. (230)

The smaller point about the assimilating of ends and values is established by the glossing of "general ends" by "involved values" that are "abstract" in the sense specified. The larger point is the function of ends or values as "general ideas" that "are used as intellectual instrumentalities."

What must never be lost sight of is the movement from the specific to the general and back to the specific. The process for Dewey was always one that began and ended in the immediate. Intellectual tools, whether they be hypotheses, theories, ends, values or ideals, are products of a deliberative process, as well as tools. They are never self-existing. With regard to ideals, they function as aims to provide direction, but as general ends-in-view they clarify and enlarge many particular ends. One reason they can do so is because they have originated as effective ends-in-view in specific situations. They have not come out of nowhere. They have arisen in actual situations as effective tools and, with appropriate modifications where necessary, could be used as such again.

This process is clearly seen in a passage in *A Common Faith*. In attempting to establish that the formation of an ideal was "experimental and continuous," Dewey wrote: "The artist, scientific man, or good citizen, depends upon what others have done before him and are doing around him. The sense of new values that become ends to be realized arises first in dim and uncertain form. As the values are dwelt upon and carried forward in action they grow in definiteness and coherence. Interaction between aim and existent conditions improves and tests the idea; and conditions are at the same time modified. Ideals change as they are applied in existent conditions. The process endures and advances with the life of humanity" (LW 9:34). Ideals are neither fixed nor without origins in experience. They arise and are modified and used as situations require. This plasticity is important, distinguishing Deweyan ideals from the absolute values of the philosophic tradition.

·   As generalized ends-in-view, Dewey thought ideals are not to be mistaken for ends in themselves. In showing how they arise from particular ends-in-view in particular situations, Dewey connected them indissolubly with actual events, with historic occasions. He thought there could be no sliding them over into absolute ends, divorcing them from the conditions that gave rise to them.

Dewey was proposing a middle position between no values and absolute ends. His critics had charged him with lacking "poetic vision" or being all technique and no value. But this criticism begged the question of the origin and status of values; it assumed that a value must exist independent of the process in which it is employed. Dewey, however, was suggesting a third way; he was suggesting that values arise as projected aims in particular situations. When realized—however partially—and judged upon reflection to be good, they become material for future possibilites to be realized and refined.

Perhaps the point can be made by discussing Dewey's reliance on "the better" rather than "the best." Observing that morality "has to do with all activity into which alternative possibilities occur," he then declared that with such possibilities there arise "a difference between better and worse." When one determines the better course of action, he is judging that this is the good in this situation. Therefore,, "the better is the good; the best is not better than the good but is simply the discovered good" (MW 14:194). There is no "best" beyond the "discovered good" of the situation. One can determine what is better or worse than what existed at any point relative to the felt need; valuation is possible. But one need not find the best action over all, regardless of the specific problematic situation that one is trying to resolve. Such a search was pointless from Dewey's instrumentalist perspective. One must be content with the better course of action that has been discovered through deliberation. The better is all the good there is.

Better here means the course of action, among the alternatives considered, that will satisfy the felt need, the problematic situation that occasioned the inquiry. This point is crucial. Dewey denied that there could be a standard of evaluation available outside the process. The inquirer as inquirer has some problem and thus some possible resolutions of it. One of these possible resolutions will satisfy the originating demand better than the others considered. It is the task of the inquirer to determine which one is the better solution. Of course, one resolution could be the dissolution of the problem. Just as the end is not fixed, so also the problem is not fixed. It too is modifiable in deliberation.

Moreover, one does not come empty to these deliberations; one draws upon previously established goods, using them as tools in new, problematic situations. Some tools prove their worth over time, surviving as principles or standards of conduct. Such a tool was Dewey's ideal of democracy as ordered richness. He found continuing value in promoting structures that made richness possible. The error is not in using past intellectual products in present situations, but in forgetting their status as products and tools. In so doing one subverts their effectiveness. The point of fashioning the intellectual tools is to discover the better course of action relative to the problematic situation. By treating the instrument as fixed, and hence a sort of an end in itself, one stops the growth, having determined in advance that the experience will conform to an antecedent existence. Dewey once remarked, "Standardizations, formulae, generalizations, principles, universals, have their place, but the place is that of being instrumental to better approximation to what is unique and unrepeatable" (LW 1:97).

Growth from Within Experience

Clearly, Dewey valued growth in richness of experience, and he thought the method of intelligence better promoted this growth than did other methods of regulating conduct, such as tradition or happenstance. But this is precisely what troubled some of his critics. It is at this point that they thought he was begging the question. A method that eschewed fixed ends was itself invariably recommended by Dewey in the service of what appeared to be an absolute—growth in fuller and richer experience. Therefore, there appears to be a double begging of the question. Both method and the ideal it serves seem to be functioning as absolutes, as ends in themselves. Such an objection regards Dewey's operational end, as well as his recommended method, as having greater fixity than he did. To be sure, Dewey regularly invoked the value of growth and the method of intelligence as the means of fostering it, but he never claimed for them the status that his absolutist opponents claimed for their values.

The fullest justification for both a method and an ideal is found in their usefulness, not in their correspondence to reality. (Of course, to be an ideal—and not just a fantasy—it must not be too removed from existence.)

An ideal, including the ideal method, is justified by how well it functions as a means to the resolution of the problem that has been identified.

Dewey thought that if one considered the requirements for human development one would realize that what is required are conditions of continuous development. To the objection that one could "grow into a highly expert burglar" Dewey once replied with questions that indicated he thought this was a very narrow sort of growth that did not constitute the open-ended sort of development he thought was essential (LW 13:19–20). A related example that better illustrates his thinking was his discussion of "a gang of thieves" as a "social group" in *Democracy and Education*. Such a gang exhibits community life in a minimal sense, for "we find some interest held in common, and we find a certain amount of" cooperation. "From these two traits," Dewey wrote, "we derive our standard. How numerous and varied are the interests which are consciously shared? How full and free is the interplay with other forms of association?" By transforming the traits of commonality and cooperation into standards, Dewey was able to evaluate the "criminal band," finding that "the ties which consciously hold the members together are few in number, reducible almost to a common interest in plunder; and that they are of such a nature as to isolate the group from other groups with respect to give and take of the values of life." Therefore, the development of such a group will be "partial and distorted" (MW 9:89).

The group could become a better band of criminals, but there would be definite limits to its growth. Moreover, to the extent that it extended its common interest beyond plunder and broke out of its isolation, it would risk becoming something other than a criminal society. Continuing, Dewey contrasted the deficient social group with one that better exhibited the two desirable traits of a society: "If we take, on the other hand, the kind of family life which illustrates the standard, we find that there are material, intellectual, aesthetic interests in which all participate and that the progess of one member has worth for the experience of other members—it is readily communicable—and that the family is not an isolated whole, but enters intimately into relationships with business groups, with schools, with all the agencies of culture, as well as with other similar groups, and that it plays a due part in the political organization and in return receives support from it. In short, [for an ideal group] there are many interests consciously communicated and shared; and there are varied and free points of contact with other modes of association" (89). Such a group exhibits "ordered richness," better fulfilling the characteristics of a group than, say, a criminal band. But the latter—as a group—has the potential to be one marked by commonality and cooperation.

It is not the case that one needs a value from outside the experience of a group to identify these idealizable traits. Even from within the experience of a criminal band one can locate and develop the traits of commonality and cooperation, expanding their operation and scope and transforming the band into a richer and fuller community. Hence Dewey's value of ordered richness was one that he felt arose from within experience and could be used to evaluate and enrich experience.

This process can be seen in Dewey's claim that the idea of "democracy is not an alternative to other principles of associated life. It is the idea of community life itself" become an ideal in the sense that it is "the tendency and movement of some thing which exists carried to its final limit" (LW 2:328). Democracy is the logical and ideal end of associated living. When one reflects upon "community life" one comes to understand that the ideal form of such a life—democracy as ordered richness—is one that provides for the development of commonality and cooperation. Such a life will be not an undifferentiated whole, but an ordered richness that values "liberty" as "that secure release and fulfillment of personal potentialities which take place only in rich and manifold association with others: the power to be an individualized self making a distinctive contribution and enjoying in its own way the fruits of association" (LW 2:329). One of these "fruits of association" is "equality," the share each one has as a distinctive individual regardless of "physical and psychological inequalities" (329–30).

These examples of naturalistic generation of ideals should not only meet the objection of those, such as Bourne, who thought Dewey lacked ideals, but it should also blunt the criticism of those who thought his ideals were arbitrary. Even if one might not be satisfied with Dewey's particular account of the origin and justification of such ideals as freedom and equality, the point is that he attempted to develop them from within experience without recourse to antecedent reality. To be sure, he begins from an understanding of "life" as "a self-renewing process" (MW 9:12), but this reality is not antecedent to the reality in which Dewey and we find ourselves. The view that life is an ongoing process, capable of transformation, is an understanding grasped from within the continuing process.

Dewey confronted this criticism directly in a discussion of the relation between custom and morality in *Human Nature and Conduct*. To those who objected that his theory made morality dependent on custom he countered with the example of language, contending that language had just happened; it had not been designed: "Men did not intend language; they did not have social objects consciously in view when they began to talk, nor did they have grammatical and phonetic principles before them by which to regulate their efforts at communication. These things come after the fact and because of it. Language grew out of unintelligent babblings, instinctive motions called gestures, and the pressure of circumstance." But once developed language has normative dimensions, even features that permit it to go beyond its originating conditions: "Language once called into existence is language and operates as language. It operates not to perpetuate the forces which produced it but to modify and redirect them. . . . Literatures are produced, and then a vast apparatus of grammar, rhetoric, dictionaries, literary criticism, reviews, essays, a derived literature *ad lib*. Education, schooling, becomes a necessity; literacy an end. In short, language when it is produced meets old needs and opens new possibilities" (MW 14:56–57). What is true of language is true of other institutions as well. Indeed, this is what human life has become, a culture composed of all sorts of practices that are continuing to evolve. Moreover, each of these cultural institutions—family, property, law, and so forth—carries within "demands, expectations, rules, standards."

We cannot identify the source of these norms in the sense of an originating authority. We can, however, recognize the value of culturally developed norms, for they are a part of and contribute to living well, and we can modify them as needed. As Dewey wrote: "The only question having sense which can be asked is *how* we are going to use and be used by these things, not whether we are going to use them. Reason, moral principles, cannot in any case be shoved behind these affairs, for reason and morality grow out of them. But they have grown into them as well as out of them. They are there as part of them. No one can escape them if he wants to. He cannot escape the problem of *how* to engage in life, since in any case he must engage in it some way or other—or else quit and get out." Life, with its various practices, is our inheritance and our lot. But, while one has no choice except to participate in life or not, this is not the important choice. The crucial question, as Dewey insisted, has to do with the manner of our participation. We can participate uncritically, or we can choose to act intelligently (57–58).

Dewey started in the middle of things, whether life, customs, practices, habits, or desires. But he saw being situated within experience as but a beginning. One is then able to criticize one's situation, discovering the conditions that make the present situation what it is, surveying the consequences that flow from it, and identifying the possibilities that could improve it. Although within experience, one is not bound by any particular situation; one is free to modify it within limits. There is usually sufficient wiggle room to improve it in a direction that is more satisfying. At least this was Dewey's expectation based on his experience.

INSTRUMENTALISM AND IDEALS IN DEWEY

One cannot completely separate Dewey's instrumentalism, his democratic ideal, and his understanding of experience; they are continuous. In the previous section I attempted to situate his ideal of ordered richness within his view of experience. In this section I will show the continuity between his method and his ideals, closing the section with another look at the political technology issue. The solution to the latter problem lies in the ends-means continuum that is central to Dewey's instrumentalism. The solution to the former problem is found by considering this question: If one employs Dewey's method of cultural instrumentalism, will one develop and embrace his values—values such as democracy and equality—to select the two values that Campbell (*Understanding John Dewey*, p.141) identified?

Dewey's Method and the Human Situation

With the method of instrumentalism comes the understanding of experience that it presumes. Beginning with problematic situations and transforming them into satisfactory ones, the method is but an elaboration of the process of reestablishment of equilibrium. Experiences are either satisfactory or not. If the latter, one can locate the difficulty, translate this felt need into a desired end-in-view, and proceed to remake the situation into one that is satisfactory. Note the relation of problem and proposed solution. When fully elaborated this continuum will include ends-in-view and even generalized ends-in-view or ideals. Therefore, there is no break between method and ideals, for the latter are tools in the resolution of the problem. Nor is there a break between the method and the needs that lie behind the ideals, for the method of intelligence is the better way of meeting the needs. One does not choose the method arbitrarily; one inquires in Dewey's sense—transforming a problematic situation into one that is more satisfying—in order to do just that, solve the problem. One employs intelligence because it is effective in solving problems.

But this is also the limitation of intelligence as a method. Since it is designed to resolve difficulties, specifically human difficulties, it accepts the value of such difficulties. We can explore these human difficulties, enriching our understanding of them. But since the method takes these very difficulties as valuable, we cannot then use it to justify the worth of a human situation independent of that situation. Dewey, it will be recalled, demanded of philosophy that it become "a method, cultivated by philosophers, for dealing with the problems of men," not "the problems of philosophers" (MW 10:46).

Instrumentalism can be broadened into a cultural instrumentalism that is not only aware of itself as a method, but makes full use of the culture in which it operates. As a cultural instrumentalism it can employ a rich variety of meanings and ideals. But, as a method used to resolve human problems, it cannot answer wholesale the question of the value of these problems independent of them. To the extent that it takes this question seriously, it is affirming the worth of the question. In other words, it cannot assume a stance outside the human situation to ask if it is worthwhile for humans to exist. A pragmatist can ask about the value of human life, but can do so from no standpoint external to the human situation. The very asking of the question, on an instrumentalist account of inquiry, is an attempt to meet a *human* need. William James, in denying that "purely objective truth" is possible, insisted that what is called true is called so "for human reasons," concluding, "The trail of the human serpent is thus over everything."[15] Even if pragmatists are wrong about the possibility of objective truth, *they* cannot consistently seek it. Their method, beginning with human problems, limits them to inquiries that deal with human predicaments.

This, of course, poses no problem for pragmatists. Since they understand philosophy to be a form of intelligence cultivated to deal with human problems, pragmatists gladly stand convicted of having a method that does no more than that. They never asked for anything more. However, this frustrates those who do not share the pragmatic presuppostion. It would become a problem for pragmatists only if they were to shift their perspective, treating some method or ideal as if it were independently valuable. But Dewey, despite charges that he did so, did not do this. His justification for his instrumentalism was precisely that it enabled human beings to solve their problems better than the alternatives—custom, political or religious authority, or happenstance. He did not appeal to any standard outside the framework of human life and its development. He thought an ideal, including an ideal method, is justified insofar as it contributes to the resolution of the felt need, either by reconstructing the need or by remaking the situation so that the originating need is satisfied.

Human needs are not absolute; they can be contextualized and modified. They certainly were not taken by Dewey as givens or without qualification. He understood subjectivity as a beginning point or something to be taken into account, but not as a bare fact. He thought, as we have seen, that it makes all the difference what sort of subjectivity is embraced. A person can take as his or her standpoint "impartiality"—that is, "a standpoint which gives a rich and ordered landscape rather than . . . one from which things are seen confusedly and meagerly" (LW 6:14–15). The problem is not with subjectivity itself, but with the sort of subjectivity that is embraced. Dewey recommended an enhancing subjectivity rather than an impoverishing one.

Useful Ideals

Deweyan ideals are not absolute, either. They are constructed by us to solve problems. One generalizes an "end-in-view," making it an ideal. Ideals do not have antecedent existence; nor are they valuable in themselves. Human beings develop and deploy them because they are useful in transforming problematic situations into ones that are more satisfying.

Ordered richness is an idea that is worth implementing, because it helps to create a situation in which individuals can flourish. If there were a better way to enhance the lives of individuals, Dewey would have been required to embrace it. But as far as he could determine the better situation is one in which the needs of individuals and the needs of the community are balanced. Too much individualism and there is chaos; too much order and individuals suffer. What is needed is sufficient order for individuals to flourish and sufficient diversity for the community to develop. Such reasoning regards ideals as tools. Whether the ideal be democracy or equality or ordered richness, the case for the ideal is that it functions as a generalized end-in-view in the resolution of a problematic situation. It meets a human need. If it does not, Dewey thought it ceases to be valuable.

Consider Dewey's repeated insistence that the pervasive problem of modern society is that we continue to hold certain values despite their lack of relevance to our current needs. Once useful, many of these inherited ideals are no longer so. An outstanding example of this is seen in Dewey's analysis of individualism in *Individualism, Old and New*. He acknowledged the value of the older form of individualism at the time at which it was developed. For instance, the "earlier economic individualism" served the purpose of freeing people from "legal restrictions" (LW 5:78). But in his lifetime he thought a new social individualism was needed, one that went beyond the simple opposition of the new corporate society to "the rugged individual" (LW 5:84–86). Since life is not static, ideals cannot remain fixed. They need to be continually developed to remain useful.

There is no ideal, then, that is valid for all time. Ideals are relevant to situations. Therefore, the question of the truth of an ideal is ultimately not the right one for Dewey; the important question has to do with the usefulness of an ideal. This is what makes Dewey a pragmatist. Ideas and ideals are valuable insofar as they meet the needs of those involved. Correct opinions are obviously valuable, but the important question is not ultimately one of descriptive accuracy. Usefulness is what finally counts for Dewey.

Gail Kennedy captures this idea in the penultimate paragraph of his article "The Hidden Link in Dewey's Theory of Evaluation."[16] To be fully appreciated this article needs to be read in the context of a continuing controversy about how to understand Dewey's distinction between what is desired and what is desirable, but I am excerpting the following portion in order to show the relation of truth and value in Dewey.[17] Kennedy wrote: "If the question is raised, 'Why this alternative rather than another?' the answer is, 'Because it is a more adequate solution of the problem.' Since what the situation demands—the claim made by it—is the most adequate solution possible, it follows that whichever proposed alternative does seem more adequate is within that context the better—it is the 'good' *of* that situation or it is the 'right' thing to do *in* that situation. And whether this proposed alternative is in reality the better means can be tested by reference to factual knowledge" (94).

Kennedy thought that Dewey had not been explicit on this point; therefore, it was a "hidden" rather than a "missing" link in Dewey's theory of evaluation. Perhaps Dewey could have been more explicit at times, but in the *Ethics* he clearly defined "the Good" as "that which satisfies want, craving, which fulfills or makes complete the need which stirs to action," then proceeded to note that "not every satisfaction of appetite and craving turns out to be a good," concluding: "The task of moral theory is thus to frame a theory of Good as the end or objective of desire, and also to frame a theory of the true, as distinct from the specious, good. In effect this latter need signifies the discovery of ends which will meet the demands of impartial and far-sighted thought as well as satisfy the urgencies of desire" (LW 7:191). Dewey must always be read as trying not just to satisfy our desires, but to fulfill or enlarge them through deliberation. Intelligence is both the effective way to satisfy needs and the way we transform them into that which is truly good.

Dewey's critics want either to reduce him to a mere opportunist who settled for any sort of need-satisfaction or to accuse him, when he resorted to talk of "a theory of the true, as distinct from the specious, good," of smuggling in an absolute value. In fact, he was attempting to use a third strategy. The good, to be a good, must satisfy some need. This good will be constructed by us to meet that need; therefore, it is not an absolute. It is a useful ideal, a good-for-something, not an end-in-itself. But neither is the need that this constructed good satisfies an absolute. It is itself reconstructible through inquiry. Needs, ends-in-view, ideals—all are modifiable. What is fixed are the specific relationships of conditions and consequences.

Given some situation with its need, end-in-view, and ideal, the particular conditions and consequences are set and open to empirical investigation. Truth, then, is locally important, but as to ideals the questions are whether they are realizable and whether they are useful.

Dewey's instrumentalism, far from being a narrow concentration on methods, was an attempt to relate means and ends, particularly those involving intellect. Therefore, ideals were neither remote nor platonically "Real," but useful tools. This attention to ideals as tools is what saves Dewey's instrumentalism from being the crassly opportunistic program that some take pragmatism to be. Dewey was able to work within existing situations, seizing the opportunities available, but—and this is crucial—moving the situation in a direction that improved it. He could do this because he sought to hold together means and ends, practice and theory. Indeed, his instrumentalism was centered in his use of theory to inform practice with the theory to be tested by the resulting informed practice.

Deweyan Political Technology and a Society of Ordered Richness

A qualified answer must be given to the question of the adequacy of Dewey's political technology. Dewey was generally correct in his insistence that practice, including political practice, could be improved through deliberation about ends and means. Moreover, his employment of intelligence in resolving public problems is suggestive. But, as he acknowledged in his response to Randall, he did not develop a theory that was sufficiently detailed in its specification of appropriate means that it could be considered an adequate political technology. There is no Deweyan manual to political action.

Toward a Theory of Democratic Social Change

Nevertheless, we can sketch such a theory, or at least provide some guidelines for democratic social change: The aim of a democratic political technology is to create a social order that liberates individuals; it is not mere political victory. Politics may be about power, but a democratic politics must be about the widespread distribution of power, not its concentration. The way to distribute power widely is by intelligizing practice. To intelligize political practice we should (1) Be wary of both idealists and political operatives, for both separate ideals and methods. The one unduly idealizes the situation; the other is contemptuous of ideals. The immediate problem is not one of vision or technique alone, but of employing the available (or devisable) techniques in service of one's feasible ideals. We should also (2) realize that neither the existing situation nor some supposed alternative is

absolute. The present situation was constructed by human activity; therefore, it can be reconstructed. Similiary, one's ideal, having been generated
from ends-in-view, is open to revision. To intelligize practice we should also
(3) employ social inquiry to identify both the practice to be changed
(including its conditions and consequences) and the end-in-view to be realized. This will involve experimentation and not just discussion. Deweyan
inquiry is not just a mental questioning; it is a transformation of an existential situation with attention to the mental aspects. Further, we should (4)
use social inquiry to create a public. Publics need to become self-consciously
so. This can be done through social inquiry. Publics are neither given nor
found; they are created through informed, open communication and self-
identification in reference to common needs and purposes. Publics are
made, not born, and they are made through inquiry. Hence, we should (5)
look for middle ground—that is, commonalities. There are one or more
sharable values that makes a public a public. These shared values must be
identified and strengthened. In spite of forces that set people apart, a
Deweyan political technology will emphasize what people have in common
in a situation. Since ends and means are continuous, we should (6) employ
democratic means to realize democratic ends. One develops a society characterized by ordered richness by engaging in practices that are constitutive
of both order and richness.

Although each of these guidelines is traceable to Dewey, as this and the
preceding chapter have shown, Dewey nowhere presented such a package.
At least he did not do so in a systematic way comparable to what he did for
art in *Art as Experience* or scientific method in *Logic: The Theory of
Inquiry*. His writings on politics, as is well known, stopped short of discussion of the forms needed for a democratic society. Even these guidelines do
not constitute a technology. At best they are second-order tools, tools for
making tools to change society. For better or worse, Dewey, in spite of what
the term *instrumentalism* may suggest to most, was not one to fashion tools
for political change. He was more comfortable considering the concepts
employed in social change, placing efforts to effect social change in historical perspective, identifying obstacles to reform, evaluating programs for
social action, and even engaging in political activity than he was inventing
and assembling an array of techniques for social change.

Society's Failure?

The most charitable explanation of Dewey's failure to complete his
instrumentalism in this way is that, as he often contended, social and political practice had not achieved the success that scientific practice had. His

thinking, in spite of much attention to social reform, was programmatic. He continually called for the application of instrumental thinking to social problems, citing science as a model to be emulated. This was precisely Randall's criticism—a criticism, as we have seen, that Dewey acknowledged. After citing several passages from *Liberalism and Social Action*, Randall wrote (and I quote again, in part): "This is not the place to question or to defend the adequacy of Dewey's program for our present conflicts. If he be right, if it be true that history itself generates change in the method of directing social change, then surely the most insistent problem today is precisely this one of political education. And the achievement of the political intelligence to persuade men to use the intelligence we do as a society possess must be the conscious focus of our philosophies. Instead of many fine generalities about the 'method of coöperative intelligence,' Dewey might well direct attention to this crucial problem of extending our political skill" (Schilpp, 90–91). The point I want to make here in recalling this critique is the need for a change in the environing conditions that would make possible the development of an adequate political technology.

It may have been that in Dewey's time there had been sufficient experience with directed social change to permit the development of a political technology. Dewey observed or participated in various nineteenth-century reform efforts, but also participated in several efforts that carried over into the twentieth century—the Progressive Movement, women's suffrage, the union movement, and educational reform. But the point remains: Science and technology had achieved greater success than had democratic reform. While there was some experimentation in the 1930s, Dewey and other advocates of increased democracy were often on the defensive, confronted as they were not only with corporate capitalism and jingoistic Americanism, but with fascism and communism.

As Dewey clearly understood, a fully articulated methodology for transforming society required a transforming society—that is, a society that was employing practices that would deliberately transform it. Without this intelligized social practice there could not be an adequate theory of social transformation. As Dewey also understood, this was not an either-or matter. One did not need a fully developed theory before the process of transformation could begin. Indeed, there were many elements of a transforming society already in place. What was needed was an enhancing of these democratic practices. With this extension there could be in time a theory that both grew out of and returned to democratic practice for verification and use. If Dewey's instrumentalism is correct, one cannot have a theory that is very far from the practice. Since the ideas that make up the theory are drawn from—idealized from—the experience of particular agents at particular times and are referred back to such experiences for validation in use, these ideas cannot be too ideal. If so, they fail to be useful. As an instrumentalist, Dewey could not have what the experience of his time and place failed to provide. Admittedly, an instrumentalist is not so bound to his or her situation as to be a prisoner of it. Change is possible. But a theory—if it is to be a useful and experiential one in Dewey's understanding of these terms—cannot run too far in advance of the experience of the people involved.

In Dewey's view, effective practice requires a continuity between ideal, next steps, and present situation. The social practice of Dewey's time and place was not as effective as he thought it needed to be in order for individuals to live freely and fully. As he continually argued, it lagged behind the best intelligence of recent centuries, the intelligence found in scientific practice. Hence, there could be no adequate theory of social change. Dewey thought he knew the way to make the transition, and he never ceased to offer informed opinions about how to proceed. But he continually insisted that he could not say what the far side of the transition would look like. Only the developing experience of a society that deliberately sought to order and promote richness could provide that sort of detail. Therefore, he provided guidelines for taking the next steps and urged the development of a political technology, for he believed that "in the concrete the invention of such a technology" was "the heart of the problem of intelligent action in political matters" (LW 14:75 n.). But Dewey himself neither invented nor assembled such a technology.

Dewey's Achievement

What Dewey did do, however, must not be overlooked. By insisting on the consideration of reciprocal means and ends, he avoided the mistake of isolating and effectively absolutizing either one. Means and ends are distinguishable, but not completely separable. Nor is one to be privileged over the other. Admittedly, this advice to hold means and ends together is not the detailed sort of help that some expect. But it is useful nevertheless. Its usefulness consists in matching means and ends, but also in refusing to make the search for either one the most significant problem.

No doubt Dewey's theory of cultural transformation could be filled out. In addition to his proposals about how to go about being intelligent one could supply not just examples of effective social action, but a theory of when to do what, a political technology. One product of such a comprehensive theory could well be a manual of social and political intelligence that could include rather specific advice about how to go about social change.

Dewey did everything but write such a manual. He had a theory of human nature set within a philosophy of existence. He had accounts of what it was to be intelligent and proposals for specific programs for social reform. What he did not provide was a set of operational instructions for the would-be social-political change agent.

The conclusion to be drawn from this admission is not all that damning. It points to no inherent flaw in Dewey's intellectual project. As Dewey indicated to Randall, what was left to be done was to develop such a political technology. His project did not need to be abandoned; it needed only to be rounded out. To expect a philosophy to be complete for all time is unrealistic; it is to hanker after the certainty that Dewey condemned in *The Quest for Certainty*. To expect a philosophy to meet the needs of its time and place is more realistic. By this standard Dewey's project is seen to be at worst incomplete. The appropriate response, then, for those who are attracted to his philosophy is at some point to get on with the task of developing a democratic political technology. Fortunately, those who would attempt this have two advantages: One, as I have been arguing, they have only to extend Dewey's work; they do not have to start from scratch. Two, they have a half-century of additional democratic change efforts, as well as social science, from which to learn. Since Dewey's death there have occurred the most visible stages of the civil rights movement, an additional wave of the women's movement, the environmental movement, the Vietnam War protest, efforts for gay and lesbian rights, liberation movements in the Philippines, Latin America, and South Africa, as well as the democratic movements in eastern Europe and the former Soviet Union. Even this list is not exhaustive. One could talk of efforts to establish workplace democracy and ensure public access for those who use wheelchairs. In addition to this considerable experience, there are many intellectual attempts to understand these developments. Therefore, there is much upon which one could draw in attempting to develop a democratic political technology.

Giving Dewey's Project Some Practical Help

I will turn now to a recent important book—Randy Shaw's *The Activist's Handbook: A Primer for the 1990's and Beyond*[18]—which enables an advance of Dewey's political technology. I will do so both to illustrate my point that the decades since Dewey was active have given us additional social democratic practice upon which to reflect and to show one area in which a Deweyan political technology has been developed. Shaw and other law students founded the Tenderloin Housing Clinic in San Francisco in 1980. The book grows out of his reflection on this and others' experiences in democratic social change. Organized in eight substantive chapters, Shaw's book begins with a statement of his general approach—activists should not just react to crises, but should use them to organize strategically. He then proceeds to treat several topics that any activist organization will face: how to deal with elected officials, the role of coalitions, the use of ballot initiatives, dealing with the media, the role of lawyers, the use of direct action, and how to get started.

Shaw's book is Deweyan in that it articulates a form of pragmatic, deliberative democracy. It is pragmatic in that it is meliorative, process-oriented and consequentialist; it is deliberative in that Shaw shows that the people affected by decisions must be included in the planning—not just on principle but because deliberation contributes to success.[19] In the initial chapter Shaw discusses what he regards as his "best experience of how tactical activism can transform a defensive battle into a springboard toward accomplishing a significant goal" (8). The low-income Tenderloin District learned in 1980 of plans by Holiday Inn, Ramada Inn, and Hilton Hotel to build "three luxury tourist hotels." The threat was clear: "The encroachment of these big-money corporations would surely drive up property values, leading to further development and gentrification and, ultimately, the obliteration of the neighborhood" (8–9). Yet there did not seem to be any legal or political way to stop the construction.

Rather than be immobilized, the residents and those organizing them came up with a mitigating proposal that, if successful, would also accomplish two strategic goals: recognition of the Tenderloin as "a residential neighborhood" and, subsequently, the establishment of the zoning protections accorded such neighborhoods (9). Some would have defined the hotel fight as an antidevlopment effort, but the organizers "understood . . . that development projects are rarely stopped and are at best mitigated" (9). Shaw concludes, "'No hotels' was not a solution to the neighborhood's problem—rezoning was" (10).

The Luxury Hotel Task Force was organized and succeeded in winning several concessions, including a contribution from the hotels that resulted in the distribution of over $300,000 per year for twenty years "for low cost housing development," as well a total of $600,000 in community service projects, participation by the hotels as sponsors of a grant to acquire and renovate four low-cost residential hotels, and their agreement to good-faith efforts to employ Tenderloin residents (11).

Shaw stresses that the success of the task force was dependent in no small way on the deliberative democratic process employed: "The decision to use this defensive battle to achieve a critical goal resulted entirely from continual discussions of strategy and tactics among the thirty to forty residents who regularly attended Luxury Hotel Task Force meetings" (11). He then adds: "These time-consuming and often frustrating internal discussions enabled residents to understand that they did not have to accomplish the impossible (i.e., prevent approval of the towers) to score a victory. Without this understanding, the city's ultimate approval of the hotels could have been psychologically and emotionally devastating. Instead, the Planning Commission's approval did not diminish residents' feelings that they had achieved a great triumph in their own lives and in the history of the neighborhood" (11–12). It took several more years to accomplish the rezoning goal, but , as Shaw writes, "the Tenderloin rezoning proposal was signed into law on March 28, 1985. Its passage culminated nearly five years of strategic planning that had involved hundreds of low-income people in ongoing tactical discussions" (13).

Shaw's method throughout the book is to deploy case studies in a systematic way to illustrate the tactical activism he is recommending. Although the book is not organized as a reference book, a democratic change agent could use as a handbook the stories Shaw tells and his analyses of the events, activities, strategies, and tactics depicted, for the stories illustrate the issues Shaw systematically addresses.

Shaw indicates that he had "no awareness of Dewey,"[20] but his social democratic orientation fits nicely with Dewey's similar progressive orientation, which of course is situated in his larger philosophy. Dewey came to politics and social change as a philosopher; Shaw clearly is a lawyer and organizer who is reflecting on his and others' political activities.

More than Education—Social Service Plus Political Action

The issue is not whether Dewey had a political technology. He did not. However, he did have a philosophy that needs to be and can be partially filled out by the work of Shaw and others. Moreover, Shaw has done so in one of the most difficult areas of social-political life—the enhancement of the lives of urban people of low and moderate income.[21]

More than he realizes, Shaw has rounded out Dewey's social-political thought by providing us with systematically situated instances of effective (and ineffective) action. He has shown the importance of public discussion and concerted effort—and he has identified and discussed the techniques employed. These techniques range from strategic planning to paying attention to politicians' performances (and not their promises), forming coalitions, bringing lawsuits, and taking direct action. Shaw's discussion of tactics for dealing with reporters is one of several must-reads for any activist.

He also has a carefully-worked-out set of criteria for evaluating possible ballot initiatives. In instance after instance one can learn from Shaw's discussions how to implement democratic change.

Shaw has done what Dewey did not do: He has specified the instruments of democratic social change for local organizations. But Shaw is not a political philosopher; he is well aware of the importance of what he has worked out for American society, but he does not develop the theoretical significance of either the model implicit in his own practice or the techniques of this practice and the organizing activities of either. With his brief references to the organizational setup of the Tenderloin Housing Clinic, Shaw has allowed us to glimpse a model for ongoing organization of low-income people, but he does not firmly identify this structure or generalize it. His focus is on the progressive activist's strategy and tactics. Moreover, Shaw is not aware of the Deweyan character of his unarticulated model, a model that exemplifies the Deweyan insistence that we intelligize practice rather than practicallize intelligence.

To practicalize intelligence is to start with reason and attempt to make it useful. The procedure advocated by Dewey is the reverse. He started with situations or ongoing practices and tried to make them more intelligent. To put the distinction starkly in terms of social change: Many advocates for social justice start with a rationally generated ideal and demand that an existing situation be replaced by one that conforms to their ideal. Dewey, who was not without his ideals, would seem to side with the political operatives, the political "pragmatists," in requiring that any suggested change take the existing situation into account and work from there. One moves the current practice toward an ideal, modifiying both situation and ideal as needed, through a process of deliberative change. This change is deliberative in two senses: It is slower than many activists would like, and, more to the point here, it is a process of social intelligence, a process involving the affected parties in ongoing discussion of problems, means, and ends. (Of course, this collaborative problem- and people-oriented approach distinguishes Dewey from many nonidealistic power-for-power's-sake political operatives.) I have already referred to Shaw's emphasis on grassroots decision making. I now want to make explicit the organizational model employed by him, a model that makes use of existing societal forms, modifying them in politically effective ways.

Shaw makes his living as a lawyer who defends low-income tenants on a fee-for-service basis. Therefore, the money for his legal practice is generated by his socially recognizable skill as a lawyer.[22] But, given the nature of his practice, he cannot effectively defend his clients by dealing with them one-on-one. He and his colleagues in the Tenderloin Housing Clinic need to organize the neighborhood in order to serve the interests of their clients. Unfortunately, Shaw does not describe how his organization works; he alludes to its setup in a few places, providing his readers only a glimpse of its structure. But we can infer what he has achieved, particularly when we read him alongside a book that Shaw mentions in an endnote—Robert Fisher's *Let the People Decide: Neighborhood Organizing in America*.[23]

Shaw refers his readers to Fisher for an explanation of the contradictory approach of neo-Alinsky groups that are populist yet embrace right-wing solutions that some think run counter to the interests of their constituencies (282, n. 17). But what interests me here is Fisher's analysis of three types of neighborhood organizing: social work, political activism, and neighborhood maintenance. The first is instanced by the settlement houses of a century ago or the community centers of recent years. The second is exemplified by the work of Saul Alinsky in the 1940s and 50s or that of various activists in the 1960s. The third is the less radical, often reactionary approach of the neighborhood improvement associations that attempt to protect or restore their privileged positions.

More recently a hybrid model has been developed, one that connects social action to service delivery. "Its roots," observes Fisher, "lie in the feminist movement ('the personal is political') and the development of a feminist practice in social work community organizing during the 1980s and early 1990s" (203). Fisher offers several examples of empowerment and service delivery, such as organizing around AIDS, homelessness, or health care, but he does not mention the sort of empowering legal services that the Tenderloin Housing Clinic apparently provides. Clearly, a more general model is available, and the Tenderloin Housing Clinic, if I am understanding it correctly, fits this model. If so, we have the makings of a model for social change that can employ in a sustainable way the social and political technology described by Shaw that would contribute to the completion of Dewey's social intelligence proposal.

Neither the model nor the techniques are fully worked out, although Shaw's discussions of the latter are full enough to guide an imaginative, resourceful organization. What is most needed is the intellectual development of the service-plus-empowerment model that I have identified in Shaw and Fisher. Several examples need to be identified, how they work needs to be analyzed, and then the resulting model needs to be displayed in a how-to book. Then, with a little more development of the techniques discussed by Shaw, we would have a Deweyan social-political technology for local democratic social action. This, in turn, could encourage the development of large-scale models and techniques. But at least a more fully developed local model and techniques would show that Dewey's work was not wrongheaded; it was just incomplete.

When I worked as an organizer in low- and moderate-income neighborhoods I found myself pulled in two directions. Tempermentally I was inclined to be accommodating, "realistic" in approach. But my sense of social justice was such that I was attracted to more extreme, confrontational approaches. Dewey, Shaw, and Fisher now help me understand that one can be pragmatic without being coopted by the existing situation. I left organizing for two reasons: One, I had questions that could best be answered by pursuing a Ph.D. in philosophy, and two, the federal money that was funding our efforts in the 1960s and 70s was drying up; we needed a new source of funding. Shaw and Fisher provide a way to find this funding.

One finds a practice that meets people's needs in ways that they can understand—and someone is willing to pay for. This could be a homeless shelter, spousal abuse shelter, tenant law practice, or some other social service. One meets people where they are in terms they can understand. Then one builds into this social or legal service-delivery model an organizing or political education dimension. This is not an add-on that is driven by the personal convictions of the service providers; it is an integral component that is included because organizing, while it initially may be outside the clients' experiences, is necessary for the continued delivery of services in a comprehensive manner. One meets a constituency's needs one-on-one only if the particular need is an isolated one. This is seldom the case. A more comprehensive approach is usually required. Most often the clients' personal difficulties are exacerbated by their socioeconomic situations. Confronting the structural dimension along with providing personal assistance helps to change the conditions that contribute to the personal difficulties. The social service–plus–political organizing model effectively meets this need in a sustainable way. It is not entirely dependent on politically vulnerable funding sources who are reluctant to finance efforts to effect social change. Nor does it suffer from the notorious defect of an organizing-only strategy—namely, grassroots organizations are difficult to sustain over time. Rather, the service-plus-empowerment model locates itself at the edge of what is politically and economically sustainable, delivering needed services and employing the techniques displayed in Shaw's book. In so doing, it points the way to an effective local change technology for Dewey's social intelligence proposal.

But a theoretical context and a model for local democratic action drawn from actual experience do not constitute a tranformed political situation. Nor, to recall Rorty's contention cited in the previous chapter, does participatory democracy as the goal of "the mainstream of American political rhetoric" and "American intellectual life." I will even grant that most politicians, political observers, and vocal citizens value access and participation in public life. But democracy as understood by Dewey, Westbrook, Shaw, and Fisher involves organized activity. These thinkers believe that democratic participation will involve the participants in a sustained, organized effort. Moreover, this organizational engagement will not be over against representative democracy, but will—and this is what separates them from the mainstream advocates of representative democracy—modify conventional representative democracy to include active, sustained, direct engagement. This reconstructed form of representative democracy is what Dewey envisioned and Shaw has described in practice.

Looking Ahead: A Matter of Faith

A less than full theory of a transforming society was not the only incompleteness with which Dewey had to live. Also open was the very feasibility of a democratically self-transforming society. Dewey was confident that a deliberately transforming democratic society was achievable, but realized that such a society had yet to be realized in practice. His faith in democracy was just that—a confidence based on experience upon which he was willing to act, but nevertheless a faith. He thought—and argued—that this faith was well founded. Others did not think so; they thought that his faith in social intelligence and democratic processes was misplaced. He was under continual attack from absolutists of all sorts who thought his confidence in an open society that could deliberately transform itself was naive.

Dewey responded to these attacks in a variety of ways, but the one that I want to single out here is his belief that constructive change was possible and that such a change could not be determined in both senses of *determined*. One could not know what would actually happen, and what would eventually happen was not entirely fixed by the present course of events.

In "I Believe," an essay published in 1939, Dewey argued that the danger at that time was that his society would attempt to overcome "the evils of private economic collectivism" by plunging into "political economic collectivism" rather than turning to the "cooperative voluntary" society that he advocated. He defended his hope that a society of voluntary associations voluntarily chosen could be brought about by criticizing the two then-prominent alternatives to mass society capitalism—communism and fascism—and by appealing to history: "For if history teaches anything it is that judgments regarding the future have been predicated upon the basis of the tendencies that are most conspicuous at the time, while in fact the great social changes which have produced new social institutions have been the cumulative effect of flank movements that were not obvious at the time of their origin." Dewey then recalled the failed prophesy of Herbert Spencer in the latter part of the nineteenth century, "during the height of expanding competitive industrialism," that the effect of this increasing industrialism "would be a future society of free individuals and of free nations so interdependent that lasting peace would be achieved." Indeed, given the events of the Great War and the depression and the impending world war that would turn the former one into World War I, Dewey could observe that "the actual result has been the opposite": the consequence of competitive industrialism was not increased freedom (LW 14:94–96).

After comparing the call for a collectivized industrialism based on an extrapolation of tendencies present at the time to this earlier failed prediction, Dewey noted: "Nevertheless those who can escape the hypnotic influence exercised by the immediate contemporary scene are aware that movements going on in the interstices of the existing order are those which will in fact shape the future. As a friend of mine puts it, the last thing the lord of the feudal castle would have imagined was that the future of society was with the forces that were represented by the humble trader who set up his post under the walls of his castle." He then closed the essay by expressing his confidence that "the ultimate way out of the present social dead end" was to be found in the development of "voluntary associations of individuals, which are even now building up within the cracks of a crumbling social order." As Dewey wrote: "Individuals who have not lost faith in themselves and in other individuals will increasingly ally themselves with these groups. Sooner or later they will construct the way out of present confusion and conflict. The sooner it is done the shorter will be the time of chaos and catastrophe" (LW 14:96–97).

Here we find an interesting mix of experiential checking (the appeal to history), political and cultural critique (the analysis of capitalism and its alternatives), an appeal to Dewey's ideal of ordered richness (a voluntary society), and a faith in the possibilites of human nature (both the appeal to the open future and the confidence in "individuals who have not lost faith in themselves and in other individuals").

Dewey may not have had a finely tuned political technology, but he certainly was capable of evaluating his present society and its alternatives. He was an informed critic, calling attention to "voluntary associations" that were even then "building up within the cracks of a crumbling social order," who could deliberate publicly about the next steps to be taken in the light of an overarching vision, even if he could not offer a detailed plan of this society of voluntary associations voluntarily achieved. He did know, however, that such a society could be achieved only through the experimentation implicit in his reference to the existence of "voluntary associations . . . within the cracks" and the public deliberation in which he was continually engaged. Such a democratic society could be achieved only by the democratic means of free deliberation and experimentation. Or so he believed.

Faith-talk smacks of religion, and Dewey was willing to use religious language to express his core proposal. In the "I Believe" essay we have a rather mild example of his faith in social intelligence and the possibilites of social reconstruction. But even here we find what, upon reflection, appears to be a quite astonishing affirmation for a philosopher who takes the scientific method as a model for intelligence. He argued for his voluntary-society ideal not only on the basis of history and as an alternative to what was not working, but also came very close to arguing (if he did not in fact do so) on the basis of what would come about: "Individuals who have not lost faith in themselves and in other individuals will increasingly ally themselves with these groups. Sooner or later they will construct the way out of present confusion and conflict." He thus appealed not just to what could be—that is, an attractive possibility—but to what he claimed *would come about*, a high probability if not an outright prediction. Dewey had what some have taken to be an unshakable faith in democracy.

Religious language, particularly when used in nontraditional ways, is open to misinterpretation. Dewey's talk of faith in democracy as an ordering richness and his talk of the coming voluntary society were no exceptions. His efforts to express secular understandings in religious or quasireligious language met with a mixed reaction. With his participation in a public discussion of the nature of God in the *Christian Century* in 1933 and the subsequent publication of *A Common Faith* the following year, Dewey found himself embroiled in controversy as he attempted to reconstruct religious beliefs and thus harness religious impulses for the democratic way of life. Some welcomed his embrace of the religious in experience; some were bewildered; others were amused. I will address the former reactions in the next chapter. As for the amused reactions, I will cite here one example. In April 1933 his friend and fellow participant in the debate about God in the *Christian Century*, the philosopher Max C. Otto, wrote Dewey about the latter's efforts: "In the back of my consciousness there has been a smile, most of the time, as I have said to myself: I'll bet he didn't know what he was letting himself in for when he agreed to review the debate" (quoted in LW 9:448). Whether Dewey knew what would happen or not, he continued to speak of his deepest convictions as a faith in democracy. To understand this faith and Dewey's religious proposal will be my aim in the next chapter.

5

❖

DEWEY'S RELIGIOUS PROPOSAL

While the conflict of traditional religious beliefs with opinions that I could myself honestly entertain was the source of a trying personal crisis, it did not at any time constitute a leading philosophical problem. This might look as if the two things were kept apart; in reality it was due to a feeling that any genuinely sound religious experience could and should adapt itself to whatever beliefs one found oneself intellectually entitled to hold. . . . In consequence, . . . I have not been able to attach much importance to religion as a philosophic problem; for the effect of that attachment seems to be in the end a subornation of candid philosophic thinking to the alleged but factitious needs of some special set of convictions.

—John Dewey, "From Absolutism to Experimentalism"
(LW 5:153)

DEWEY'S RELIGIOUS PROPOSAL, as found in *A Common Faith* (1934, LW 9), is a philosophical elaboration of his own faith in intelligence and democracy and of his commitment to the principle of continuity, a working out of what he had come to believe through critical inquiry and was willing to recommend to others. In the previous chapters I have spelled out much of the content of this faith, particularly Dewey's social concern; now I turn to the problematic character of Dewey's faith and his controversial proposal to reconstruct religion in accordance with it both in terms of content and form. We will find that his intended strategy was characteristic of his overall approach. He neither accepted nor rejected religion as he found it. Rather, he attempted to transform it, developing a third option, one that made use of some features of the various religions—notably faith, piety, the idea of a god, and some of the humane values associated with various traditions—but rejected or made no use or limited use of many elements that are often thought central to religion, including revelation, prayer, immortality, separate institutions, and even a distinctively religious experience. Dewey denied that there is a referent for the term *religion*, arguing that there are only the various religious traditions. Religion per se does not exist. Nevertheless, his proposal is a radical reconstruction of what he took to be valuable in the religious traditions. Therefore, Dewey did not reject the religious in experience completely. He found something of value within the cultural heritage of his audience and attempted to build on this in ways that accorded with his own secular approach.

Handling Dewey's Religious Proposal with Care

This reconstructive insight is crucial to understanding Dewey's proposal. If the heritage of his readers had been different, his borrowings and reconstruction would have been different. We must not focus too much on what he had to say about "God," to take the notable, controversial example, for Dewey was attempting to articulate his essentially secular project in language congenial to those who wished to be both religious and secular. The language he used in *A Common Faith* was responsive to the needs of his audience; it was never intended to be timelessly expressive of his understanding of experience.[1] To think that it was is to think that 'Dewey's little book on religion' is in some sense superior to the extensive secular writing that he produced. Also, while *A Common Faith* may be in many ways a good summary of Dewey's approach, it is not definitive. One must bear in mind that Dewey was not one to write systematic treatments; as an instrumentalist he preferred to speak to specific problems or situations. *A Common Faith* is just what it appears to be—a series of lectures delivered at Yale University in 1934 by a prominent secular philosopher on the significant human topic of religion, talks that nevertheless reflect what he had been saying for years. Therefore, *A Common Faith* is of interest, but it is not one of Dewey's major books in terms of either length or the attention he gave it.

Dewey's recommendation to intelligize practice can be considered religious, but only in a restricted sense. If a practice is intensively and extensively intelligent, Dewey and many others would regard it as religious, for it would reflect the commitment and integration associated with religion. But this thoroughly intelligized experience will seem to still others to be a less than robust form of religion. As George Santayana is reported to have quipped, "'A Common Faith'? A very common faith indeed!"[2]

My hope is that by coming to this discussion of Dewey's religious proposal after an extensive consideration of his core project of intelligizing practice we can appreciate the instrumental—that is, broadly ad hoc—character of his proposal. Perhaps in this way we can avoid the mistake of reading into his language content that he never intended and even sought to guard against.

There is an opposing difficulty. Secular interpreters sometimes pay no attention or little attention to *A Common Faith*, regarding it as a small book with its own significance, but one that is not as central a work as some of Dewey's other writings. Unlike his metaphysics, method, education, or politics, it can be safely ignored or, as Dewey himself often did with the subject of religion in many of his books, relegated to a few sentences or pages.[3] This neglect can be explained, in part, by the special focus of some interpreters. Thomas Alexander and Larry Hickman are concerned primarily with Deweyan aesthetics and technology, respectively, although both, of course, are concerned also with Dewey's thinking as a whole. But this explanation will not do for the authors of two other recent, major, valuable books on Dewey, Ralph Sleeper and J. E. Tiles. Nor will it do for Richard Bernstein, author of the well-regarded *John Dewey* (New York: Washington Square Press, 1967).

Bernstein makes the remarkable claim that Dewey's "treatment of the religious attitude and quality is the culmination of his entire philosophy" (161), yet he confines his exposition of Dewey's religious proposal to a few pages (161–65). Bernstein qualifies his claim in two ways: One, he understands *A Common Faith* to be "an expression of . . . Dewey's 'natural piety'"; and two, "interpreted in this manner, Dewey is making explicit [in *A Common Faith*] what is implicit in his entire philosophy" (161). The latter qualification is largely correct; the former, in my view, is too narrow. "Natural piety" is not sufficient to cover Dewey's faith, for it says nothing about intelligence and democracy. It is very difficult to do what Dewey himself did not do: present his philosophy in a way that integrates the religious in experience throughout the exposition.[4] I have not done so either; nor do I think it should be done. Given the connotations of religious language, one cannot use this language to express a secular outlook without being misunderstood. The religious interpretation of Dewey in a limited sense of *religious* that includes Dewey's understanding of the religious as a quality of experience is best left to those who will take the time and trouble to appreciate its refined use. The time is still not right for a secularly religious interpretation. It was not so in Dewey's lifetime, as we shall see, nor is it so now.

The contrast of my approach with that of Bruce Kuklick is striking.[5] For Kuklick "Dewey's thought," even as a mature philosopher, was "shaped" by the "Andover Liberals," who were Dewey's theological allies when he was a young philosophy instructor and still active in the

Congregational Church in the 1880s (255). Therefore, Kulick believes that "*A Common Faith* elaborated Dewey's view of religion and, unsurprisingly, recapitulated in his new [scientific] conceptual framework earlier notions connected to his defense of [the Andover Liberals'] Progressive Orthodoxy" (251). The clear impression is that Dewey's thinking, even in the 1930s, was religious or even theological to a significant extent and was being expressed in the scientific language of instrumentalism.

My own approach is the reverse of Kuklick's. I interpret Dewey, as do most, as a pervasively secular thinker. But, unlike most of Dewey's secular interpreters, I tackle head on the religious character of Dewey's philosophy. His approach can be regarded as a religious one.[6] My hesitation in making this claim is that one who fails to observe the qualified ways in which Dewey uses religious language and the rather limited way in which I understand his project to be religious will take me to be saying that Dewey's philosophy is religious in a conventional sense. Clearly, it is not. What separates me from many interpreters of *A Common Faith* is that I think it is possible to use only secular language to articulate any aspect of the mature Dewey's thinking and yet recognize the way in which his project to intelligize practice can function religiously. To grasp this we will have to pay careful attention to the way Dewey reconstructed religious beliefs and practices and not allow these reconstructions to slide back into unreconstructed ideas.

Also, as I will argue, the assertion that in some sense Dewey's philosophy is religious may not amount to much. Given the restricted sense that Dewey gave the religious, one may be making an empty claim. It is important to realize, as Ryan shows, that Dewey's use of religious language appealed to his reading public in the first part of the twentieth century. But there may not be anything left once one discounts the rhetoric. The hard truth for partisans of a religious interpretation of Dewey's philosophy is that he so reconstructed the religious as to make it almost indistinguishable from the nonreligious. For the most part, if he were not advertising his commitments as a faith and suggesting that the way of life he recommended could be understood in a religious sense, very few interpreters would notice anything religious in Dewey's philosophy. Indeed, as I have already indicated, most have not. The irony of my approach is that after criticizing others for too often paying only lip service to the religious in Dewey I will conclude by stating that, for the most part, in our time Dewey is best interpreted almost entirely in secular terms.[7]

To develop this very nuanced understanding of Dewey's religious proposal I will first pay particular attention to the reworked understanding of faith that was his inheritance as a pragmatist. (There is no question that

Dewey had faith in intelligence and democracy and the natural conditions that made these ideals realizable, but there is considerable question regarding just what having faith meant for Dewey.) Then I will turn to the occasion for the Terry Lectures that were published as *A Common Faith* before dealing with the book itself. My treatment of the book will specify in ways that others have not done what Dewey means by the religious in experience. Finally, I will consider some of the reactions to the book. These reactions, we will find, exemplify one of the problems with Dewey's melioristic approach to philosophy. Dewey took practices as he found them and stretched them in ways that he thought desirable, but not so far as to seem a radically new approach to all observers. Yet some of his readers fail to notice what is distinctive in his reconstruction. Lacking dramatic markers, his readers tend to reduce his view to one or the other of the two options of the dualism that he had attempted to transform into a third choice, one he thought was a genuinely new way that borrowed from the dualism's two options, but advanced beyond them. This risk holds true everywhere with regard to Dewey and his critics, but it is particularly evident with regard to his religious proposal.

Dewey's proposal to intelligize practice can, under certain conditions, be embodied in a way of life that can be described as religious, although it will be, as I shall continue to point out, a reconstructed type of religion. Just as a Deweyan change agent or educator will be both like and unlike a conventional politician or traditional lecturer, a Deweyan religious practitioner will be both similar to and different from a conventional religious adherent. But a qualification needs to be made. Religious beliefs and practices, perhaps even more than those of politics or education, are invested with traditional meanings that are difficult to reconstruct. The old ways die hard. Therefore, Dewey's transformations have not always worked. Some of his readers have received the new wine in old bottles, assimilating Dewey's radical proposal to their traditional beliefs and practices. Like the proverbial camel who gets its nose under the tent, religion, if given an opening, can soon take over the whole enterprise. *A Common Faith* has, upon occasion, become the camel in some Deweyans' tents.

Dewey's Faith

Dewey was not reluctant to talk of his faiths in human nature, the possibility of intelligence in ordinary people (and thus the possibility of education), science, equality, democracy, and voluntary activity. These various faiths are, of course, related; they are "a cluster of faiths," to use

Campbell's phrase.[8] The core of this faith is expressed in a passage in "Creative Democracy—The Task Before Us" that I discussed in the previous chapter. There Dewey described his faith in democracy as a threefold faith in human nature, intelligent judgment and action, and cooperative activity. Significantly, he claimed, speaking specifically of his faith in intelligent judgment and action, not to have invented this faith, but to have "acquired it from my surroundings as far as those surroundings were animated by the democratic spirit" (LW 14:227). Dewey's faith was a reworking of his cultural heritage, but a reconstruction that eliminated much of what most people would regard as religious. He retained and developed what he had "acquired" from his environment that was "animated by the democratic spirit."

One useful approach, then, is to trace the development of Dewey's faith. Steven C. Rockefeller, in *John Dewey: Religious Faith and Democratic Humanism,* has done a very fine job of this. His account of Dewey's religious growth is full and informative. He patiently works through the original material, often correcting the mistakes of previous historians.[9] He also places Dewey's religious development in context, attempting to correct for the distortion that comes from taking a single perspective. Nevertheless, he thinks that "Dewey's vision of the meaning and value of the democratic way of uniting the ideal and the actual culminates in his philosophy of the religious dimension of experience" (539). I am uncomfortable with the hierarchial model implied by the term "culminates." As I indicated earlier, I think Dewey's philosophy *can* be characterized as a religious one, but I think it is also political and educational. Perhaps one can write a thematic history and not privilege the chosen theme, but Rockefeller has not done so.[10] I am also uncomfortable with Rockefeller's characterization of the direction of Dewey's movement, implying as it does a religious orientation from beginning to end. Nevertheless, I wholeheartedly endorse the judgment that the problem of the relation between existence and value was the central problem in Dewey's thought.

But, in addition to the difficulty of writing a balanced book about Dewey that follows a single stream, no matter how contextual one might be, there is another good reason for my not tracing the development of Dewey's faith: Rockefeller has already done so. His book fills a real need. It is a full, informed account of this significant aspect of Dewey's life and work. Therefore, all I need to do is record some of the pertinent developments. This I will do indirectly by considering Dewey's recollections of these developments. Then I will examine his pragmatic understanding of what it means to have faith.

Dewey's Heritage

Dewey was reared in Burlington, Vermont, in the 1860s and 1870s, the son of an easygoing storekeeper father and pious, community-minded mother. Over time he rejected the Congregational Church of his early years, but retained and developed the small-town democratic heritage of his family. He also built upon the education he received at the University of Vermont, from which he graduated in 1879 at age nineteen, and afterward in private study with his philosophy teacher. I will deal with this last recollection first, then focus on two memories of the cultural influences on Dewey as a youth and one of his drift away from the neo-Hegelianism of his graduate school years and beyond.[11] I will deal with the philosophical shift after discussing the first cultural influence, the one having to do with religion, saving the democratic heritage recollection for last.

The Torrey Model

H. A. P. Torrey was Dewey's philosophy teacher at the University of Vermont. Not much persisted in the later Dewey of the content of Torrey's teaching, but Lewis S. Feuer cites a sentence from one of Torrey's lectures that was to become a guiding principle for Dewey: "The work of philosophy is one of continual readjustment to changing environment."[12] What Dewey remembered at age seventy was that Torrey was "an excellent teacher" who had turned Dewey's "thoughts definitely to the study of philosophy as a life-pursuit" and had freely spent time with Dewey after graduation, reading classic philosophic texts with him, as well as philosophic German (LW 5:149).

What I find striking is Dewey's memory of a theologically liberal but still orthodox Protestant who stayed within the ecclesiastical bounds set by his time and place. Speaking of his postbacculaureate study with Torrey, Dewey wrote: "In our walks and talks during this year, after three years on my part of high-school teaching, he let his mind go much more freely than in the classroom, and revealed potentialities that might have placed him among the leaders in the development of a freer American philosophy—but the time for the latter had not yet come" (149). In 1930, when Dewey wrote the autobiographical essay, "From Absolutism to Experience," from which this sentence is taken, Dewey was moving into his most radical period. He had just retired from Columbia and was becoming more active politically. He was not one to judge his teacher too harshly for having lived within the constraints of a small nineteenth-century university in northern New England. But he did see the constraints for what they were and valued the possibilities of a more liberating society. Fortunately, Dewey was able to move beyond the confinement of the society of his youth. But the way in which he did so was not that of rebellion. His radicalism evolved; he never pushed beyond the limits of what his employing institution would tolerate. But, unlike his first philosophy teacher, he found new institutions in freer environments than Burlington, Vermont.

The Christianity Dewey Left Behind

Later in this same autobiographical piece there is an often-quoted passage about what Dewey found painful about the culture in which he was reared. This text deserves study, for it describes in vivid terms Dewey's motivation for overcoming dualisms. Following a report of the influence of his graduate school teacher, George Sylvester Morris, and the Hegelianism he learned from Morris and others, Dewey spoke of the "'subjective' reasons for the appeal that Hegel's thought made" to him as a Johns Hopkins University Ph.D. student:

> It supplied a demand for unification that was doubtless an intense emotional craving, and yet was a hunger that only an intellectualized subject-matter could satisfy. It is more than difficult, it is impossible, to recover that early mood. But the sense of divisions and separations that were, I suppose, borne in upon me as a consequences of a heritage of New England culture, divisions by way of isolation of self from the world, of soul from body, of nature from God, brought a painful oppression—or, rather, they were an inward laceration. My earlier philosophic study had been an intellectual gymnastic. Hegel's synthesis of subject and object, matter and spirit, the divine and the human, was, however, no mere intellectual formula; it operated as an immense release, a liberation. Hegel's treatment of human culture, of institutions and the arts, involved the same dissolution of hard-and-fast dividing walls, and had a special attraction for me. (LW 5:153)

I will have more to say a bit later about the Hegelian "deposit" (LW 5:154) that persisted in Dewey's thinking as a result of his graduate school liberation, but I want to concentrate here on the sort of culture that he rejected.

Following Dewey's death in 1952, Sidney Hook recalled Dewey once telling him "in a rare, reminiscent mood . . . something of his religious development, and some embarrassing episodes when he was a boy." One such embarassment was this: "My mother was converted to Evangelism which in practice was something worse than Puritanism. She was continuously asking me and my brother—sometimes before others—'Are you right with Jesus? Have you prayed to God for forgiveness?' It tended to induce in us a sense of guilt and at the same time irritation because of the triviality of the occasions on which she questioned us."[13] Jane Dewey, in her biography of her father, mentioned her grandmother's intensity and missionary zeal, but also noted that, while Lucina Dewey "was stricter with the boys" than "her easy-going husband," she also "had more ambition for them," for "it was largely due to her influence that the boys broke with family tradition and obtained a college education" (Schilpp, 6).

Another qualification must also be registered. Lucina was not the only religious influence on Dewey. His mother's family were Universalists, and Dewey often spent summers with his maternal grandfather.[14] Also, the minister of First Congregational Church in Burlington when Dewey was a teenager was Lewis O. Brastow, a liberal evangelical who was to leave Burlington in 1884 to become a professor of practical theology at Yale University. Therefore, the religious influence on Dewey was broader than Hook's transmission of Dewey's recollection of his mother's regular interrogation might indicate. Nevertheless, the divisions that Dewey remembered were also present in the teaching of those more moderate than his mother.

Many other intelligent, sensitive young men responded to these divisions and the challenges of modern science by coming to stress God's immanence rather than his transcendence and by encouraging human development rather than demanding conversion from sin. Speaking of the liberals of "the Golden Age of Liberal Theology," the period from just before the turn of the century until just after World War I, Sydney E. Ahlstrom observed that they sought to unify things, avoiding disjunctions: "They preferred to combine or merge the romantic inclination to see man and nature as alike infused with divinity and the Darwinian tendency to relate man to the natural world in a scientific way. Similarly, man and God were brought together." They were more inclined than conservatives to think of God as being immanent rather than transcendent. "The supernatural and the spiritual tended to be identified; and the spiritual in turn was identified with consciousness—the conative, intellectual, emotive side of man. Finally, the ancient disjunctions between the subjective and objective, between the mental world and the 'real' or 'objective' world, were minimized philosophically by theories of reality which stressed the ideal nature of things and by intuitional or idealistic theories of knowledge."[15] As Kuklick shows, Dewey was a part of this liberal religious movement. As a neo-Hegelian philosopher in the 1880s and an active member of the Congregational Church in Ann

Arbor and on the University of Michigan campus, Dewey contributed to the liberalization of Christianity in America in the late nineteenth century.

But Dewey came to recognize the persistent dualism in even the liberal attempt to overcome the divisions he had felt keenly as a youth. Increasingly during the 1890s Dewey went beyond Christian liberalism, becoming a secular person and thinker. Ryan claims that Dewey "unobtrusively lost his faith in 1891." This may be, but Ryan is on firmer ground in calling attention to the boldness of the 1892 address "Christianity and Democracy" (EW 4:3–10), in which Dewey was dismissive of institutional religion, attempting to locate the ongoing revelation of God and Christianity in science and democracy.[16] As this address shows, if Dewey had lost his faith by 1892 he was still willing to couch his defense of science and democracy in Christian terms.

But the significant question is not the backward-looking one of how much Christianity was still clinging to Dewey as he was ending his stay in Ann Arbor and moving to Chicago. The real question has to do with where Dewey was headed not so much in terms of religion, but in reference to philosophy, culture, and life generally. Whatever happened in the early 1890s, whether there was a decisive event or a slow transformation, Ryan is correct to call attention to the secular turn in Dewey's life and thinking. He is also correct to note that Dewey continued to express his thinking on occasion in religious language even when "arguing for a view of the world that is commonly thought to be squarely at odds with religion" (20). I would not express it as Ryan does, but there is some truth in his observation that "Dewey brought off the delicate rhetorical trick of investing his views with the mystique of modernity and science at the same time that he persuaded his hearers that they were firmly linked to tradition and the ways of everyday common sense" (206).

Dewey was a *via media* thinker. Although he ceased to be Christian in the 1890s and religious in any conventional sense, he continued to use religious terms as needed. But we must not mistake his speaking in an idiom with which he had long been familiar and which may have assisted his audience in accepting his sometimes radical proposals with a continuing commitment to the faith of his youth. Recall that Hook said that Dewey recollected his mother's religious influence "in a rare, reminiscent mood." There was not much drag on Dewey; his life was marked by "openness and growth," to use the phrase and concur with the judgment with which Coughlan ends his book (162). What is interesting is that during the forty-five or so productive years remaining to Dewey in the 1890s he became the naturalistic and pragmatic philosopher that is worthy of continued study.

The young liberal Christian philosophy professor did not make it out of Michigan.

The Hegelian Deposit

Parallel to Dewey's move beyond Christianity was his gradual moving away from Hegelianism. In "From Absolutism to Experimentalism" he wrote, "I drifted away from Hegelianism in the next fifteen years; the word 'drifting' expresses the slow and, for a long time, imperceptible character of the movement."[17] Then he added: "I should never think of ignoring, much less denying, what an astute critic occasionally refers to as a novel discovery—that acquaintance with Hegel has left a permanent deposit in my thinking" (LW 5:154).

Jane Dewey, in her biography of her father, refers to this statement and then adds another statement from him. I quote the entire paragraph because of its significance for understanding this "Hegelian deposit." Worthy of special notice is the precision of Dewey's recollection; there is little of the qualification and vagueness of which Dewey is often accused:

> Hegel's idea of cultural institutions as an "objective mind" upon which individuals were dependent in the formation of their mental life fell in with the influence of Comte and of Condorcet and Bacon. The metaphysical ideal that an absolute mind is manifested in social institutions dropped out; the idea, upon an empirical basis, of the power exercised by cultural environment in shaping the ideas, beliefs, and intellectual attitudes of individuals remained. It was a factor in producing my belief that the not uncommon assumption in both psychology and philosophy of a ready-made mind over against a physical world as an object has no empirical support. It was a factor in producing my belief that the only possible psychology, as distinct from a biological account of behavior, is a social psychology. With respect to more technically philosophical matters, the Hegelian emphasis upon continuity and the function of conflict persisted on empirical grounds after my earlier confidence in dialectic had given way to scepticism. There was a period extending into my earlier years at Chicago when, in connection with a seminar in Hegel's Logic I tried reinterpreting his categories in terms of "readjustment" and "reconstruction." Gradually I came to realize that what the principles actually stood for could be better understood and stated when completely emancipated from Hegelian garb. (Schilpp, 17–18)

Dewey's recollection is that he took from Hegel the principle of continuity and the recognition of the role of conflict, retaining them "on empirical grounds." This is the "naturalized Hegelianism" that has proved troublesome to his critics. Historians of Dewey's development have difficulty marking the shift from idealism to instrumentalism.[18] More difficult philosophically is the claim that Dewey never really abandoned Hegel, continuing to be a closet idealist.[19] Therefore, his philosophy is compromised, many think, by a contradiction between his lingering Hegelianism and his professed naturalism. But Dewey thought there was no latent idealism. He is very clear that what he had retained from Hegel had been completely reconstructed.

I think Dewey successfully naturalized Hegel, finding a third way—instrumentalism—beyond the idealism of his earlier years and the then-competing realism of his contemporaries.[20] It has been my concern throughout this book to show the integrity of Dewey's novel approach and the difficulty he had in articulating it in conventional language, as well as the tendency of his critics to interpret him in terms of the existing dualisms. But I will finally confront this matter directly in the last chapter, "The Secularity of Deweyan Criticism." For now what needs to be noted is that Dewey understood that he eventually rejected objective idealism and transformed some features of it, developing a naturalistic philosophy that was neither idealist nor realist. Recognizing this naturalism is important in understanding his faith in democracy and intelligence, for it provides an account of the conditions in nature that support these cooperative, life-transforming activities.

The Democracy Dewey Transformed

In 1929, at age seventy, Dewey returned to the University of Vermont to participate in a commemoration of the publication of James Marsh's introduction to Coleridge's *Aids to Reflection*. Marsh, the university's fifth president, was the one who had established the curriculum that was still in place when Dewey was a student. His address, published as "James Marsh and American Philosophy," contains this rare personal reference: "I shall never cease to be grateful that I was born at a time and place where the earlier ideal of liberty and the self-governing community of citizens still sufficiently prevailed so that I unconsciously imbibed a sense of its meaning." This meaning, which he primarily articulated in what follows in terms of the historicity of governmental institutions, could also be developed in terms of other cultural beliefs and practices, as the foregoing reference to liberty shows. Continuing, he recalled, "In Vermont, perhaps even more than elsewhere, there was embodied in the spirit of the people the conviction that governments were like the houses we live in, made to contribute to human welfare, and that those who lived in them were as free to change and extend the one as they were the other when developing needs of the human family called for such alterations and modifications" (LW 5:194). The later ideal of freedom, the one that "eclipsed" the individualism of Dewey's youth, was one that exalted "individuals free from social relations and responsibilities" (193). But what he "unconsciously imbibed" was a constructive notion of democracy that felt "free to change and extend" government as necessary to meet the "developing needs of the human family." Governments, like houses, were useful, but not sacred.

Dewey was fully aware of the constrictions of his childhood society, as we have already seen in his comments about his university philosophy teacher and as we see at the end of the Marsh essay. In the last paragraph he observed, "The period was not favorable to far-reaching thought which always demands a certain audacity lacking both to the period and to Dr. Marsh's temperament" (196). Dewey was under no illusion that the nineteenth century in Vermont was a golden age of democracy. What he treasured and developed was a sense of freedom and self-governance that valued community, but did not freeze the governmental forms. This freedom was both an individualism and a willingness to alter institutions as necessary. However, this freedom did not extend to the same degree to religious thought and institutions, nor to philosophy. This was so in spite of a reforming, if not radical, tendency in the thought of Coleridge that Marsh was transmitting to his American readers. Marsh, Dewey observed, was "conscious that he was coming into conflict with the ideas which dominated not only American society but the churches themselves"; therefore, he "restricted" his philosophical activity. It was left to Emerson and others to bring out the liberating tendencies in Coleridge's thought (184).

Dewey ended his address with this final observation: "The underlying substance [of Marsh's thought] is a wistful aspiration for full and ordered living" (196). The latter phrase recalls Dewey's own understanding of democracy as "ordered richness." But the characterization of Marsh's aspiration as a wistful one should keep us from attributing a robust valuing of diversity and freedom to him; his life and times were more "ordered" than "full." One cannot trace Dewey's mature understanding of democracy as an ordering richness that values free inquiry and creative conflict to an idyllic democratic Vermont; one can, however, see something of the later ideal if not in the earlier period, at least in Dewey's recollections of the influences on his youth.

An important transition for Dewey was marked by his move in 1894 from Ann Arbor to become chairman of the department of philosophy at the

University of Chicago. Dykhuizen reports, "Democracy in all its phases—political, economic, social, cultural—came to claim Dewey's strongest allegiance and to command his deepest loyalties; interest in social aid and social reform groups began to replace his interest in the Church." This shift in interest had institutional implications: "Dewey's formal connection with organized religion ended when he left Ann Arbor. A few years after settling in Chicago, he withdrew his membership from the church in Ann Arbor and did not ask for a letter of transferral to a church in Chicago. 'Dismissed without letter' is the last notation under Dewey's name in the records of the Congregational Church in Ann Arbor" (*Life and Mind*, pp.. 73–74). Dewey ceased to be not just a church member, but a Christian, somewhere around the turn of the century, if not when he moved to Chicago then perhaps by the time that he left in 1904 for New York City and Columbia University. Unlike during the Michigan years, Dewey's involvments in New York were largely secular, with no supportive involvement whatsoever in conventional Christianity. Clearly, the Chicago years were transitional in terms of religious affiliation and identification.

That which persisted and came to be characteristic of Dewey as a philosopher and a person was a deep and extensive commitment to the ideals of democracy as an ordering richness and intelligence as a creative, critical activity. What is less evident is his "natural piety." Therefore, Randall is able to summarize Dewey's faith as follows: "Piety toward nature is as deep-seated for him as spiritual devotion to the community that intelligence is to create" ("The Religion of Shared Experience," 123). This summary is too neat and suggests wrongly that intelligence is the condition for community. I think, rather, that democracy and intelligence were mutually dependent on one another for Dewey.

What is even more unclear at this point is the nature of Dewey's commitment—whatever its content. Just what does it mean to say that Dewey's faith included devotion to intelligence and democracy, as well as natural piety? The latter notion involves considerations that can be better handled once we consider *A Common Faith* and introduce Santayana's distinction between piety and spirituality, an analysis that Dewey more or less adopted. For now we can concentrate on the more generic idea of faith.

Faith as a Revisable Tendency to Action

A persistent criticism of Dewey, one that we have seen before, is that Dewey's faith in intelligence and democracy was possibly not just religious in the sense that he intended, a sense that we will examine later in this chapter, but was unwarranted by experience, and thus religious in a sense he would not accept.[21] The alleged inconsistency between his metaphysical naturalism and his "ultimate values," a problem raised by Rockefeller, must wait until we have discussed Dewey's reconstructed notion of God. For now I want to limit the discussion to his understanding of faith.

The Problem

Dewey the self-professed naturalist was possibly a believer in a utopian and therefore unrealizable form of democracy. Some think that he refused to face up to the mounting evidence in his own lifetime that the democratic way of life in which he believed was not a realistic possibility; he persisted in believing in what could not be. Therefore, one could infer that he was religious not just in the *A Common Faith* sense of having a deeply held self-transforming confidence, but in the sense that he had criticized. For example, the professed experimentalist refused to read the results of the tests to which his form of democracy had been put. Therefore, he had no right as a pragmatist to believe in democracy, for it was not, to cite one of the three criteria stated by William James in "The Will to Believe," a live option. Dewey's democratic faith was like the schoolboy's faith that James cited as a "misapprehension" of what he recommended: "Faith is when you believe something that you know ain't true."[22] Clearly, Dewey as a philosopher of experience could not embrace what he knew (or should have known) "ain't true." To do so would have been not only to engage in the sort of religion he condemned, but, to quote James once again, "patent superstition" (32).

There are passages that support the view that Dewey persisted in believing in something that he knew could not be. One is his discussion of democracy as "the idea of community life itself" in *The Public and Its Problems*. As an ideal, he wrote, democracy is "the tendency and movement of some thing which exists carried to its final limit," but "democracy in this sense is not a fact and never will be" (LW 2:328). From this passage, taken by itself, one could infer that Dewey believed in something that could never be. This would make Dewey like the supernaturalists that he constantly criticized. But to read him in this way is to distort his use of a nonexistent possibility, ideal democracy, into a belief in the actuality of such an ideal in a way comparable to the way one believes in the existence of empirical objects. This is not a promising line of attack.

Robert Westbrook, in a review of Campbell's book on pragmatic social thought[23] and in an autobiographical statement initially read at the 1993 meeting of the Society for the Advancement of American philosophy[24], speaks of Dewey's attitude toward democracy—and particularly participatory democracy—as a faith. Westbrook thinks that Dewey failed to spell out this faith in politically effective practices and that events have not shown it to be warranted either in his own lifetime or since. Coming from the author of a well-received intellectual history, *John Dewey and American Democracy*, this charge must be taken seriously. From time to time others have also thought Dewey religious in a compromising sense, but Westbrook's opinion has an authority based on years of careful research. Although I challenge the claim in the two *Transactions* pieces, I want to make my respect for Westbrook's book clear. His is an informed history of Dewey as a publicly engaged democratic thinker. Westbrook may be wrong here and there, and perhaps he could have done more.[25] But what he has done is impressive and valuable.

Faith for Dewey

As Dewey saw it, faith is not a belief in *X*, that *X* exists, so much as it is a tendency to action. It is a tendency to act upon a revisable ideal, or "generalized end-in-view" (LW 13:226). As an end-in-view an ideal is something that does not already exist; it is a possibility arising from existent situations. But an ideal is no fantasy; it is a possibility. In *A Common Faith* Dewey noted that his view of ideals was sometimes thought to leave "the ideal wholly without roots in existence and without support from existence." But he said, "What I have tried to show is that the ideal itself has its roots in natural conditions; it emerges when the imagination idealizes existence by laying hold of the possibilities offered to thought and action" (LW 9:32–33). Ideals, then, are action-guiding possibilites. They arise, guide action, and are revised in an ongoing reconstructive process. Over time some ideals, such as democracy, gain considerable stability. But as generalized *ends-in-view* they never escape their origins in temporal conditions. They are not outside of experience.

Dewey opened his essay "What I Believe" (1930) with the observation, "Faith was once almost universally thought to be acceptance of a definite body of intellectual propositions, acceptance being based upon authority— preferably that of revelation from on high." Then he quoted William James: "Faith is tendency toward action,"[26] and commented, "Faith in its newer sense signifies that experience itself is the sole ultimate authority" (LW 5:267). In the next-to-last sentence of the essay he wrote, "A philosophic faith, being a tendency to action, can be tried and tested only in action" (278).

This willingness of Dewey's to modify a "tendency to action" is illustrated by the shift that occurred during the 1930s in his attitude toward voluntary action. Nine years after he wrote "What I Believe," in the follow-up essay "I Believe" he called attention to the change of emphasis in his beliefs regarding the significance of individuals, and he explained why his emphasis had changed. First he acknowledged the challenge posed by "the rise of dictatorships and totalitarian states and the decline of democracy" and the accompanying "loud proclamation of the idea that only the state, the political organization of society, can give security to individuals." Then he said that in response to this threat he had rethought his position and been "led to emphasize the idea that only the voluntary initiative and voluntary cooperation of individuals can produce social institutions that will protect the liberties necessary for achieving development of genuine individuality" (LW 14:91–92).

It is precisely this change in views that is discussed by Hu Shih (and confirmed by Dewey) as an instance of the operation of what Hu called "the principle of relativity" in Dewey's instrumentalism (as I discussed in chapter 3). Dewey not only held that faith as a tendency to action should be modifiable by experience, but, as the last citation shows, he revised his beliefs, specifically his understanding of and attitude toward the ideal of individuality. Note that this pragmatic understanding of faith as a modifiable tendency to action was correctible by his instrumentalist method. Dewey pointed to the specific problematic situations—the rise of totalitarianism in the 1930s and the implications of this development for his understanding of the role of the state—and his deliberative revision of his political ideals. A wedge cannot be driven between Dewey's faith and his instrumentalism.

A Critical Faith

Other examples of Deweyan revisions can readily be found. I have discussed in a limited way the development of Dewey's liberal Christian faith and his subsequent abandonment of it. Also relevant is his embrace of neo-Hegelian idealism and the consequent replacement of it with instrumentalism. Late in life, in attempting to write a new introduction to *Experience and Nature*, Dewey considered abandoning the term *experience*.[27] There is no more significant term in the Deweyan vocabulary than this, yet he was willing to give up the term (but not what he meant by it). Dewey was a restless thinker, continually open to new developments. He wrote of himself in "From Absolutism to Experimentlism": "I seem to be unstable, chameleon-like, yielding one after another to many diverse and even incompatible influences; struggling to assimilate something from each and yet striving to carry it forward in a way that is logically consistent with what has been learned from its predecessors" (LW 5:155). Where others have found unwavering loyalties, Dewey reported shifts. One possible resolution of this conflict is to note Dewey's reconstructive strategy. His changes were often changes in degree rather than complete breaks. His new, reconciling belief attempted to be "logically consistent" with what he had previously "learned from its predecessors."

Dewey's mature philosophy was experimental, but it was not experimental in a neat and tidy way. Consider, for example, what he regarded as a large-scale social experiment, nineteenth-century social idealism. In "The Democratic Faith and Education" (1944) Dewey identified several articles of faith of the "ardent and hopeful social idealist of the last century or so" that have "been proved so wrong": prospects of the abolition of war, the general development of enlightenment and rationality with increased education, the withering away of the state, and improvement in the general standard of living "to a point where extreme poverty would be practically eliminated" (LW 15:251–252). This social experiment was not a laboratory experiment, but there was an identifiable body of beliefs that was eventually discredited by events. Haphazard and extended over time, it was nevertheless an instance of a social experiment. (This hardly provides comfort for those who think Dewey advocated the importation of laboratory methods into human affairs.)

Dewey, it should be noted, did not think that the opposing view, realism, was thereby vindicated: "If 'idealists' were misguided in what they failed to do, 'realists' were wrong in what they did. If the former erred in supposing that the drift (called by them progress or evolution) was inevitably toward the better, the latter were more actively harmful because their insistence upon trusting to natural laws was definitely in the interest of personal and class profit" (253). Characteristically, Dewey called for a third way, one that relied on the use of intelligence and democracy.

Dewey thought this newer, more realistic social idealism was developed through criticism, a term more descriptive of his method than experimentalism.[28] He identified "the omitted premise" of both the realists and idealists, a belief that "science" and "technology" was "an impersonal cosmic force," replacing it with an understanding of science and technology as "transactions in which man and nature work together and in which the human factor is that directly open to modification and direction" (253–54). He then called for the development of "large-scale collective planning" and discussed the needed changes in education (254–59).

Dewey closed with a reference to the "democratic faith" and the need for courage. But lest this be taken as a blind faith, note that he added: "If our courage is to be intelligent rather than blind, . . . successful maintenance of democracy demands the utmost in use of the best available methods to procure a social knowledge that is reasonably commensurate with our physical knowledge, and the invention and use of forms of social engineering, reasonably commensurate with our technological abilities in physical affairs." Once again, there is occasion for misunderstanding. By "social engineering" Dewey did not mean what that phrase has come to mean, for he would have insisted that ordinary people participate in the experimentation by choosing both ends and means. In the next paragraph he quickly noted the need to "humanize" both science and technology that they "may be rendered servants of the democratic hope and faith" (260).

Dewey did have a "democratic hope and faith." Sometimes, as we saw at the end of the last chapter, he overstated this hope, expressing confidence that individuals who have not lost faith in social cooperation will ally themselves with one another and "will construct the way out of the present confusion and conflict" (LW 14:97). He was warranted in thinking that a socialized intelligence could be a constructive way out of the "present social dead end"; he was not justified in asserting that it would happen. I choose to regard this as an overstatement, correctible by criticism. If it were called to Dewey's attention, he would realize that he had gone beyond the evidence. The future, by his own admission, was more open than his statement allowed. What he should have said is not that advocates of social cooperation *would* construct a more viable future, but that they *could* do so. But even this latter assertion would be too much for some; they would insist that it was beyond human capability to construct a more humane future. The issue could then be joined, each side citing evidence for their respective claims. I am confident that Dewey would take into account the criticisms brought forth and would adjust his claim accordingly.

But this is precisely the complaint. Some see a fundamental belief in intelligence and democracy that is essentially invulnerable to criticism. At the margins it can be modified, but at the core it persists. Therfore, Dewey might acknowledge, as he in fact did in *Freedom and Culture:* "It is no longer possible to hold the simple faith of the Enlightenment that assured advance of science will produce free institutions by dispelling ignorance and superstition:—the sources of human servitude and the pillars of oppressive government" (LW 13:156). But then, as we have seen, he would modify this Enlightenment faith, taking into account the ways in which this faith was too simple. Reworking it, he would make it more realistic. Therefore, the content might shift, but the basic commitment would remain.

Was there some point at which Dewey would abandon intelligence and democracy the way he abandoned Christianity and idealism? I do not think so, but this hardly means that his persistent belief in intelligence and democracy was the sort of faith based on unprovable realities that he condemned. Given who he was and what he had come to believe, there is little or no chance that he would abandon his core beliefs. But he would modify them. Therefore, his faith was not blind, nor were his beliefs simple empirical claims. His faith was a third option, a set of enduring beliefs that ran beyond the evidence available at any given time, but that remained correctible by continued experience. The mature Dewey would not abandon the good ship "Intelligence and Democracy" as he had "Christianity and Idealism," but he was continually working on the vessel, making it, he thought, more seaworthy and attractive to others.

Dewey's faith was similar to his subjectivism. The latter, as we have seen, was no narrow bias. Dewey embraced the ideal of a wide and impartial perspective, but he did not do so because it was "objective" in the sense of being unbiased. Rather, he thought a subjectivity that sought to overcome "partisan prejudice" was preferable, because it provided "a rich and ordered landscape." The choice was between subjectivitites and not between subjectivity and objectivity (LW 6:14–15). Similarly, Dewey's faith could never be replaced by what was empirically verifiable at any given time, but he did expect that it would be open to modification by experience over time. The evidence was that it was. Dewey was never one to be unmoved by new developments or new insights.

A COMMON FAITH

Dewey was seventy-three years old when he agreed to deliver the lectures that became *A Common Faith*. He had been reluctant as a philosopher, in spite of his personal faith, to take up the problems of religion before. But once he did his views became a matter of vital concern to many. I will first discuss his reticence, then report his reason for agreeing to write the book. Then I will discuss the book's religious proposal.

Dewey's Reluctance to Turn to Religion as a Philosophic Problem

By Dewey's own admission in "From Absolutism to Experimentalism," he was reluctant to deal intellectually with the problems of religion, noting that he had "been frequently criticized for undue reticence about the problems of religion." The first explanation he provided was his suspicion of the critics' motives: "It seems to me that the great solicitude of many persons, professing belief in the universality of the need for religion, about the present and future of religion proves that in fact they are moved more by partisan interest in a particular religion than by interest in religious experience."

He gave the second reason in the next paragraph: "Social interests and problems from an early period had to me the intellectual appeal and provided the intellectual sustenance that many seem to have found primarily in religious questions" (LW 5:154). Earlier he had noted that he had "not been able to attach much importance to religion as a philosophic problem" (153). So Dewey's lack of philosophic interest in the topic, coupled with the greater appeal of "social interests and problems" and his suspicion of the partisan motives of his critics, made him reticent about engaging in philosophic discussions about religion.[29]

The change came in the early 1930s. Increasingly, Dewey became involved in public discussions of religion.[30] First he made the comments about his religious development and inattention to religion as a philosophic problem in "From Absolutism to Experimentalism" (1930; LW 5:147–60). Then he articulated his faith in the essay "What I Believe" (March 1930, LW 5:267–78) and his humanism in "What Humanism Means to Me" (June 1930, LW 5:263–66). Entering even more into public controversy, Dewey agreed to review *Is There a God? A Conversation*, a 1932 book by Henry Nelson Wieman, Douglas Clyde Macintosh, and Max Carl Otto, with an introduction by Charles Clayton Morrison, editor of *The Christian Century*, the journal in which this conversation originally appeared. This review, published in February 1933, embroiled Dewey in a public discussion through April (LW 9:213–28, 412–22). Then, following the publication of *A Common Faith* the next year, the discussion continued in *The Christian Century* (LW 9:294–95, 426–40). Dewey was also attacked from the left by Norbert Guterman in a review in *The New Republic*, to which Dewey responded sharply (LW 9:293, 423–25).

The occasion for the publication of *A Common Faith* was James R. Angell's invitation during the initial *Christian Century* discussion to deliver the 1934 Terry Lectures at Yale University. These three lectures became the three chapters of *A Common Faith*. Angell, the president of Yale, was Dewey's former student at Michigan and colleague at Chicago and the son of James B. Angell, the president at Michigan when Dewey taught there (Dykhuizen, *Life and Mind*, 56). The older Angell, moreover, had been president of the University of Vermont when Dewey was a boy (3). He is celebrated in Jane Dewey's biography as "the ideal college president, one who increased the stature of his institution by fostering a truly democratic atmosphere for students and faculty and encouraging the freedom and individual responsibility that are necessary for creative education. His personal charm and geniality created a general atmosphere of friendliness to newcomers and to students" (Schilpp, 19). The younger Angell is mentioned by

Robert L. McCaul as one of "Dewey's closest friends on the [Chicago] faculty."[31] Perhaps this warm personal association helped Dewey overcome his reticence to speak publicly about religion. But perhaps not, for in 1933 Dewey also signed *A Humanist Manifesto*, which was published in *The New Humanist*.[32] With the *Christian Century* discussion, the signing of the humanist manifesto, and his Terry Lectures, Dewey demonstrated that he was clearly willing to take up religion in a public and even (with the exception of the manifesto) philosophical way.

Rockefeller, without citing any documentary evidence in Dewey's writings other than *A Common Faith* itself, usefully suggests that the book was Dewey's response to several developments in the late 1920s and early 1930s, including the rise of fundamentalism with its strident rejection of modernity, the publication of Joseph Wood Krutch's *The Modern Temper* (1929) with its gloomy secular humanism, the development of religious modernism and religious humanism, and Niebuhr's combination of neoorthodoxy and political radicalism. Many of these developments touched Dewey personally. Krutch sent Dewey an inscribed copy of his book (455); some of the modernists made use of Dewey's work (455); the religious humanists counted Dewey as one of their own (456–59), particularly following his signing of their manifesto; and Niebuhr attacked his political ally Dewey directly in *Moral Man and Immoral Society* (461–63). Apparently, in the 1930s religion had become for Dewey, if not an intellectual problem directly, certainly one indirectly by becoming a social and political problem. His reading audience was getting contradictory messages from Krutch, Niebuhr, and the religious humanists. Dewey decided to become involved.

Why Dewey Wrote *A Common Faith*

Dewey was very clear about his reasons for writing *A Common Faith*. Primarily, he wrote for those who had abandoned traditional beliefs and were not in the churches, yet still considered themselves—or wished to be—religious. Secondarily, he wanted to help the liberals "realize how inconsistent they are." He did not address the book to those who were comfortable in their traditional religions. Dewey stated his reasons in a 1935 letter to Otto, which is quoted in Anne Sharpe's textual commentary: "My book was written for the people who feel inarticulately they have the essence of the religious with them and yet are repelled by the religions and are confused—primarily for them, secondarily for the 'liberals' to help them realize how inconsistent they are" (LW 9:455).

In his 1939 rejoinder in the Schilpp volume Dewey expanded on the primary reason after first noting those to whom he had not addressed the book: "*A Common Faith* was not addressed to those who are content with traditions in which 'metaphysical' is substantially identical with 'supernatural.' It was addressed to those who have abandoned supernaturalism, and who on that account are reproached by traditionalists for having turned their backs on everything religious. The book was an attempt to show such persons that they still have within their experience all the elements which give the religious attitude its value" (LW 14:79–80).

Although Dewey did not "address" the traditionally religious, in places he did argue against their views. At one point he defended science against religious apologists (LW 9:27); at another he was critical of those who identified "the existence of ideal goods with that of a Person supposed to originate and support them" (31); at still another he charged the churches with having devoted "their chief attention in social affairs to moral *symptoms*, to vices and abuses, like drunkenness, sale of intoxicants, divorce, rather than to the cause of war and of the long list of economic and political injustices and oppressions. Protest against the latter has been mainly left to secular movements" (46). Dewey was also critical of "militant atheism," charging it with a lack of "natural piety" (36).

Clearly, Dewey's audience was neither the conventionally religious nor those who were antireligious. He was concerned instead with those who valued both religion and modernity. He did not want them to emulate the religious liberals who sought to modernize their religious traditions in a way Dewey found inconsistent. The liberals were closest to Dewey's position in some respects; therefore, it was important that he distinguish his view from theirs. This he did by showing that the religious liberals were attempting to maintain an "unstable equilibrium" (49) of two realms, the sacred and the secular, by affirming that there was a religious experience distinct from the scientific, one not subject to the methods of science. They needed, Dewey thought, to abandon the idea of a distinct religious sphere and its untenable dualism, not only because it was dualistic and thus unintegrated, but also because their argument was fallacious. They argued that something positive existed (religious experience) because science had not explained religious phenomena. Such an argument was vulnerable to future scientific advances (see 8–9, 24–27 and 48–49).

But Dewey thought there was still a way to be religious without being supernaturalistic. This third option was not a new religion, but the emancipation of the religious elements within ordinary experience. These "elements," it must be stressed, were not a distinct sort of experience, but aspects of our common experience. On this point much of Dewey's proposal turns. He sought to identify just enough of the religious in experience to be able to make his proposal, but not so much that there could be a religious characteristic that could constitute a distinct religious sphere.

The Religious in Experience

The religious liberal cannot become a thoroughgoing secularist because of his claim that there is some area that is not be to be touched by science. Dewey, if he was to distinguish his position from that of the "inconsistent liberals," must avoid this error. But "militant atheism" lies in the other direction. He was unwilling to completely eliminate the religious from experience. Therefore, he felt he must navigate between what he took to be inconsistency on the one hand and impiety regarding nature on the other hand.

The Religious Distinguished from Both Religion and Religions

In the first chapter of *A Common Faith*, "Religion versus the Religious," Dewey was concerned to break the conventional identification of the religious with the supernatural, an identification made by both the traditionally religious and the antireligious. If he could do this and yet show that the religious was a quality within experience, he would be able to find a middle way between the traditionalists and the extreme atheists without resorting to the liberals' two-realms strategem. Accordingly, he undercut the conventional view of religion as expressed in the *Oxford Dictionary*'s definition, "Recognition on the part of man of some unseen higher power as having control of his destiny and as being entitled to obedience, reverence and worship" (LW 9:4), by showing that there was no significant common referent in the various religions in terms of "unseen powers," "obedience and reverence," and morality (5–6). Dewey thought the variety among the many religions is too great for the term *religion* to be anything more than "a strictly collective term" for a "miscellaneous aggregate" (7).

There is, however, an effect claimed by the religions that Dewey thought can be identified and brought about apart from them. He wrote: "It is the claim of religions that they effect" a "generic and enduring change in attitude," one that can be called an "adjustment." Sometimes we "accommodate" ourselves to existing conditions, conforming to them. This is a partial and passive response. Sometimes we are more active, "adapting" the existing conditions, as when we remodel a house. Adjustment is the more general process, for it is inclusive of both these partial responses, active or passive as the occasion requires. Upon this flexible way of interacting with the environment Dewey built his notion of the religious: The "inclusive and deep seated" changes that are a part of this adjustment "relate not to this and that want in relation to this and that condition of our surroundings, but pertain to our being in its entirety. Because of its scope, this modification of ourselves is enduring. It lasts through any amount of vicissitude of circumstances, internal and external. There is a composing and harmonizing of the various elements of our being such that, in spite of changes in the special conditions that surround us, these conditions are also arranged, settled, in relation to us." Whenever such a "change takes place there is a definitely religious attitude" (12–13). It is not the case, however, that this adjusting attitude, this harmonizing of the self with the world in terms of both passive and active changes, constitutes an entirely distinct attitude. Dewey was insistent that he was talking about a quality of experience rather than a separable experience.

Unlike the religious liberals, who "hold to the notion that there is a definite kind of experience which is itself religious," one "that is marked off from experience as aesthetic, scientific, moral, political," Dewey held that the "religious" is "a quality of experience" that "signifies something that may belong to all these experiences. It is the polar opposite of some type of experience that can exist by itself" (9). Not a distinctive kind of activity, but a quality of these various sorts of activities, the religious is, in Dewey's proposal, a certain way or manner in which one conducts oneself. As Ryan adroitly observes, Dewey's intent "was to rescue religious life from his youthful faith" (242). He wanted the attitude and the behavior that he found attractive in religious traditions, but without the "historic encumbrances" (LW 9:6).

Specifying the Religious in Experience

Dewey was very clear about what distinguished a religious practice or attitude from a nonreligious one. The religious was the pervasive adjustment of the self and its environment (14). As a faith, it was not "a substitute for knowledge," but a faith with "a moral and practical import" (15). But not "all moral faith in ideal ends is by virtue of that fact religious in quality." The difference, once again, has to do with a difference in degree, not in kind. To see this we need to turn to Dewey and Tufts' *Ethics*, revised in 1932, for in the discussion of moral faith in *A Common Faith* Dewey does not explain what he means by a *moral* faith. In the latter his concern was to show that moral ideals should not be converted into existences that become items in "an intellectual creed" (16). Moral faith as a faith does not require that one's ideals exist.

In chapter 15 of the *Ethics*, "The Moral Self," Dewey argued that the self is constituted by its actions (LW 7:288)—or, better, by its interests (289–92), the most inclusive of which is the social (298–303): "The final happiness of an individual resides in the supremacy of certain interests in the make-up of character; namely, alert, sincere, enduring interests in the objects in which all can share" (302). The moral person is moral in both a descriptive and an honorific sense. In the sense that one's actions constitute the person, one's actions are moral rather than nonmoral. Therefore, the moral self is the self produced by one's choices. A choice is a moral one if it affects the development of one's character. But, normatively, those actions are truly moral that make one a person "in which desires and affections centre in the values which are common; in which interest focuses in objects that contribute to the enrichment of the lives of all" (302–303). The moral agent, then, in the honorific sense, is the one whose life-forming interests include wide, enduring ends-in-view—that is, moral ideals.

Returning to *A Common Faith*, we find that Dewey thought the religious is similar, if not identical, to this honorific sense of morality. It is distinguished from morality (in the usual sense) by a greater intensity of emotion, more inclusive ends, and self-unification (not mere self-constitution): "The religious is 'morality touched by emotion'[33] only when the ends of moral conviction arouse emotions that are not only intense but are actuated and supported by ends so inclusive that they unify the self" (LW 9:16–17). Or, as Dewey expressed it in a formulation in the second chapter: "I should describe this faith as the unification of the self through allegiance to inclusive ideal ends, which imagination presents to us and to which the human will responds as worthy of controlling our desires and choices" (23). Like morality in the honorific sense, the religious is marked by intense emotion or "allegiance" and "inclusive ideal ends" and results in "the unification of the self."

Supporting the interpretation that Dewey thought the religious is a difference in degree rather than a difference in kind from moral faith are several considerations. One, we have Dewey's direct statement that indicates that the religious is one sort of moral faith (16). Two, there is a relevant paragraph in the third chapter in which he contended that there is "no opposition" between intelligence and emotion: "There is such a thing as passionate intelligence, as ardor in behalf of light shining into the murky places of social existence, and as zeal for its refreshing and purifying effect. The whole story of man shows that there are no objects that may not deeply stir engrossing emotion. One of the few experiments in the attachment of emotion to ends that mankind has not tried is that of devotion, so intense as to be religious, to intelligence as a force in social action" (52–53). What is telling is the aside, "so intense as to be religious." This is not a free-floating emotional intensity, but one that finds expression in "devotion . . . to intelligence as a force in social action." Although Dewey singled out emotion here, we must not be reductionistic. Clearly, elsewhere Dewey linked intense emotion to inclusivity of ends and self-unification. All three are necessary to distinguish the religious from moral faith that is not "religious in quality." As Dewey made clear later in the paragraph in the first chapter (and this is the third consideration): "The religious attitude signifies something that is bound through imagination to a *general* attitude. This comprehensive attitude, moreover, is much broader than anything indicated by 'moral' in its usual sense" (17).

The force of this generality and its greater breadth than "'moral' in its usual sense" is brought out in Dewey's discussion of "natural piety," the topic to which he immediately turned. *Piety* was the term Santayana used to designate "man's reverent attachment to the sources of his being and the steadying of his life by that attachment."[34] He distinguished piety from "spirituality," regarding the former as "retrospective" and the latter as prospective, for it "looks to the end toward which we move," whereas "piety looks to the conditions of progress and to the sources from which we draw our energies" (193). Dewey accepted the piety side of this distinction, but, significantly, he chose to speak of "faith" rather than "spirituality," avoiding the otherworldly connotations of the latter term. Randall calls attention to the similarities rather than the differences, observing, "For both [Santayana and Dewey], the essential reconstruction of the religious tradition lies in the separation of piety, as respect for the sources of our being and our good, from spirituality, as devotion to the ends toward which we move. And for both there is a common insistence that the ideal has a natural basis and can be realized only by a proper respect for the natural conditions of its attainment."[35] But Rockefeller brings out the differences (496–97): Santayana's "spirituality" is more poetic and less worldly and practical than Dewey's "faith," which, as we have seen, is an intense and inclusive, self-transforming way of life.

For Dewey this reverence for the sources of one's being involved a balancing of "a just sense of nature as the whole of which we are parts" and a recognition that "we are parts that are marked by intelligence and purpose, having the capacity to strive by their aid to bring conditions into greater consonance with what is humanly desirable" (LW 9:18). Therefore, for Dewey the religious involved a proper appreciation of one's place in the universe, as well as a self-transforming commitment to inclusive ideals.

In the midst of the paragraph on natural piety, there is this negative characterization of the religious: "The essentially unreligious attitude is that which attributes human achievement and purpose to man in isolation from the world of physical nature and his fellows" (18). This emphasis on a contextual understanding, as we know, is a partial characterization of the religious. Dewey was concerned to hold together, in addition to the need for inclusive ideal ends, two additional criteria: emotional intensity and self-transformation. Moreover, the three were related in a very specific way: The religious person was the one who was strongly committed to wide interests to such a degree that she or he was unified as a self in the process.

A Secular Religiosity

The implication for conduct is clear. Since the religious is both a broadening and a deepening of one's life-transforming interests, there are no special, set-apart interests. There is no need for distinctive rituals, revelations, or prayers and for churches, synagogues, temples, or shrines. The religious occurs in the heightened, widened way one goes about living. There is no justification for nonsecular pursuits or institutions.

But Dewey did not draw this radical conclusion; he pulled his punch. In the third chapter of *A Common Faith*, "The Human Abode of the Religious Function," he allowed that religious institutions could continue to exist, provided they were reconstructed along naturalistic lines and became more socially minded (54–55). The burden of the third chapter was to move beyond fundamentalism and religious liberalism to a stage in which dualisms would be overcome and the values of justice and community formerly associated with the supernatural would be found "in the matrix of human relations" (47). It is somewhat jarring, then, to find Dewey making room for religious institutions in this newly integrated, secular society.

The shock is lessened when one realizes that Dewey gave these institutions a very limited, even precarious role. He would have had them surrender all "claims to an exclusive and authoritative position," renouncing any assertion of "a monopoly of supreme values and motivating forces" (55). Their role would be a double one of celebrating common values and stimulating social action.[36] Regarding the celebrative role Dewey wrote: "The fund of human values that are prized and that need to be cherished, values that are satisfied and rectified by *all* human concerns and arrangements, could be celebrated and reinforced, in different ways and with differing symbols, by the churches." Regarding the social action role, he urged that "the churches take a definite stand upon such questions as war, economic injustice, political corruption," stimulating "action for a divine kingdom on earth" (54–55).

Although Dewey thought that "the transfer of idealizing imagination, thought and emotion to natural human relations would not signify the destruction of the churches that now exist" (54), many traditionally religious persons would regard this sort of reconstruction as tantamount to destruction. Still, his allowance for secularized religious institutions seems to be a temporizing move, falling short of the naturalized reconstruction of the religious that he developed in the first chapter and extended to society in the third. The logic of his proposal to deepen and broaden existing secular practices would not seem to require the continuing of any distinctive religious institutions, for all significant, worthwhile practices would become religious in the Deweyan sense. Every praiseworthy institution's activities and goals would be pursued with an emotional intensity and wideness of purpose characteristic of the religious. And they would have the desired transformative effects upon those who participated in them.

This typically Deweyan move to mediate between extremes comes out even more clearly in his willingness to use the term *God* in a reconstructed naturalistic way. Not many people paid attention to his proposal to remake the churches, but everyone noticed that Dewey was willing to make room for "God" in his common faith.

God and the Idealizing Imagination

Dewey was willing to use the term *God* because he thought his target audience, the unchurched secularly religious, would like to be able to do so in good conscience. But what he did not count on was the attention his use would draw, an attention that obscured for many his more substantive point about the idealizing imagination. Rockefeller has a fine account of Dewey's use of the term and the controversy it provoked (512–27); therefore, I will limit myself to a brief exposition of Dewey's reconstructed meaning for the term, concentrating instead on the point that almost got lost in the controversy.

A God for Nontheists

In the discussion in 1933 following Dewey's review of *Is There a God?* Dewey made the limited range of choices regarding the nature and existence of a divinity quite clear in a letter to the editor of *The Christian Century*. He began with the distinction between the religious in experience and the question of God's existence that he would develop the following year in the first two chapters of *A Common Faith*: "Separating the matter of religious experience from the question of the existence of God (as for example those as far apart from one another as the Buddhists and the Comtean Positivists have done), I have found—and there are many who will corroborate my experience by their own—that all of the things which traditional religionists prize and which they connect exclusively with their own conception of God can be had equally well in the ordinary course of human experience in our relations to the natural world and to one another as human beings related in the family, friendship, industry, art, science, and citizenship." Then he presented a choice, italicizing it to emphasize his point: *"Either then the concept of God can be dropped out as far as genuinely religious experience is concerned, or it must be framed wholly in terms of natural and human relationship involved in our straightaway human experience"* (LW 9:224).

These alternatives are extremely limited. Both lie within the narrow middle way between militant atheism and a theistic religious liberalism. Unlike adherents to the extreme forms of atheism, Dewey was insistent on the value of the religious in experience. Unlike the theists, he required that, if the term *God* were used, it had to be understood within naturalistic and social limits. Therefore, the only question for Dewey had to do with whether the term was used or not. Dewey developed the second alternative in the second chapter of *A Common Faith*, but conceded that this was "a matter for individual decision" (LW 9:35). His religious proposal would permit either; he chose to use the term *God*, provided that the concept was "framed wholly in terms of natural and human relationship involved in our straightaway human experience."

Dewey's decision was not a casual one. He had already experienced the difficulty of distinguishing his view from Henry Nelson Wieman's. The above-quoted disjunction was posed in reply to Wieman's March 1, 1933, letter to the editor of *The Christian Century* (LW 9:412–17). Both before and after the publication of *A Common Faith* Wieman attempted to read more unity into Dewey's naturalistic divinity than Dewey intended. Dewey had contended that there is a collection of natural and social forces making for good, but that these forces are "unified only in their functional effect" (LW 9:221). Wieman tended to locate the unity in the forces themselves, not just their functional effects (see LW 9:413 and 431).

Dewey's former student, Sidney Hook, who worked with him to prepare the manuscript of *A Common Faith* for publication, also objected to his use of the term *God*. Hook, a Marxist in the early 1930s, recalls in "Some Memories of John Dewey: 1859–1952," written shortly after Dewey's death, that his objection had to do with the lack of commonality between Dewey's concept and some of the more prominent conceptions in western thought, including that of his fellow pragmatist William James. According to Hook, Dewey gave four reasons for using the term *God*: One, "the term had no unequivocal meaning in the history of thought." Two, "there was no danger of its being misunderstood," presumably because Dewey would specify the sense in which he was using the term. Three, "there was no reason why its

emotive associations of the sacred, profound, and ultimate should be sur-
rendered to the supernaturalist." Four (and this reason squares with
Dewey's other statements about his intended audience): "Besides there are
so many people who would feel bewildered if not hurt were they denied the
intellectual right to use the term 'God.' They are not in the churches, they
believe what I believe, they would feel a loss if they could not speak of God.
Why then shouldn't I use the term?" (*Commentary* 14:253).

The first, second, and third reasons are in tension with one another. To
the extent that there are the specified "emotive associations," there is not
the desired latitude implied in the lack of an unequivocal meaning. It is
because of the connotations of sacredness, profoundness, and ultimacy in
the various meanings that some read into Dewey's use what he thought his
specified meaning prohibited. As Ryan remarks, "We may wonder whether
in fact, it is possible to have the *use* of religious vocabulary without the
accretion of supernaturalist beliefs that Dewey wishes to slough off."[37]

Dewey's Divine Union

Dewey thought Wieman had located the unity to be found in Dewey's
god in the forces themselves rather than in the way these forces function "in
human experience in its religious dimension" (LW 9:294). Dewey's initial
formulation in the 1933 letter to the editor of *The Christian Century* of
what he was willing to call divine could be interpreted in this way. But a
careful reading of this formulation and his later statement in the second
chapter of *A Common Faith*, "Faith and Its Object," reveals his humanistic
orientation. His humanism, as we have already seen, was a cosmically contextual one. The dispute with Wieman has to do with how much emphasis
one places on the human element and how much one puts on the forces in
nature that support human goods. Perhaps a different chapter title would
have been less misleading. There is a single object of the faith that Dewey
was proposing, but it is a unity that is more a collection than the word
object suggests. As it is, this chapter title unintentionally reinforces the
dualism of subject and object that Dewey spent much of his life trying to
overcome.

In *A Common Faith* Dewey first defined his god as "the unity of all ideal
ends arousing us to desire and action." Distinguishing it from "a particular
Being," he was concerned at this point to stress the ideality of his conception. This god was "imaginative in origin," but no less effective for this reason than the traditional conception, for "the reality of ideal ends as ideals is
vouched for by their undeniable power in action" (LW 9:29–30). But these
imaginative possibilities that are unified by us into a conception of the

divine are not "without roots in existence and without support from existence": The ideal "emerges when the imagination idealizes existence by laying hold of the possibilities offered to thought and action. There are values, goods, actually realized upon a natural basis—the good of human association, of art and knowledge. The idealizing imagination seizes upon the most precious things found in the climacteric moments of experience and projects them. We need no external criterion and guarantee for their goodness. They are had, they exist as good, and out of them we frame our ideal ends" (32–33). The unity of these ideals, these projected goods drawn from experience, is what Dewey regarded as divine.

But then Dewey shifted the focus from this unity and the role of imagination in creating the ideals that make up the divine unity to the interaction of these ideals with "existent conditions." He wrote: "The sense of new values that become ends to be realized arises first in dim and uncertain form. As the values are dwelt upon and carried forward in action they grow in definiteness and coherence. Interaction between aim and existent conditions improves and tests the ideal; and conditions are at the same time modified. Ideals change as they are applied in existent conditions. The process endures and advances with the life of humanity." This process, "this *active* relation between ideal and actual," is that which he was willing to call "God" (34).

Dewey repeated this interactive formulation in the next paragraph. But first he said that he "would not insist that the name *must* be given," noting, "There are those who hold that the associations of the term with the supernatural are so numerous and close that any use of the word 'God' is sure to give rise to misconception and be taken as a concession to traditional ideas." (Among those who would have been making this objection, as we have seen, would have been Hook, who was assisting Dewey in the preparation of the manuscript.) He then acknowledged, "They may be correct in this view," and offered this justification: "But the facts to which I have referred are there, and they need to be brought out with all possible clearness and force. There exist concretely and experimentally goods—the values of art in all its forms, of knowledge, of effort and of rest after striving, of education and fellowship, of friendship and love, of growth in mind and body. These goods are there and yet they are relatively embryonic. Many persons are shut out from generous participation in them." Despite "forces at work that threaten and sap existent goods as well as prevent their expansion," what is needed is a "clear and intense conception of a union of ideal ends with actual conditions [that] is capable of arousing steady emotion" (pp.34–35). Dewey thought the term *God* was helpful in developing a "clear and intense conception" of these nascent goods. But his examples leave little doubt about the scope of his divinity; he clearly had in mind social goods within a naturalistic setting. Moreover, in the last sentence he restated his understanding of the divine as "a union of ideal ends with actual conditions." Therefore, his final formulation was less dualistic than the initial formulation, the chapter title, and his use of the word *God* suggest.

The Non-necessity of God-talk

Although Dewey had his reasons for invoking a name that would run the risk of "misconception," he may well have thought better of his choice later. Rockefeller reports that Jerome Nathanson told him in an interview in 1972 that "some time after 1942" Dewey told Nathanson "that he would omit the word 'God,' if he were to write another book along the lines of *A Common Faith*." This recollection is given plausibility not only by the miunderstandings that Dewey encountered, but also by the partial failure of his stated purpose and his characteristic willingness to change his mind. Evidence for the failure of purpose is also provided by Nathanson, who told Rockefeller that John Lovejoy Elliott, another leader of the New York Society for Ethical Culture, had once said, "I will never forgive John Dewey for using the word God in *A Common Faith*."[38]

The significance of this is that the ethical culture movement founded by Felix Adler, a colleague of Dewey's in the philosophy department at Columbia University, later came to understand itself as a form of ethical humanism. Rockefeller reports, "Increasingly during the twentieth century, the majority of Adler's small but dedicated following found his idealist philosophical speculations and religious vision obscure, and many came to fall under the influence of Dewey's naturalistic humanism" (458). Elliot and other religious humanists were among those for whom Dewey intended his religious proposal. For some of them to object to his use of the term *God* would have indicated to him that perhaps he had misjudged his audience. (Of course there were many other religious humanists who were encouraged by Dewey's willingness to use traditional religious language.)

Documentary evidence of Dewey's second thoughts comes from the correspondence between Corliss Lamont and Dewey in 1935. Lamont had been one of Dewey's harshest critics the year before. The titles for his two articles in the *New Masses*, "John Dewey Capitulates to 'God'" (July 31) and "The Right Reverend Re-Definer" (October 2), indicate his sarcastic tone and dismay at Dewey's use of the term *God*.[39] Responding to Lamont's query, Dewey wrote: "What I still don't get about your reaction to my book . . . and the same is true of reviews from the conventional religious angle—is

why there is so much more concern about the word 'God' and so little attention to that which I said was a reality to which the word *might* be applied."

Lamont then replied that Dewey's use of the term was "new and star-
tling." People had not expected him as an opponent of "supernaturalism
and the old-time religion" to use this word. Moreover, "the parsons . . . saw
in your definition of 'God' their one chance to make capital out of you on
behalf of *their* religion." Dewey responded with this weak defense: "Thanks
for your note which explained something I hadn't been able to understand. I
suppose one of the first things I learned in grammar was the difference
between *will* and *shall*, and the consequent difference between *would* and
should. But nevertheless I made a bad slip which accounts for the fact that
you thought I was making a recommendation. The meaning in my mind
was essentially: If the word 'God' is used, this is what it *should* stand for; I
didn't have a recommendation in mind beyond the proper use of a word."
But lest we make too much of this revisionist account, note that in 1941
Dewey was back to his old defense. Chiding Lamont for "'squeamishness'
about the use of the word 'God,'" Dewey declared: "I think it important to
help people to realize that they can save what it actually meant to them free
from superstitious elements."[40] This, of course, is the question: Can one
invoke the word *God* without evoking connotations of supernaturalism?

As noted, there were others who were appreciative of Dewey's use of
traditional language. In a January 14, 1935, letter to Otto Dewey reported
that he knew "from letters and conversations" that he had been able to
reach many "who feel inarticulately" that "they have the essence of the
religous with them and yet are repelled by the religions and are confused"
precisely on this point about the divine, as his next remark indicated. He
had been able "to bear up between Wieman on one hand and Corliss
Lamont on the other" because of the reception his book had gotten
("Textual Commentary," LW 9:455).

But ultimately this controversy is beside the point. Dewey complained to
Lamont, as we have seen, that many readers paid too much attention to a
word and not to the reality to which it was intended to refer. Earlier in 1934
he had made a similar point in the letter to Otto: "I didnt [*sic*] want to get
drawn further into the Christian Century discussion, because their assumption is that I am primarily interested—as they are—in 'God' when in fact my
reference to it was purely incidental, and the real meaning is in just the paragraph to which you refer." The paragraph to which Otto referred was found
on page 51 of the Yale University Press edition (LW 9:35), and I quoted it
almost in full above. It was Dewey's statement that the naturally occurring
goods are "relatively embryonic" and that "many persons are shut out from

generous participation in them." What was needed, then, was a "clear and intense conception of a union of ideal ends with actual conditions" that would be "capable of arousing steady emotion." Nowhere in this paragraph did Dewey use the "G word." The emphasis was on the "reality" to which he thought "the word *might* be applied." Of course this paragraph is bracketed by his two declarations of his personal willingness to use the word *God* and his insistence that its use is a matter "for individual decision."

The Necessity of Inclusive Idealization and "Steady Emotion"

What was not dispensable for Dewey was the process of inclusive idealization and the role of an agent's interests, including his or her emotional involvement. In the previous chapter I tried to make clear the role of ideal formation in my discussion of generalized ends-in-view in furthering an agent's concerns. Earlier in this chapter I cited a passage in Dewey's development of the concept of what he regarded as divine. This process, the one to which Dewey was willing to refer to as "God," was an entirely secular one. To quote the text again: "The idealizing imagination seizes upon the most precious things found in the climacteric moments of experience and projects them. We need no external criterion and guarantee for their goodness. They are had, they exist as good, and out of them we frame our ideal ends" (LW 9:33). The "idealizing imagination" is the activity of intelligence, a secular intelligence. It is certainly not reason as traditionally understood and is thus not divorced from desire. Literally, from Dewey's point of view a project is a projection that will meet an agent's need. One has an interest in this project because it is a proposed way of satisfying a felt need. It is in his or her interest to do so. Therefore, there is no necessary opposition between desire and intelligence. From Dewey's point of view they are intertwined and potentially reinforcing.

In the chapter "Desire and Intelligence" in *Human Nature and Conduct* (1922, MW 14:177–81) Dewey observed, "The separation of warm emotion and cool intelligence is the great moral tragedy." He then declared, "The intellect is always inspired by some impulse." Offering two examples, he continued, "Even the most case-hardened scientific specialist, the most abstract philosopher, is moved by some passion." The mistake is not to be found in a mixing of desire and intelligence, but in an unnatural separation of ideals and goal-oriented thinking. The "association of idealism with emotion and impulse" must be maintained, for "every end that man holds up, every project he entertains is ideal. It marks something wanted, rather than something existing. It is wanted because existence as it *now* is does not furnish it." Dewey thought that the mistake of some idealists is to harden the ideal "by thought . . . into some high, far-away object. It is so elevated and so distant that it does not belong to this world or to experience. It is in technical language, transcendental; in common speech, supernatural, of heaven not of earth."

What is needed, Dewey thought, is a naturalistic understanding of the process of idealization, one that will appropriately combine desire and thinking and will grasp the larger whole of which one's efforts are a part. Intelligence and contextualization are bound up with one another: "The 'ends' that are foreseen and utilized mark out a little island in an infinite sea." We select an aim from an "indefinite context of consequences." This selected aim then "enters into the *present* meaning of activity. The 'end' is the figured pattern at the centre of the field through which runs the axis of conduct. About this central figuration extends infinitely a supporting background in a vague whole, undefined and undiscriminated. At most intelligence but throws a spotlight on that little part of the whole which marks out the axis of movement." This is a deflationary account of both "reason" and ideals. Reason becomes intelligence, the selection of some organizing aim whose selection can be defended, but not absolutely justified. Moreover, some other selection could also be defended depending on the agent and his or her circumstances. Ideals, as we saw in the last chapter, also lose their cosmic justification. They are but generalizations from our ends-in-view. They never lose—or at least should never lose—their connection with the agent's aspirations, with all the subjectivity that this implies.

But Dewey's deflationary account did not completely eliminate the moral currency. He was also concerned to show that the selected aims that get built up into action-guiding ideals are a part of "a supporting background in a vague whole." It is "conceit" that "persuades us that cosmic difference hangs upon even our wisest and most strenuous effort. Yet discontent with this limitation is" also "unreasonable," for "in a genuine sense every act is already possessed of infinite import." Dewey continued in this poetic vein: "The little part of the scheme of affairs which is modifiable by our efforts is continuous with the rest of the world. The boundaries of our garden plot join it to the world of our neighbors and neighbors' neighbors. That small effort which we can put forth is in turn connected with an infinity of events that sustain and support it. The consciousness of this encompassing infinity of connections is ideal." It is ideal in the sense that that to which it aspires does not yet exist and indeed will never exist, for "this ideal is not a goal to be attained. It is a significance to be felt, appreciated." Moreover, it cannot be precisely stated: "Though conciousness of it cannot become intellectualized (identified in objects of a distinct character) yet emotional appreciation of it is won by those willing to think" (MW 14:177–80).

Dewey then rounded off this discussion of idealization, desire, and intelligence with a closing comment about religion. But before I follow him in this relevant, significant connection I want to note the characteristic way in which Dewey tied together what many would normally oppose—desire and intelligence. Much rides on the success of Dewey's transformations. Recall that his definition of *inquiry* in the *Logic* was the transformation of indeterminate situations into unified wholes (LW 12:108). Time after time we see Dewey reorganizing opposing positions into new ones that he claimed successfully combined the old partial positions into new, integrated ones. His critics then attempted to reduce his new position to one or the other of the positions that Dewey had sought to overcome. Desire and intelligence was one of these dualities; indeed it was central to Dewey's pragmatism and instrumentalism. It is because desire and intelligence are bound up with one another that Dewey thought that there was no problem either with motivation or objectivity. We are inclined to pursue our interests. We can grasp the import of these interests, revising them as needed. There is no necessary conflict. Moreover, it is through a naturalized idealization—an imaginative projection of our desires and deliberation concerning the conditions and consequences of these projections—that we can successfully hold together desire and intelligence.

Ironically, the subjectivity embraced by the pragmatist and the objectivity disclaimed by him turn out, at least in Dewey, to be less than willful. Dewey was a dispassionate celebrant of interest-cultivating individuality. In fact, one of the continued criticisms of him is that one of his strengths—his placid, untemperamental, philosophic disposition—was also a weakness: he lacked angst. Note also his counterexamples to the claim that desire and intelligence necessarily oppose one another—"the most case-hardened scientific specialist" and "the most abstract philosopher" (MW 14:177–78). It apparently did not take much passion for Dewey to be able to detect it. Where others would see only intellect, Dewey saw a mix of desire and intelligence. The "steady emotion" aroused by a "clear and intense conception of a union of ideal ends with actual conditions" (LW 9:35) did not have to cross a very high threshold to count as religious for Dewey. This is an important consideration in assessing his proposal regarding the religious in experience—indeed, in assessing his philosophy as a whole as being religious. At the end of this chapter I will contend that Dewey's religiosity is almost, if not entirely, indistinguishable from nonreligiosity. But first I need to develop the unifying function of the religious in experience, for it contributes to the development of the "steady emotion" Dewey recommended and is itself an additional criterion for the religious.

The Unifying Function of the Religious in Experience

Dewey began the last paragraph of the chapter on desire and intelligence in *Human Nature and Conduct* with the claim that it was "the office of art and religion to evoke" the sort of "appreciations and intimations" that form the consciousness of ideals, "to enhance and steady them till they are wrought into the texture of our lives." But then he proceeded to talk only of the religious, silently omitting continued discussion of the role of art. I will partially correct this failure by referring to two passages in *Art As Experience* where Dewey related art to religion. In this way I hope to lessen the temptation to make religion too special, too set apart in Dewey's philosophy, showing rather that what has historically been understood to be religious in Dewey can find expression in the secular.

There are two places in *Art as Experience*, which was published in the same year as *A Common Faith* but based on the inaugural William James Lectures delivered in the spring term of 1931, in which Dewey explicitly connected art and religion. The first was in a passage in which he made a point similar to the one in the text in *Human Nature and Conduct* just discussed about "the undefined pervasive quality of an experience . . . that . . . binds together all the defined elements, the objects of which we are focally aware, making them a whole." It is this "sense of an extensive and underlying whole" that provides coherence, yet the setting for any particular experience is at its outer edges "indeterminate." In the next paragraph Dewey declared, "A work of art elicits and accentuates this quality of being a whole and of belonging to the larger, all-inclusive, whole which is the universe in which we live." At times of "intense esthetic perception," Dewey thought, this sense of a whole can be a "religious feeling": "We are, as it were, introduced into a world beyond this world which is nevertheless the deeper reality of the world in which we live in our ordinary experiences. We are carried out beyond ourselves to find ourselves." Indeed, our sanity depends on this sense of connectedness, "for the mad, the insane, thing to us is that which is torn from the common context and which stands alone and isolated, as anything must which occurs in a world totally different from ours" (LW 10:198–99).

The last statement serves as a reminder that we must not take the language in the previous citation—"a world beyond this world"—literally. Dewey spoke less misleadingly in his immediate qualification—"which is nevertheless the deeper reality of the world in which we live in our ordinary experience." He thought that art and religion provide us access to this deeper, broader world. They are not the only sorts of experience that do this, for ordinary experience also gives us "a sense of things as belonging or not belonging, of relevancy." I take it that the latter comment is inclusive of ordinary experience, for Dewey describes this as "our constant sense of things" (198). But art and religion are particularly adept at eliciting this sense of wholeness.

Later in *Art as Experience* Dewey returned to the problem of isolation and noted the value of art for communication. Art, he claimed, is "the most universal and freest form of communication." Even "apart from literature" it has this quality. Then occurs the statement that is relevant to our discussion of the religious in experience: "The sense of communion generated by a work of art may take on a definitely religious quality. The union of men with one another is the source of the rites that from the time of archaic man to the present have commemorated the crises of birth, death, and marriage. Art is the extension of the power of rites and ceremonies to unite men, through a shared celebration, to all incidents and scenes of life. This office is the reward and seal of art. That art weds man and nature is a familiar fact. Art also renders men aware of their union with one another in origin and destiny" (275). Here Dewey seemed to have almost completely transferred the religious function to the esthetic. He first said that "a work of art may take on a definitely religious quality." He then noted the religious activities that "commemorate" various transitions in life. But he concluded by celebrating the way in which art as "the extension of power of rites and ceremonies" can perform the religious functions of uniting humans to one another and to nature. If so, this is a good example of the complete secularization of the religious.[41]

But usually Dewey gave to both art and religion this ability to generate a sense of wholeness. Returning to the final paragraph in the chapter on desire and intelligence in *Human Nature and Conduct* we find him, as I said earlier, beginning with a claim about "the office of art and religion," but discussing only the latter. The point he was concerned to make there was that the religious should not be separated from morality and intelligence as some philosophers were inclined to do. He wrote that they have correctly claimed "that definite purposes and methods shade off of necessity into a vast whole which is incapable of objective presentation," but "they have falsified the conception by treating the religious consciousness as something that comes *after* an experience in which striving, resolution and foresight are found." The truth is that "there is a point in *every* intelligent activity where effort ceases; where thought and doing fall back upon a course of events which effort and reflection cannot touch." At some "point *in* deliberate action . . . definite thought fades into the ineffable and undefinable—into emotion." But it is not a matter of "alternation," for then the "function of religion" would be "caricatured rather than realized" and "morals, like war," would be "thought of as hell, and religion, like peace, as a respite." No, the religious is within experience, within action, enabling us to act. "The religious experience," Dewey contended, "is a reality in so far as in the midst of effort to foresee and regulate future objects we are sustained and expanded in feebleness and failure by the sense of an enveloping whole." This sense of peace occurs "in action not after it," and "it is the contribution of the ideal to conduct" (MW 14:181). The better way "to foresee and regulate future objects" is intelligent action. One engages in it most constructively when one is "sustained and expanded in feebleness and failure by the sense of an enveloping whole." But this difficult-to-specify sense is not separable in activity; it is an aspect of it.

We must note the carefully qualified place Dewey gave to the religious. It is not a distinct experience, and it functions as a condition within intelligent behavior to sustain those who would "foresee and regulate future objects." It is a quality of intelligent action. To be religious is to persist and grow in one's intelligent actions by the means of an awareness of a very wide context. Or, as Dewey put it negatively in *A Common Faith:* "The essentially unreligious attitude is that which attributes human achievement and purpose to man in isolation from the world of physical nature and his fellows" (LW 9:18). There is nothing otherworldly here; it is entirely naturalistic or secular. Moreover, this very wide contextual awareness is constitutive of intelligence. It has an important role to play, but it is only a part of intelligent action and subordinate to it. Also, it is discriminable only upon reflection; it is not a discrete activity that can become an intrinsic object of concern. In pursuing worthwhile objectives one notices that one is aided by an awareness of one's relationships to the natural and social world. One cultivates this "sense of an enveloping whole" as a constitutive dimension of intelligent conduct—not as an intrinsic end.

Therefore, Randall Auxier is doubly mistaken. One, he understands Dewey's "God" to be inclusivity, and two, in so doing he makes inclusivity an intrinsic object of cultivation. Auxier runs together Dewey's statements about God as "the unity of all ideal ends" (LW 9:29) and as the "*active* relation between ideal and actual" (34) into this malformed statement: "God is the union of the actual and the ideal."[42] This makes Dewey's god almost everything there is, but not quite (for it leaves out unideal possibilities), and it permits the notion that Dewey encouraged a faith in inclusivity.

Certainly Dewey thought we should be inclusive, but his sense of a whole was in the service of (and therefore an instrument of) his recommended object of devotion—intelligence.

Shared Miscommunication

Auxier's mistake is encouraged by the looseness of Dewey's language. For instance, the sentence in *Human Nature and Conduct* is so constructed that one is led to believe that Dewey is going to say what religious experience is, and, sure enough, standing in the climactic position in the sentence is what appears to be what Dewey promised—"the sense of an enveloping whole." But, as I have tried to show, this sense, important as it is, was understood by Dewey to be constitutive of the humanistic aim of living well. One who is attempting to accomplish one's aims is aided by the sense of a whole. The religious dimension is subordinate to experience and its possibilities. Verbally very close to Auxier's understanding—"God is the union of the actual and ideal"—is Dewey's "union of ideal ends with actual conditions" (LW 9:35). But in the context of the paragraph in which it occurs this latter formulation is clearly not as inclusive as Auxier's "union of the actual and the ideal." Dewey's phrase should be taken as a reference to specific "union[s] of ideal ends with actual conditions"—art, knowledge, work, rest, education, and so forth. These specific goods, found in ordinary life, unite both ideals and existing conditions.

Here we have crystalized the problem of Dewey's religious proposal. He clearly had in mind attitudes and processes that occur "in the ordinary course of human experience in our relations to the natural world and to one another as human beings related in the family, friendship, industry, art, science, and citizenship" (LW 9:224). But readers as sympathetic, astute, and even untraditional in their religious sensibilities as Wieman and Auxier take Dewey's expression of these secular activities in traditional religious language—"faith," "God" and "piety"—in ways that are more philosophically idealistic and personalistic than naturalistic and humanistic. They, like Rockefeller, push Dewey toward the world-view and commitments of his early manhood and away from the secularity of his maturity. But the access for this retrogressive push was provided by Dewey himself. His occasionally imprecise use of selected religious language opened the way for misinterpretation. But even when he was exact misinterpretation can occur. In our culture religious sensibilities are such that one has trouble circumscribing the religious. Dewey's comment to Otto is very revealing. He reported, "I didnt [*sic*] want to get drawn further into the Christian Century discussion, because their assumption is that I am primarily interested—as they are—in

'God' when in fact my reference to it was purely incidental, . . ." (LW 9:455). But one cannot casually refer to God in our society. Invoking him evoked more than Dewey wished to continue to be concerned with.

RELIGION: NOT DEWEY'S PROBLEM

If the function of the religious, along with art, is to provide the sense of a whole that is essential to experience that is satisfying, Dewey's quest for wholeness was a religious one, as well as an aesthetic one. As I noted at the beginning of this chapter, Bernstein claims that Dewey's *A Common Faith* is "an expression of what might be called Dewey's 'natural piety.'" So interpreted, "Dewey is making explicit what is implicit in his entire philosophy." Therefore, his "treatment of the religious attitude and quality is the culmination of his entire philosophy" (161). Jerome Soneson, as I also noted, makes a similar claim, but with—in my opinion—better justification. For Soneson, Dewey is "fundamentally a religious thinker," because "what informs and motivates all his thinking is his abiding concern for meaningful orientation and human fulfilment" (127). His "meaningful orientation" I take to be the sense of a whole that I have been discussing, and "human fulfilment" could be the self-transformation that comes from one's intense and comprehensive commitments. If so, the religious for Dewey would not only be the search for meaning, but also self-realization. This reasoning, however, makes it difficult to separate Dewey as a religious thinker from Dewey as a philosopher.

By a series of steps one can get from the traditionally or conventionally religious to Dewey and can with some plausibility refer to his untraditional approach as religious. One may, while one is going through the twists and turns, think that the two are similar, but in actuality there is not much resemblance between the two. Whatever Dewey's thought was, "religious" does not capture it except in a very restrained sense. (Some would deem it an impoverished sense.) Saying Dewey was religious is like saying Dewey believed in God. As we have seen, the latter assertion must be heavily qualified—so much so that not much survives of the assertion. Similarly, once one makes the necessary qualifications there does not seem to be much point in calling Dewey religious.

This is true unless, of course, the person doing the calling has a real stake in considering Dewey religious. Such seems to be case with Rockefeller. His is a fine account of Dewey's religious development. Moreover, he is very well aware of the "danger in pursuing" a "reconstruction of Dewey's idea of the divine," for, as he continues his explanation, "some will use it to reassert all the old dualisms of ideal and real, natural and spiritual, religion and culture that Dewey devoted his life to overcoming and that are fraught with negative consequences." Rockefeller thinks that he can avoid this mistake by not treating "the eternal One" as "a being, an it, an object." Yet in identifying it as "the ground of personality and the wellspring of human goodness and ultimate meaning," he comes close—too close in my view—to finding more extra-human unity in the interaction of ideal and actual than I think Dewey would. Rockefeller appears to have made the move that Dewey found objectionable in Wieman's interpretation; his reconstructive suggestions may cross the line into theism. Rockefeller thinks not. But the issue here is not the adequacy of Rockefeller's understanding of the "divine presence" (pp.538–39); it is a matter of understanding Dewey's proposal to intelligize practice and the wisdom of casting this proposal in religious language.

I think Dewey's willingness to use the language of faith and even the word "God" is counterproductive. Despite his stipulations, this use with its connotations of, to cite Hook's words, "the sacred, profound and ultimate,"[43] invites misunderstanding. Moreover, there is nothing in Dewey's writings that cannot be expressed in secular language. If there were, his philosophy would be deeply inconsistent. As he himself said on more than one occasion, the use of religious language was optional. He also said, as I have noted, that religion never constituted for him a "leading philosophical problem."

But once again it is important to understand what motivated Dewey. He was trying to find a middle way between his secular sensibility and the conventional religious heritage of his reading public. This heritage was not one in which they were comfortable, but the new culture of modernity, informed by secularism, science, technology, and individualism, was not one in which they were completely at home either. Dewey was trying to integrate their common religious and moral inheritance with their newly developing culture. I do not think his mix worked. But this is not to say that an integration of our lives as lived and our values does not need to be articulated in a meaningful way. It is only to say that Dewey failed to achieve all that he set out to do—express a common faith. In a world still divided in multiple ways this may not be possible. But surely the effort to *integrate* and *embody* our values is a worthy one.

In our culture the effort to incarnate our ideals in tangible ways is an aesthetic and religious one. Therefore, Dewey's reconstructive project can be viewed as a religious one. There was another reason for Dewey's project as well. His entire project is, if not religious, then quasireligious in terms of its ability to provide meaning and promote self-development. If one can think in wholly naturalistic terms, one can grasp that Dewey's notion of adjustment (see LW 9:12–13)—the transformation of experience that affects both the agent and the environment—is thoroughly secular and yet has important similarities to the way in which religions function. But thinking of his project as a thoroughly secular yet religiously functioning one is difficult to sustain. It is extremely difficult for even knowledgeable interpreters of Dewey to combine what most take as opposites, much less maintain the balance. I think Deweyans need to concede failure and try a different approach.

Although one may worship a god or engage in a religious practice for intrinsic reasons, one often becomes a devotee for its beneficial effects—better living or salvation either in this world or in some other. Dewey's proposal is in fact a competitor to religious devotion in this arena. He is unyielding in his insistence that the life of inquiry enables one to interact with others and nature in a more satisfying way than do less intelligent ways. But, as I have been concerned to show, his willingness to enter the arena with his religious competitors is easily misunderstood. Therefore, I think that the Deweyan process of adjustment, of transforming experience, is better understood as intelligence generally or specifically as the secular form of cultural criticism that he understood to be philosophy. In the next and final chapter I will take up directly this simultaneously mundane and distinctive form of philosophy.

6

❖

THE SECULARITY OF
DEWEYAN CRITICISM

*There are those who look upon philosophy as a revelation of something
foreign to everyday experience, or as a key that opens a door to realms
otherwise inaccessible which have a supreme and final value. There
are those who have once believed they found this ultimate revelation
and this powerful key in religion, and who, having been disillusioned
there, search in philosophy for what they have missed. When they do
not find what they are after, they turn away disappointed or invent a
system of fantasy according to their wishes and label it philosophy.
But philosophy is not a special road to something alien to ordinary
beliefs, knowledge, action, enjoyment, and suffering. It is rather a criticism, a critical viewing, of just these familiar things.*
—John Dewey, *Construction and Criticism* (LW 5:141)

ESPITE HIS USE of religious language, Dewey made a clean break
with traditional religion. If one understands the religious concepts
embraced by Dewey—faith, the religious in experience, piety, and
God—in the ways specified by him one will have nothing that is non-naturalistic or goes beyond Dewey's cultural instrumentalism as found in his
mature work. Indeed, the secularity of Deweyan criticism must be understood if one is to appreciate his proposed solution of what he took to be the
outstanding problem of modern society—the relationship of science and
value—or, in its more general formulation, the relationship of existence and
value. Deweyan criticism—either as everyday intelligence, the specific disciplines, or philosophy, which is the criticism of these various criticisms—
reworks our practices to make them more satisfying than they have been or
would otherwise be. It is a process of valuation that existentially transforms
the situations of our lives. These transformations are secular in two respects:
Both the means employed and the ends sought are within experience. One

170

needs neither ends nor means that are extranatural—taking *natural* to be inclusive of human conduct and institutions.

DEWEY'S SECULAR APPROACH

Deweyan criticism requires and reinforces secularity. Therefore, Dewey's method of inquiry, loose though it may be, is not completely indeterminate. His cultural instrumentalism is conducive to neither conventional religion nor authoritarian practices. Certainly it is antithetical to thoughtlessness or happenstance. Expressed positively, Deweyan criticism values science, technology, democracy, and growth. There is thus a continuity between Deweyan criticism and these secular values.

It is my aim in this chapter to elucidate this secularity. I will begin by considering the critique of John Herman Randall, Jr., that Dewey should have made more use of traditional religion. This discussion will contribute to the explanation of the contrast between Dewey's less-than-accommodationist approach to religion and his more accommodating stance in politics. Dewey may have been a *via media* thinker, but this does not mean that he always took a course half-way between the extremes. In political matters he was more willing to accept the prevailing situation; in religion, less so. It is his commitment to secularity that explains these divergent responses. His philosophy of experience required him to work with the existing political realities, but to reject conventional religion with its extraexperiential commitments.

Deweyan criticism, or intelligence, is neither just splitting the difference (compromise) nor simply improving some traditional practice. Rather, with regard to social practices, it is the remaking of our common—that is, shared—and secular practices in ways that are more emancipating (liberating), yet still shared and secular. In terms of our personal practices it is the recognition that the satisfying of our needs or desires depends on our shared and secular practices. We grow or stretch the present, making use of what we have and are in the service of what we would like to have and become. The better way to remake experience—better than the traditional methods of authority and simple coercion—is through criticism.

In this chapter I will focus on the materials of criticism—the ordinary, mundane stuff of our lives—as well as the critical activity that develops this stuff into more satisfying experiences. Dewey's commitment to the common, to what is shared, enables us to understand his willingness to remake political practices and to abandon conventional religion. His divergent treatments of politics and religion, which I have examined in the preceding chapters, serve as two large examples of what he meant by criticism or intelligence, enabling us to understand his commitment to what is shared as a function of his secularity. "Thoughtful valuation" (LW 1:326) is not as innocuous as it appears. Over time the criticism of one's practices will lead to their secular reconstruction.

Dewey's Secular Orientation

For a democratic socialist Dewey was clearly expedient in his politics. He had a vision of democracy that was more radical than that of conventional politics, but he continued to engage in public life using the means available to influence American society. No matter how much he might have been at odds with politicians and voters, he continued to engage in electoral politics and other efforts to influence public opinion and policy. He disengaged himself, however, from conventional religious life, declining to participate in religious institutions. His metaphysical naturalism would not permit him to be active in supernaturalistic religious institutions. The only religious institutions that he would accept were those that reconstructed themselves naturalistically (LW 9:54–55).

But Dewey's abstention from conventional religion did not go unchallenged. His younger colleague at Columbia, John Herman Randall, Jr., among others, questioned both Dewey's ability to free the religious in experience from the "historic encumbrances" of institutionalized religions and the wisdom of such an "emancipation."[1] I will treat these issues in reverse order, showing why Dewey had to seek an alternative to traditional religion and then explaining how he proposed to do so. The discussion of this secular alternative will raise an additional problem: In resisting religious sectarianism, it is charged, Dewey may have fallen into a secular sectarianism. The sympathetic musings of Randall have indeed been pushed by Dewey's critics—even if, for the most part, they are unaware of Randall's critique—into the charge that Dewey is an advocate of a rival religion—secular humanism. In extricating Dewey's cultural instrumentalism from this charge, I will show how one can be simultaneously pragmatic and secular without being sectarian, at least not in the sense feared by Dewey.

An Exception for Non-Natural Religion?

In his essay on Dewey's religious proposal, "The Religion of Shared Experience,"[2] Randall pointed out that Dewey attacked "the very notion of a particular religion" as being "anti-religious" (135), in Dewey's sense of religious, citing Dewey's statement in *A Common Faith:* "A body of beliefs and practices that are apart from the common and natural relations of mankind must, in the degree in which it is influential, weaken and sap the force of the possibilities inherent in such relations" (LW 9:19). The possibility of irony did not go unnoticed by Dewey's friend, Max Otto. Commenting on Dewey's distinction between actual religions and the religious in experience, Otto observed in his review of *A Common Faith:* "This is so sharply drawn that it almost seems as if Mr. Dewey were saying that every activity in the world may take on a religious character, excepting religion."[3]

This quip, of course, overstates Dewey's objection. In the last chapter of *A Common Faith,* as we have seen, Dewey allowed for the possibility of secularly oriented religious institutions. But Dewey's rejection of the vast majority of traditional or conventional religious institutions was nevertheless regarded as an anomaly by Edward L. Schaub. Noting that Dewey normally regarded existing institutions as "centers of possibilities" for reconstruction, Schaub then observed: "But in envisaging things and existences as possibilities, Dewey made an exception—and apparently the only one—in the case of the existing religions. As to them he bade us . . . to eschew reformation and reconstruction, and to acquiesce cheerfully in an expected demise."[4] Schaub—by overlooking Dewey's exceptions—thus found an inconsistency where Otto had noticed an irony.

Dewey's rejection of traditional or conventional religion was an anomaly, however, only if Dewey's approach is taken to be one of always beginning with existing institutions and attempting to reform them. Clearly, as the example of religion shows, Dewey was sometimes willing to break with current practices and not just try to bend them in the right direction. The reason is that Dewey thought that organized religion, on the whole, was committed to a non-naturalistic approach (see LW 9:19 and 55). The overwhelming majority of religious institutions were fundamentally opposed to Dewey's project of working within experience to develop our shared values.

Dewey thought that, as long as religious institutions remained otherworldly in their orientation, they could not be stretched in the right direction; they must be abandoned. An entirely different orientation and a fundamentally different approach were needed. This approach was the one that Dewey consistently advocated in making the proposal that we intelligize our practices by making use of the goods that arise naturally in interactions with one another and the physical environment. Therefore Dewey, with his commitment to work within experience alone, could not consistently accept institutions predicated on a bifurcation of existence into the natural and the supernatural.

Randall and other naturalists, however, thought Dewey should have been more appreciative of traditional religion. Horace Friess, to whom Randall dedicated one of his books,[5] raised the question of a Deweyan "blind spot" regarding religion in "Dewey's Philosophy of Religion."[6] Friess, coauthor of a survey of world religions,[7] first questioned whether Dewey's "strictures on the way religious institutions harden and become devitalized do enough justice to the actual roles of cult in relation to community" (210). Then, noting Dewey's criticism of religious institutions' orientation toward the supernatural, Friess observed: "How far such a judgment involved a blind spot in Dewey, besides chronic lassitude and indirection in much theological thought, remains an open question. But it must be noted as a fact that, among the friendly critics and the followers of Dewey in ways of naturalistic philosophy, there were those who found his treatment of 'religion' seriously lacking in unprejudiced empirical consideration of the religious arts" (210). A footnote then directed the reader to Randall's review of *A Common Faith* and an article and book by Willard E. Arnett, a Columbia Ph.D. and student of Justus Buchler.

I will begin with Arnett's article, "Critique of Dewey's Anticlerical Religious Philosophy,"[8] in which he argued that Dewey's moralism "blind[ed] him to the more positive aspects of the religions" and prevented him from appreciating "religion as a significant moral force." While acknowledging "the crimes of the religions," Arnett nevertheless maintained that these "are hardly sufficient justification for the destruction of the church as a means and medium of encouraging the religious life" (257). Therefore, he missed Dewey's point that it is the non-natural orientation of religious institutions and not the fallibility of human beings that makes religious institutions unsuitable as means for the realization of the religious in experience. Arnett thought that if Dewey had been more sensitive to this pervasive human activity he would have been more appreciative of the various religions' actual and potential contributions.

Similarly, but with more appreciation of Dewey, Jerome Soneson thought that Dewey did not grasp the possibilities of reform within religious traditions. Dewey's rejection of traditional religion "would seem . . . [to] make [him] a poor resource for thinking about religious problems in general and problems in Christian theology in particular." But Soneson acknowledged that this "assessment" was "premature," for Dewey's functional interpretation of religion made "it possible not only to see the continuity among religious traditions but also to evaluate those traditions." But this "positive point" was "one that Dewey did not himself see."[9]

Dewey did not understand that religious traditions could be "highly significant resources for religious transformation" (134). They contain within themselves the normative possibilities that permit a "criticism and reconstruction" of these same traditions: "For example, once we see that the aim of religiousness is to find wholeness of meaning amid the tragedy of life, we have a perspective for examining the actual means at work and for criticizing and reconstructing those means in relation to their capacity for making wholeness of meaning possible." That Dewey could not see this Soneson found "somewhat surprising" for this reason: "It is the same argument for the relationship between the descriptive and the normative that he makes in his *Logic*" (135). The reference in the 1938 *Logic* that Soneson apparently had in mind was to the process whereby standards are developed out of actual practices. Dewey's words, at the beginning of the section cited by Soneson, are: "All logic forms . . . arise within the operation of inquiry and are concerned with control of inquiry so that it may yield warranted assertions" (LW 12:11).

Dewey did not, however, have a failure of sight, for he thought that inherently extranaturalistic institutions could not pursue naturalistic ends. It is Soneson who failed to recognize that there is a fundamental difference between traditional religions and every other human enterprise, including logic. The other human enterprises are not fundamentally diverted from attention to the secular. Of course it was possible for the religions to transform themselves. But the point is that in order to do so they would have had to reverse themselves! They would have had to deny the orientation that had shaped them up to that point. Soneson was concerned with using Dewey as a resource "for thinking about religious problems in general and problems in Christian theology in particular." However, Dewey rejected both the general and the particular aim. He did so not because he lacked knowledge or sensitivity, but because he realized that his secular orientation required him to reject nonsecular problems and institutions. He was not interested in reconstructing the unsecular religious traditions precisely because he thought that the way forward must be secular.

The Secular Option

Randall, the most significant of Dewey's religious naturalist critics, accused Dewey of indulging "in much loose talk about ridding religious experience of 'all historic encumbrances.'" Then, effectively embracing Schaub's complaint of an anomaly in Dewey, Randall commented that this was "an aim hardly appropriate from one usually so insistent on the continuity of human institutions and cultures."[10] I have tried to remove the sting of this inconsistency by suggesting that Dewey was not an indiscriminate reconstructor of human practices, but one whose understanding of and adherence to metaphysical naturalism required that he draw the line at those institutions that were non-naturalistically oriented.

Randall then raised the major objection against Dewey's project: As long as one wants, as Dewey said he did, to be religious, one must embrace the material conditions, so to speak, of this intention. There can be no instantiation of the religious in experience without religious institutions. As Randall himself wrote: "To free the religious attitude from institutional embodiment in any religion sounds suspiciously like freeing art from embodiment in any particular work of art; and the religious man who never goes near a religious institution suggests the musical person who never touches a muscial instrument" (137). Similarly, John E. Smith exclaimed, "It is absurd to suppose that religious institutions can be discarded as if they performed no distinctive functions of their own."[11] Thus Randall and Smith affirmed what Dewey denied—that there is a distinctive human activity, the religious, that is appropriately practiced in distinctive institutions, the various religions.

The significance of this criticism is immense. Dewey had failed to persuade his younger Columbia colleagues and their students of the wisdom of his religious proposal. As the foregoing criticism indicates, they did not accept his crucial distinction between the religions and the religious. Randall acknowledged that Dewey had attempted "to disentangle religious feeling and sentiment from any particular kind of institutionalized behavior," but then explained that effort as a function of Dewey's allegiance to his own culture's anticlerical tendencies (137–38). He thought that Dewey had sided with the unchurched, apparently giving "philosophic expression to all that is Protestant—in the sense of being "against a professional priesthood with its claims and orthodoxies" (138), provincial, and merely American in the religious degeneracy of our times" (107). A bit later I will deal with the possibility that Dewey's rejection of sectarianism in the interest of commonness was itself a sectarian stance. Now I want to show that Dewey's location of the religious in nonreligious institutions was both feasible and necessary.

Dewey's naturalistic critics thought they had him in a bind. To the extent that he embraced the religious he must also embrace religious institutions. The analogy was to art or politics: One cannot be artistic without producing or interacting with works of art. One cannot be political without engaging in political activities, such as voting or running for office. Similarly, to be religious is to pray, congregate with other believers, or engage in some recognizably religious actions.

Such a criticism, in identifying the religious with traditional or conventionally religious activities, both missed the point of Dewey's religious proposal and begged the question against that proposal. Dewey attempted to break this link, identifying the religious, as I indicated in the previous chapter, with those attitudes in any experience that were sufficiently intense and comprehensive to unify the agent. He thought the interactions can occur in a variety of settings: political, artistic, or educational; they do not have to occur in institutions set apart as religious. Indeed, some if not most religious institutions, in being oriented toward the supernatural, inhibit the scope of one's life-transforming attitudes and activities. They lack the comprehensiveness and intensity that Dewey found (at least potentially) in the secular: "The objection to supernaturalism is that it stands in the way of an effective realization of the sweep and depth of the implications of natural human relations" (*A Common Faith*, LW 9:53). From Dewey's point of view the trouble with supernaturalism was that it was irreligious!

With regard to the pervasive quality of the religious, Dewey could have developed an analogous claim with regard to the political and the educational. One can certainly be political in a variety of settings ranging from the family to the school to the workplace. Similarly, one can learn in a deliberate, directed manner in all sorts of activities in or out of school. These are adumbrations of Dewey's point, but he carried it farther with regard to religion. He chose to free the religious from exclusive identification with religious traditions because he thought that the usual non-natural orientation of these traditions denied the religious possiblities of the secular. Only when the public or common areas of our lives could be invested with the passion of the religious could the needed progress be made. What was needed was emotion wedded to intelligence, a "passionate intelligence" that would shine light into "the murky places of social existence" (LW 9:52). Dewey broke the exclusive link between the religious and the supernatural in order to establish a link between the religious and the natural.

Dewey thought that only by working from within experience could one bring about the needed transformation of experience, for commitment to the supernatural "stands in the way of using the means that are in our power to make radical changes in" the natural human relations. He argued: "It is certainly true that great material changes might be made with no corresponding improvement of a spiritual or ideal nature. But development in the latter direction cannot be introduced from without; it cannot be brought about by dressing up material and economic changes with decorations derived from the supernatural. It can come only from more intense realization of values that inhere in the actual connections of human beings with one another. The attempt to segregate the implicit public interest and social value of all institutions and social arrangements in a particular organization is a fatal diversion" (LW 9:53). The sort of change Dewey valued must not be embellished with supernatural decorations; it could be brought about only by enhancing "the values that inhere in the actual connections of human beings with one another." Dewey thought that to locate these values "in a particular organization is a fatal diversion" from where they should be properly found—in the common spaces of our lives.

Dewey's younger Columbia colleagues affirmed his naturalism, but not his extensive critique of existing religious institutions. They failed to sense the need to choose that Dewey did. He wrote at the end of the first chapter of *A Common Faith:* "The opposition between religous values as I conceive them and religions is not to be bridged" (LW 9:20). Randall, Friess, Smith, and others thought a bridge was needed; indeed it was Dewey's insensitivity toward those human practices designated as religious that kept him from seeing the need for a bridge. A bridge was needed, they thought, because it was only by means of distinctive religious institutions that one could be religious.

Dewey thought there was no need for a bridge for two reasons: One, there is no chasm to be bridged, no other side to be reached. And two, the secular space that we inhabit is sufficently rich in resources to satisfy our needs, including our religious needs. We can enhance the interactions that constitute experience in such a way that the full range of our needs can be met. What is required, he argued, is that the "faith and ardor" usually associated with the traditional religions be directed toward "verifiable realities." He wrote: "Human beings have impulses toward affection, compassion and justice, equality and freedom." What is now needed is the intelligent, passionate enhancement and extension of these natural impulses "to larger human purposes" (53–54).

One does not need to choose the supernatural alternative, Dewey thought, because human life, appropriately situated in its natural, both physical and cultural, setting, is sufficiently rich to enable human beings to live well. Moreover, the supernatural option distracts our attention from the natural one. Indeed, the situation in the 1930s was such that Dewey thought society's efforts must be focused on the enhancement and expansion of the values found in common life. This was the work of social intelligence.

Social Intelligence and Secular Humanism

That Dewey was a secular humanist in some sense has, of course, not gone unnoticed. Dewey freely acknowledged his antipathy toward conventional religion and supported humanist organizations. The issues that must be addressed here are two, and they are related. The first has to do with the tightness of the link between Dewey's commitment to secularity and his advocacy of social intelligence. I argue that secularity was in Dewey's view both a condition and a product of social intelligence. The second, related issue has to do with his partisanship in behalf of a secular social intelligence. Was Dewey so much of an advocate that he in effect became a sectarian secular humanist? I will deny that a Deweyan must be such a sectarian. Against Randall, I contend that Dewey was a nonsectarian advocate of a passionate social intelligence. Then I will show in the succeeding subsection that Dewey did have his sectarian involvements.

Intelligence and Secularity

Dewey thought that intelligence is both embodied and creative. As an embodied practice intelligence is the previously instituted ongoing activity that satisfies some need. As a creative practice it is the use of one's fund of experience to modify practices that have become dysfunctional. The method of reworking these practices to make them more satisfying is inquiry. Dewey was insistent that inquiry had been best exemplified to date in the practices of modern science and this sort of activity must now be established in the rest of life. In so doing one can transform experience, making it more and more intelligent.

When Dewey was speaking generally he referred to this activity of deliberate experience-transformation as "intelligence" or "criticism." But he drew no sharp line between intelligence generally and philosophy, for he regarded the latter as but a more careful, wider version of the former: "As soon as anyone strives to introduce definiteness, clarity, and order on any broad scale, he enters the road that leads to philosophy" (*Construction and Criticism*, LW 5:141). In the last chapter of *Experience and Nature* he often used the terms *intelligence* and *criticism* synonymously (LW 1:303–304), but he characterized philosophy, in a famous formulation, as "a criticism of criticisms" (298). For now I will use the term *criticism* because criticism is always criticism of something, and it is the something to which I want to call attention. The immediate object of criticism is one's present beliefs and practices or their contemplated alternatives. These "goods," Dewey continually insisted, are found in experience, the transactions between organisms and environment. They do not come from outside experience; they are fully within it.

The stuff that is criticized, the stuff that is transformed through intelligence, is wholly natural, fully a part of the secular order. We examine what we have inherited and consider ways in which we might improve our inheritance. This is an entirely secular process. Dewey's naturalistic critics acknowledged this, but they thought that just as he had embraced existing political practices, so he should have embraced existing religious practices. Dewey, however, as we have seen, thought that the latter are not improvable because of a 'false consciousness.' Traditional religious institutions understand themselves to be related to something beyond this world, not just incidentally, but necessarily. They do not exhibit the potential for growth in the direction of the public or common in the way that other practices do. They are locked into an understanding of themselves as being otherworldly.

The second feature to be noticed is that the very process of criticism is itself a secular practice. Intelligence is not a private activity. Or at least what may be initially a personal discovery becomes public property. Dewey's examples of embodied intelligence are inventions that become widely dispersed in society. For instance, in arguing in *Liberalism and Social Action* against the notion that "the average citizen is not endowed with the degree of intelligence that the use of it as a method demands," he observed: "There are few individuals who have the native capacity that was required to invent the stationary steam-engine, locomotive, dynamo or telephone. But there are none so mean that they cannot intelligently utilize these embodiments of intelligence once they are a part of the organized means of associated living" (LW 11:38; see also LW 2:366–67). Intelligence is not only criticism of the stuff of our lives; it is also the transformation of this stuff in ways that are widely available.

Further, Dewey thought that the sort of transformation that works best is the method of open, free deliberation. Here we need only recall his many discussions of science and democracy. Dewey thought that the most effective social change is that which comes about through a public process of informed give and take.

Finally, Dewey thought that this secularizing process is itself the product of secularization. In *Reconstruction in Philosophy* he noted: "Aforetime man employed the results of his prior experience only to form customs that henceforth had to be blindly followed or blindly broken. Now, old experience is used to suggest aims and methods for developing a new and improved experience. Consequently experience becomes in so far constructively self-regulative" (MW 12:134). Experience can be blind and dumb, or it can be "self-regulative." With the development of science the possibility has arisen of experience transforming itself by itself. Change takes place not from without experience, but from within experience through the methods developed by it.

Once one realizes that the past does not absolutely determine the future, that indeed the past and present are products themselves of previous humanly initiated changes, one can regard the present as modifiable. One can shift one's attention from some remote or extrahistorical future (and nonhistorical means) to a future that is continuous with the past and the present. The future is now understood to be of a piece with what has gone before it. Consequently, the methods one uses to shape the future can be adapted from those that have been used in the past to shape the past and the present. One does not need to break completely with the present or escape it. One needs only to modify it through the means, suitably refashioned, that are now in one's possession.

In *Liberalism and Social Action* Dewey made this point in arguing against his intellectual opposition in the 1930s, the reactionaries and those radicals who relied primarily on violence. Dewey pointed out that the radical who contends that "great social changes [in the past] have been effected only by violent means" shares in this regard the view of "the hide-bound reactionary who holds to the past as an ultimate fact." Both fail to grasp "the *fact that history in being a process of change generates change not only in details but also in the method of directing social change*" (Dewey's emphasis; LW 11:58).

Therefore, Dewey was a thorough-going naturalist. He had come to believe that the materials, methods, and aims of intelligence are entirely within history, which is to say that the products of intelligence and their reconstruction are entirely a secular affair. But recognition of this secularism raises a problem. Did Dewey become so much an advocate of secularity that he became sectarian—a narrow, partisan proponent of commonality?

Dewey's Possible Sectarianism

Dewey thought, as we have seen, that supernaturalism is a distraction from the business of living in this world. There was possibly an additional reason as well, one suggested by Randall, for Dewey's lack of regard for traditional religions. At times Dewey may have been motivated by his own sectarian interests. I will first examine Randall's charge, and then I will look at some of Dewey's "religious" affiliations.

Randall's Charge

Randall did not flatly declare Dewey to be a sectarian. He couched his concern in terms of a worry or a possibility rather than a flat assertion. He thought that Dewey's "religion of shared experience" came dangerously close to being a "total faith," and wrote that "it is after all hard to see how any total faith could fail to be divisive and sectarian in effect, or how any ideal end erected into supremacy over conduct could avoid conflict with the religion of common-ness and shared experience."[12]

Randall's worry was misplaced. Dewey's advocacy of a passionate intelligence never crossed the line to an uncritical faith. In the quotation in the preceding paragraph, for instance, Randall attributed to Dewey the view that an ideal can be made supreme (and thus come into conflict with what is common). But this misinterpreted Dewey's understanding of an authoritative ideal in two ways. One, no generalized end-in-view could ever be beyond criticism for Dewey. Needs, ends-in-view, means, actual consequences—all are subject to scrutiny. Two, one of the tests for an ideal is that it be "inclusive." Dewey described religious faith "as the unification of the self through allegiance to inclusive ideal ends, which imagination presents to us and to which the human will responds as worthy of controlling our desires and choices" (LW 9:23). Randall subtly but significantly changed Dewey's meaning by substituting "total" for "inclusive." Dewey, as the last part of the just-quoted definition of religious faith indicates, never lost sight of the subjectivity of human endeavors. He thought our regulative ideals should be inclusive, but he did not think a person's choices should be allowed to become a "total faith."

Dewey could be partisan and polemical, but he was not religious in the sense suggested by Randall's worry about Dewey's "religion of shared experience" in the totalizing sense. An examination of a crucial paragraph will show the difficulty with Randall's approach. Randall thought Dewey wavered between taking the religious as any way of life and "the complete unification of the whole self by ends so inclusive that they are acknowledged as supreme over conduct." With the first the religious loses "any distinctive meaning." With the second it becomes unrealistic, sounding "far more like the Idea of the Good or Green's Ideal Self than like any possibility of human living." It is with the latter possibility that Randall worried that Dewey may "have gone off the deep end, and sunk in the sea of apologetics for a particular religion." But then Randall observed that Dewey "comes up smiling after a page or two," reassuring us that Dewey did not mean for the religious to be understood in this unrealistic sense (140–41). Nevertheless, the rhetorical damage had been done. Randall had set up a false dichotomy, insinuating that Dewey came close to accepting the totalizing possibility. But Dewey never suggested that one's faith or its effects on the self should be as complete as Randall's reconstruction implies. Dewey had his sectarian involvements, as we shall see, but Randall did not show him to be a sectarian.

Dewey's Episodic Sectarianism

We must not make too much of Dewey's sectarian involvements, but candor requires that we note them. On occasion Dewey expressed his opposition to supernatural religion by affiliating himself with humanist organizations, including religious humanist groups. The issue here is not Dewey's political partisanship or philosophical polemics. Dewey was certainly capable of taking sides in politics or philosophical debates. To do so is no indication of sectarianism. But in becoming a member of a group or signing a manifesto in order to align himself with one religious group against another Dewey clearly became a sectarian in a limited way.[13]

In a letter dated August 30, 1940, Lamont confronted Dewey about the latter's reluctance to use the term *humanism* in reference to his philosophy: "Since in 1933 you signed the Humanist Manifesto . . . I am wondering why you have not used the word "Humanism" more to describe your own philosophy. Though I realize this term "Humanism" is open to misconception, it is certainly far less formidable for the average person, whom you wish philosophy to reach, than the term Pragmatism or Instrumentalism or even Naturalism. And of course these latter words have also given rise to plenty of misunderstanding."[14]

Dewey replied a week later, on September 6. In his response Dewey clearly stated the context in which he was willing to use the term *humanism*: "There is a great difference between different kinds of 'Humanism,' as you know; there is that of Paul Elmer More,[15] for example. I signed the humanistic manifesto . . . because it had a religious context, and my signature was a sign of sympathy on that score, and not a commitment to every clause in it" (58:26). The Humanist Manifesto of 1933 was an expression of a religious humanism, and from Dewey's point of view it was a salvo in the sectarian battles of the time. He did not mean for it to be taken as representative of his philosophical position, which could best be described, as he went on to point out in the response to Lamont, as a "cultural or humanistic naturalism." Even in the opening paragraphs of the revised version of *Experience and Nature*, where Dewey used the phrase "naturalistic humanism," he made clear that his intent in the book was to locate human experience or culture within nature (LW 1:10).

Lamont was not satisfied with Dewey's response, protesting in a letter the following week: "Though Naturalism is probably clearer to professional philosophers, it is certainly confusing to the average person, who considers a Naturalist one who, like John Burroughs, makes a specialty of birds and flowers. Also since Humanism as a word has real warmth and on the face of it indicates concern with humanity, I firmly believe that it would be more appealing and intelligible to the plain man. . . . You have always been in favor of bringing philosophy out of the confines of academic discussion and university circles so that it would mean something to the ordinary citizen. And I think you would have the best possible chance of succeeding in this aim with your own philosophy by calling it 'Humanism' or perhaps 'naturalistic Humanism.' . . . As a matter of fact, you are actively involved in the Humanist movement by being a member of the Advisory Board of Dr. Potter's[16] First Humanist Society" (26–27).

Dewey replied promptly, as was his habit:

> I don't see I have anything to add to what I wrote you the other day. I note that you prefer the word "Humanism" as a name for my philosophy. I do not, and have definite objection to it save as an adjective prefixed to Naturalism, and I suppose I must be the judge in the case of my own philosophy.
>
> Since it is a philosophy in question and since philosophers from the time of Aristotle—and before—have used the word "Nature" in a fundamental sense, I can't see the force of your objection about Naturalism having a philosophical sense. As to the Humanistic Society, as I told you before, I limit my acceptance of Humanism to religious matters where its meaning in opposition to supernaturalism is definite in significance. (27)

This correspondence firmly establishes that Dewey understood himself to be a philosophical naturalist, but a humanist only in a limited sense. He was willing to be associated with organized humanism in order to oppose the supernaturalists. He was not willing to call his philosophy a humanistic one. But the important point here is that in the 1930s and 1940s Dewey was willing to side with organized humanism in "religious matters where" this "acceptance of Humanism . . . in opposition to supernaturalism is definite in significance." There is no question that this is sectarian behavior. But what are we to make of this? Clearly, Dewey was no sectarian. His embrace of humanism was quite limited and specific; it was hardly the defining commitment of his life or of his philosophy. Indeed, his commitments pushed in the other direction, toward publicly informed change. Not only could one be engaged in the sort of public criticism and social change that Dewey advocated without doing so in a sectarian way; one's very involvement in public matters in a public way is a secularizing process. As it happened, Dewey was occasionally involved in sectarian behavior, but he was no sectarian.

THE LIMITATIONS—REAL AND ALLEGED—OF DEWEY'S INSTRUMENTALISM

A traditional complaint about Dewey's instrumentalism is its self-imposed secularity. By denying itself the authority of the past or transcendent truth, it allegedly confines itself to the present. A recent complainant is John Patrick Diggins in *The Promise of Pragmatism*, which truth in publishing should have required him to call "The Failed Promise of Pragmatism" or "The Limitations of Pragmatism."[17] One way in which the secularity of Dewey's project can be appreciated is by considering Diggins's charge of inadequacy, a concern of this section; in the final section of this chapter I will set forth in a more positive fashion the secular nature of Dewey's recommended method of social change.

"The Most Irritating Question of All"

Diggins begins *The Promise of Pragmatism* with a story about Dewey's failure to satisfactorily address a momentous public question. The occasion was December 7, 1941. Dewey was to speak to a crowd of hundreds in New York at the Cooper Union on the lessons from what would henceforth be known as the First World War. But Dewey, who was now eighty-two years old, declared to an audience anxious about the attack on Pearl Harbor: "I have nothing, had nothing, and have nothing now, to say directly about the [present] war." Continuing, he disclaimed a role for philosophy in interpreting current events: "Philosophy, intellectual operations, in general, are likely to come after events. This is a sort of *ex post facto* enterprise and very often by the time philosophy is formed, events have changed so much there isn't much for ideas to lay hold of" (1–2).

Diggins takes Dewey's inability to speak to the occasion as a failure of pragmatism to keep its central promise: "Pragmatism, America's one original contribution to the world of philosophy, had once promised to help people deliberately reflect about what to do when confronting 'problematic situations.'" But Dewey now knew or surely suspected, declares Diggins, that "Hegel was right to believe that philosophical knowledge could only be retrospective, and even then, like the Owl of Minerva taking flight at dusk, it arrives too late to be of use" (2).

Diggins does not immediately answer the question he then raises, "Does pragmatism itself work?" But later he raises again what he calls "the most irritating question of all," providing at one point a less-than-firm answer: "The irony lies in the awkward fact that pragmatism may be refuted not so much by logic as by its own criterion of verification: the experience of history may demonstrate that it fails to work in helping us understand history itself" (251). Later in the chapter, however, he declares himself firmly in the negative: "As early as 1908, Arthur O. Lovejoy had observed rather bemusedly a truth that sooner or later was bound to be found out: that pragmatism cannot provide useful knowledge at all. Unable to certify as truthful that which we need to know before we act, pragmatic philosophy cannot provide knowledge precisely when it is most valuable" (277).

This, as it happens, is not the first time Diggins passed a negative judgment on pragmatism. In the preceding chapter of his book, once again referring to Lovejoy, Diggins had observed: "It would be the ultimate irony to conclude that pragmatic knowledge is neither useful nor practical, but one cannot avoid Arthur O. Lovejoy's conclusion, spelled out in 'The Thirteen Pragmatisms' (1908) that Dewey's theories about the *ex post facto* criterion of truth are 'as irrelevant and redundant a thing as a coroner's inquest on a corpse is—to the corpse.'" (234). Diggins, then, is not at all reluctant to embrace the ironic conclusion that pragmatism does not work. It does not fulfil its promise to guide action by yielding useful knowledge. Dewey could not satisfy the needs of an anxious audience on December 7, 1941, because his philosophy was not what many took it to be. It was unpragmatic; it did not work.

But Diggins's treatment is flawed in several respects. He identifies pragmatism with Dewey's performance as a pale, tense old man uncertain in the midst of a confusing national crisis. Thus he fails to distinguish pragmatism as a method for cultivating intelligence from the practice of intelligence itself and from the performance of an individual on a particular occasion. It may be that Dewey at other times had something useful to say about intelligence even if he lacked the ability to exercise it on the evening of the attack on Pearl Harbor. About this I will have more to say later. But first I will attack a second flaw in Digginss' treatment, his use of Lovejoy and treatment of Dewey. This criticism of Diggins is intended to exemplify what Diggins suspects cannot be done, which is to engage in moral reflection without employing an absolute value or standard. I will criticize Diggins's treatment of Dewey within the limits of an experientially informed intelligence alone.

Diggins's Intellectual Performance

I quoted Diggins's embrace of what he says is "Lovejoy's conclusion" in "The Thirteen Pragmatisms" that "Dewey's theories about the *ex post facto* criterion of truth are 'as irrelevant and redundant a thing as a coroner's inquest on a corpse is—to the corpse'" (234). However, there are several problems with this assertion: One, Lovejoy made this statement in reference to William James, not Dewey. In fact, Dewey's name is never mentioned in the essay. Two, Lovejoy disclaimed any intent "to contribute to the determination of the truth or falsity" of any of the thirteen doctrines he disambiguated.[18] Whether he stuck to his actual resolve is, of course, another matter. But since Lovejoy declared that the claims of the thirteen pragmatisms he distinguished are logically independent of one another, he could have ruled on the truth-value of the *ex post facto* criterion and have left the other pragmatist doctrines untouched. Diggins's account, however, does not consider these possibilities. He simply takes Lovejoy's comment about one of the thirteen, one that Lovejoy discussed in connection with James, as a judgment about Dewey's pragmatic theory of knowledge. Finally, Lovejoy did criticize Dewey directly in 1920 in "Pragmatism *Versus* the Pragmatist," to which Dewey responded.[19] But Diggins discusses neither Lovejoy's actual criticism of Dewey nor Dewey's reply.[20]

One can find many instances in which Diggins mischaracterizes Dewey's views. Some appear relatively minor, such as the following assertion: "The concern of the philosopher, wrote Dewey in his seminal work, *Experience and Nature* (1925), 'is not with morals but with metaphysics, with, that is to say, the nature of the existential world in which we live'" (Diggins, 222). Dewey's actual concern was not as broad as Diggins indicates; Dewey was not referring to philosophy in general, but to a particular situation that he had discussed in the paragraph immediately preceding the one in which the above partial quotation occurred (see LW 1:45 and the preceding page).

More serious is the fact that Diggins systematically misconstrues what Dewey meant by science and the scientific method. For instance, Diggins declares that "Dewey refused to acknowledge any separation of social and natural science, assuming that the same methods of investigation could be applied to both realms" (239). Yet Dewey, in the chapter on social inquiry (in the 1938 *Logic*), while categorizing the social sciences as "branches of natural science," observed: "Social inquiry is, however, relatively so backward in comparison with physical and biological inquiry as to suggest need for special discussion" (LW 12:481). Dewey thought that there was a method common to both sciences, yet he was under no illusion that social science as it was then practiced was indistinguishable from natural science.

Again, Dewey dealt directly with the charge that he confused the two sciences in an essay he wrote in 1934. After suggesting that the method used successfully "in obtaining control over physical forces and conditions" should be tried "in social matters," he wrote: "This reference has . . . been misunderstood by critics. For it is not held that the particular techniques of the physical sciences are to be literally copied—though of course they are to be utilized wherever applicable—nor that experimentation in the laboratory sense can be carried out on any large scale in social affairs" ("Intelligence and Power," LW 9:108). Therefore, Diggins misses the point of one of

Dewey's central contentions. The experimental attitude that has proven successful in one area can be carried into another, provided one makes the
appropriate changes to deal with the different subject matter.

Similarly, Diggins reduces Dewey's understanding of "the environment" to "the natural world" (241), thus excluding society from the organism's environment. He then portrays Dewey as possessing an "ethical theory" that "involved an almost hedonistic focus on satisfaction and pleasure
and their pepetuation" (244–45). Again, he alleges: "Morality for Dewey
remained a fulfillment of the human organism, and hence judgments about
values are judgments about the conditions and consequences that 'should
regulate the formation of our desires, affections, and enjoyments'" (245).
By placing Dewey's words in the context of hedonism and biological needs,
Diggins flattens Dewey's ethics into a too-simple response to the needs of
the "human organism." Diggins ignores Dewey's own criticisms of hedonism
in the 1932 *Ethics* (LW 7:191–99 and 240–45) and his persistent concern
with culture. Although Dewey was impressed with the significance of "the
objective biological approach of the Jamesian psychology," he reported that
it "led straight to the perception of the importance of distinctive social categories, especially communication and participation" ("From Absolutism to
Experiementalism," LW 5:159).

Also distorting is Diggins's account of Dewey as having second
thoughts about or even recanting his lifelong championing of science:
"Dewey continued to believe that pragmatism could overcome all such
dualisms [matter and spirit, power and morality] and that knowledge
would be sufficient to a given 'problematic situation.' Yet in 1949, three
years before his death, he came upon [Max] Weber's writings and
acknowledged that 'one of the most distinguished sociologists of the last
century' has made us aware that modern science cannot answer to the
basic human need for 'meaning.' Quite an admission for a proponent of
pragmatism, a philosophy that once held that any idea having no potential
experimental meaning is itself meaningless" (40).

Quite an admission indeed! But when one checks the reference, as one
must with Diggins, one finds that there is no such admission in Dewey's
article, "Philosophy's Future in Our Scientific Age: Never Was Its Role More
Crucial," originally published in *Commentary*. First, Diggins omits the subtitle in his footnote, thus failing to provide one check on his interpretation.
Second, Dewey's discussion of Weber was intended to set up the problem
with which he intended to deal in his article. Dewey was reporting an intellectual development: "The passage stands as an expression of the transformation of the earlier optimism about science into fear and pessimism; and
of late the mere disillusionment with science has passed into bitter hostility

toward it" (LW 16:373). He then acknowledged that science's actual consequences have been "thoroughly ambiguous and double-faced," but that the
deeper question, "the one question worth asking is evaded: how does this
doubleness, this ambivalence, in human consequences come about, and
what, if anything, can be done about it?" (373–74). Not surprisingly,
Dewey recommended no abandonment of the scientific enterprise or what
we can learn from its methods. Instead, he continued to recommend what
he had long proposed, writing: "What has been accomplished in the develo-
ment of *methods* of inquiry in physiological and physical science now cries
out for extension into humane and moral subjects" (376).

Flatly wrong is Diggins's statement that Dewey "regarded ends as
given" (*Promise*, 242). Dewey thought ends have their origins in what
occurs in experience, but they are in no sense simply taken as ends to be
realized. Rather, they are to be formulated as ends-in-view and tested both
in imagination and in experience. One needs only to reflect for a moment on
Dewey's continual insistence on the means-ends continuum to realize that
ends can not be exempted from criticism. But one does not have to engage
in even this bit of reflection to recognize the flat-footedness of Diggins's
claim. After declaring that Dewey took ends as givens, Diggins cites Louis
Hartz's suggestion that "the reason pragmatism became so peculiarly an
American proposition is that America's Lockean political culture, resting on
the consensus of liberty, property, and opportunity, never called into question its ends" (242). Yet Dewey continually submitted to examination precisely these values, particularly in *Individualism, Old and New* (1930, LW
5) and *Liberalism and Social Action* (1935, LW 11).

Diggins's mistake is that he regularly cites evidence that supports his
critique of Dewey and ignores the counter-evidence that can readily be
found both in Dewey's own writing and in many secondary discussions. We
have already seen that Diggins ignores the actual interchange between
Dewey and Lovejoy in favor of one invented by Diggins. Moreover, he does
not use J. E. Tiles's account, an account contained in one of the major contemporary series on significant philosophers, *The Arguments of
Philosophers*. Nor, on the question of Dewey's theory of the truth of past
events, does Diggins refer to Hook's classic exposition of Dewey's thought,[21]
in which Hook defended Dewey's theory (83–86). Nor does he refer to the
discussion by Gail Kennedy in "Dewey's Logic and Theory of Knowledge"
in a standard reference book of Deweyan scholarship.[22]

Diggins and the Appropriate Critical Standard

Diggins begins one paragraph with this sentence: "One wonders about
an ethical theory that contains no hierarchy of values and has as its goal

'our' needs and desires," and ends it with the assertion that no "pragmatist has successfully demonstrated how the exercise of scientific intelligence can by itself command obligation" (245). These statements misconstrue Dewey's project. Dewey did not claim that "scientific intelligence can by itself command obligation." Such an expression reflects the model of authority that Dewey rejected. Dewey was careful to talk about using intelligence to modify our actions in ways that are more satisfying, and he took satisfaction in a wide enough sense to include a broad range of human needs and desires. Moreover, what Dewey rejected was a fixed hierarchy of values, not the presence of values embodied in our practices, some of which are more inclusive than others. He thought that it is when some practice no longer meets some need that one institutes an inquiry into the end required to meet that need and the means necessary to bring about the end-in-view. In so doing, one makes use of previously instituted values that continue to be useful to resolve the immediate difficulty.

These values, however, are not extrinsic. They are developed within experience. Take, for example, my criticism of Diggins's intellectual performance. A reader can reasonably expect an author, particularly the Distinguished Professor of History at the City University of New York, as Diggins is identified on the title page of his book, to accurately report what the person he is writing about says. This expectation is a cultural one, widely shared and appropriate for the reading of Diggins's book. Diggins employs the apparatus of quotation and footnotes as well as paraphrase, leading his readers to expect that he is using these author-reader conventions to fairly convey Dewey's thinking. Moreover, Diggins leads his readers to believe that he has thoroughly researched his subject matter. He cites not only Dewey's published works, but also much secondary literature and even collections of unpublished papers. Diggins presents himself as a distinguished intellectual historian who has gone to the trouble to ferret out information that is not easily accessible, someone his readers can trust to deal competently and knowledgeably with the materials being discussed. In other words, one does not need a transcendent set of values to judge Diggins adversely. One needs only the resources available within the contextualized situation of a distinguished intellectual historian and his readers.

Diggins, however, thinks that one needs something more. It is not sufficient to evaluate something within the confines of experience alone. He writes: "To locate the source of value in experience alone is a proposition riddled with difficulties, and no one has done more to illuminate the ironic consequences of these difficulties than the literary critic Kenneth Burke" (246). Burke, in the passage cited by Diggins, charges Dewey with an infinite regress. Each value is justified by some other value, "which must be founded upon another value, and so on." But there is no stopping point, "no key value, in the sense of its antecedent existence, its acceptance of authority." Dewey, Burke alleged, tried to meet this problem by making "intelligence" the functional equivalent of a "key value," a role for which it is ill suited, since (in Diggins's words) "to elevate intelligence to the status of authority is a circular exercise that relativizes the very concept of authority by endowing it with the power of self-legitimation" (247).

But Burke's criticism misconstrues what Dewey was doing. One, Dewey did not claim for intelligence (or employ it in) the role of key value. And two, he disclaimed the need for a key value in the sense of an absolute, central value. Dewey did think that intelligence is very valuable, as is democracy in the sense (specified in the fourth chapter of this book) of "ordered richness." He did bring certain rather large values or ideals to specific situations, but he did not claim for them the permanency or foundational character that Burke thinks is needed. The burden is on those such as Burke or Diggins to show that one needs such a key value to engage in criticism, as the burden is on Dewey and me to show that one does not need a key value.

I have done that. I have criticized Diggins for failing to live up to the requirements of the practice in which he is engaged, a practice that mandates that an intellectual historian carefully cite the words and thoughts of the person he is considering, discussing them in an informed way. Moreover, an intellectual historian who takes as his subject matter not just a text or an idea, but a text or idea within a philosophical movement, must consider the relevant discussions of this text or idea. Given a movement as prominent as pragmatism and a vast secondary literature, applying this standard is a judgment call. But I have shown that Diggins systematically selects adverse criticisms of Dewey and ignores favorable treatments. He fails, in short, to live up to the standards implicit in the practice in which he is engaged.

One does not need a timeless notion of truth to make such a criticism. All one needs is the practice in which Diggins is engaged. This practice, of course, can be called into question. But Diggins does not do that. What he does challenge is the "contextualist" history of ideas that situates texts in their historical settings. He finds this unduly restrictive, for he wants to place historical figures in conversation with one another, notably Dewey and Henry Adams. But this does not excuse him from treating those he juxtaposes fairly and fully; it simply permits him, once he has established what they did say, to, as he says, position them so that they "interrogate" one another. Although the questions may be anachronistic, the answers must still be consonant with the answers they actually gave. Diggins is not claiming to invent answers; indeed he has all the apparatus—quotation, citation, paraphrase—of a historian who tries to present what was actually said. He claims to do "history of ideas"; it is just that his form of intellectual history is not to be restricted by origin and the limitations of what actually occurred. "Ideas," Diggins thinks, "may be appreciated for their validity as well as their geneology, and when evaluating ideas for the problems they illuminate, we can use one author to interrogate another so that ideas speak to our condition as well as theirs" (7). As a philosopher I have no problem with this. Perhaps Robert Westbrook is correct in thinking that *"The Promise of Pragmatism* is a work less of history than of philosophical and social criticism."[23] Even so, Diggins is not excused from faithful exposition and careful reference. Philosophers, social critics, and historians are all bound by similar canons in this regard.[24]

Regardless of the genre confusion and the sloppiness with which Diggins goes about his business, consider what he is doing on his own terms. Notice the basis upon which Diggins criticizes pragmatism. By charging pragmatism with ineffectiveness in that Dewey was unable to successfully deal with the problems posed by the two world wars, Diggins is evaluating pragmatism not by some transcendent standard or key value, but by a value Diggins thinks is internal to pragmatism itself, the effectiveness of thinking in controlling human affairs. He thinks pragmatism fails on its own nontranscendental, experiential terms. I think Diggins has misconstrued Dewey's project, and I will show why below. For now I will call attention to Diggins's own inconsistency. To the extent his criticism of pragmatism on its own terms is successful he has shown the possibility and effectiveness of pragmatic criticism, for he has accepted to some extent pragmatic standards. One does not need something outside of experience to evaluate pragmatism. If Diggins were able to show that Deweyan pragmatism failed to deal adequately with the problems of war and peace in the first part of this century, as shown by experience, then Diggins would be able to demonstrate the relevance and usefulness of just such experience-bound criticism. Admittedly, Diggins makes reference to transcendent values and perennial, perhaps unsolvable problems. But the values he actually uses are those present in our cultural practices. And the one he singles out, the one that permits him to ask "the most irritating question of all," is the pragmatic one of effectiveness.

Giving Diggins His Due

For all of Diggins's clumsy criticism, he does provide us with an opportunity to pay attention to his picture of an inept Dewey on the evening of the attack on Pearl Harbor, thus enabling us to recognize the limits of Dewey's cultural instrumentalism. Dewey did not have useful advice for an audience anxious to know how to respond to the attack of a few hours before and America's involvement in the war. He had not been asked to speak to this, nor was he prepared to do so. Indeed, given the time differences between Hawaii and New York, there was very little notice of the event prior to Dewey's speech. He chose to stick to the message of his prepared remarks, cautioning his audience not to expect too much of philosophy.

Diggins, however, presents Dewey as being unable to speak to the breaking news event as a philosopher, writing: "Of the present war Dewey could only say in his improvised remarks that philosophy can neither discern the direction of events as they develop nor judge their meaning afterward" (1–2). He then cites the statement I quoted earlier: "Philosophy, intellectual operations, in general, are likely to come after events. This is a sort of *ex post facto* enterprise and very often by the time philosophy is formed, events have changed so much there isn't much for ideas to lay hold of" (Diggins, 2; LW 14:326).

Diggins cites not only the transcript of Dewey's remarks, but also Charles F. Howlett.[25] Once again one needs to follow up Diggins's references. A check of the body of the transcript finds Dewey declaring himself firmly on the side of controlled, liberating change: "You might say the lesson of the present war is that we've either got to go backward, in a more systematic and unified way, to old principles and standards, or we have got to face the things in modern life that are genuinely modern, and do what we can to liberate them from the burden of old and incompatible institutions that are weighing them down, that are holding them back, that are creating uncertainty, confusion, and conflict" (LW 14:328). Similarly, Howlett reports that Dewey's "voice became louder" as he concluded his address. Howlett then quotes the last sentence of the address, a sentence that in characteristic Deweyan fashion recommended a unified, internally driven approach rather than a divided one or one harmonized by "some outside power" (LW 14:334), noting, "The impact of the words was clean and hard" (*Troubled Philosopher*, 4).

Finally, a review of the complete text of the opening paragraph of the improvised remarks finds Dewey cautioning against an exaggerated role for philosophy or for intellectuals generally, but he does not deny either a role: "Speaking, however, moderately, I think history shows that philosophy has done something in connection with more important social interest movements." What it has done is "to make human beings more aware of what they are doing, and what they're trying to do, what they're trying to undo"

(LW 14:326). Philosophy, then, provides a contextual understanding that enables us to function intelligently. It does not solve all our problems, but it does help. It has a limited but significant role to play.

Dewey's philosophy is not in and of itself a way of life; nor does it enable one to make the correct decision in a difficult situation. Diggins has misrepresented what pragmatism is, portraying it as having failed as an all-encompassing response to the difficulties of modernity. But his portrait is not the one we recognize when we turn to the subject itself. Dewey's instrumentalism is neither complete nor fully satisfying; it is a limited response, limited by the bounds of secularity that it accepts. There are questions that it does not attempt to answer, for it knows its own limits within space and time. But there are also questions that it can answer. These mainly have to do with the way in which we relate to the beliefs, policies, and institutions that shape our lives. The answers, however, are often neither detailed nor direct. They frequently have rather to do with how we go about the activity of "thoughtful valuation" (LW 1:326). In asking for clear, definite, immediate knowledge of what to do, Diggins is bound to be disappointed by Dewey's deliberate response. Disappointed with Dewey's failure to electrify the Cooper Union audience with a pertinent, on-the-spot, historically situated analysis of the breaking news event, Diggins concludes that Dewey had little or nothing worthwhile to say, having, like Henry Adams, "sensed that the rush of events often left the mind grasping for explanations" (2).

Such a judgment, however, ignores Dewey's actual remarks, for Diggins is in no position to hear Dewey's nuanced, deliberate comments on modernism and authority. Dewey's actual remarks did not meet Diggins's expectations, and so he fails to pay attention to what Dewey said about philosophy, modernity, knowledge, and authority on December 7, 1941. In looking and listening for something that Dewey did not say, Diggins missed what Dewey did say regarding the subject matter of Diggins's book, as indicated by the subtitle, *Modernism and the Crisis of Knowledge and Authority*. Such is Diggins's due.

"THOUGHTFUL VALUATION" AND THE CULTURAL ORIENTATION OF DEWEY'S INSTRUMENTALISM

"Lessons from the War—in Philosophy," Dewey's December 7, 1941, speech, was part of a series of addresses. The war referred to in the title was World War I. Dewey's actual reference points were the various conflicts that had long concerned him—the dualism of the spiritual and the material inherited from the premodern era, the conflict between absolutism and experimental-experiential methods, and the split between emotion and ideas (LW 14:317). In discussing these conflicts he made reference to the war in which much of the world was then engaged, as well as ancient Greece and the development of modern science. In other words, it was a characteristic Deweyan performance, one that dealt with the problems and concepts that he had long thought troubling. What I want to call attention to now is the necessarily secular orientation of his address.

The Cultural Turn

Dewey's secularity or naturalism is obvious with regard to the first two conflicts he discussed. He rejected the dualism of both the spiritual-material split and the division between absolutism and the appeal to experience. In both cases he took as reality "the world of experience," a world to which we have access through our interactions with it. This access has been most successfully exemplified in the methods of modern science. In fact, Dewey had trouble keeping the discussions of the first two points distinct from one another, as he noted when he turned from the first to the second: "What has been said is so intimately connected with the second illustration of my main proposition that I can deal with the latter rather briefly." He then proceeded to talk about "what may be learned from experience" (LW 14:320–21), where experience is more than consciousness—it is a social and physical interaction with the world.

The third conflict had to do with a split in human nature, but this division also reflected an unnaturalistic or unsecular understanding. Dewey thought those who would separate human beings into two parts, reason and emotion, tend to identify reason with the higher or the spiritual reality and emotion or desires with the lower or material reality. Awareness of this split and its significance, he thought, was the lesson to be learned from the war (323–24). We have an immense problem in relating what are taken to be the two parts of human nature. Philosophers and scientists have too often distanced themselves from "important social issues" in order to "acquire a safe and peaceful place to work" (324). This has reinforced the split between reason and daily living. By continuing to understand human nature in this bifurcated way, Dewey's contemporaries continued to evade the issue. The solution, of course, from Dewey's point of view, was to regard human beings as a mix of emotion and thought who are situated in a physical and social world, making no appeal to a reality external to this world. Rather than understanding our situation as one in which we have to bring together thought and emotion, Dewey recommended that we intelligize our actions. This is the "other means" that he had in mind when he suggested that "we ask whether human behavior is capable of being directed by other means than either superior force, external authority, uncriticized customs, or sheer emotional outbursts not controlled by authenticated ideas" (325).

Diggins takes Dewey's perplexed state on the evening of December 7, 1941, to indicate second thoughts about his pragmatism. But when one looks at the reports upon which Diggins relies, Howlett's account and Dewey's prepared and actual remarks, one finds that what dismayed Dewey was not his own analysis or proposals, but the continuing confusions and divisions of the culture. Dewey was, according to Howlett—who relied, in part, on a letter from Roberta, Dewey's second wife—dismayed that the world had not learned from its experience in World War I. He was having difficulty "comprehend[ing] that it was happening all over again" (3–4). In his address Dewey was plainly chagrined that the conflicts—intellectual and social—that he had sought to overcome were still present. But Dewey's solution was not one that acquiesced to the status quo, turned away in despair, or appealed to some higher reality. Rather, Dewey attempted to find within the culture what was needed to transform it.

What Dewey turned to then and on other occasions was intelligence and democracy. He did not propose an alternative to these cultural practices. To be sure, his understanding of these practices was pragmatically informed and he thought there were ways each could be improved, but his effort was to direct attention back into the yet-to-be-fully-realized practices of his society. He made no appeal to a distinctly Deweyan way of life. His repeated move was to what was public and common. He turned questions that have wide consequences away from the unreachably private (or even the idiosyncratic) and the otherworldly to what was shared, open to deliberation, and susceptible to public control. He did not support any withdrawal into spheres outside of common experience. The characteristically Deweyan approach was to urge greater reliance on intelligence and democracy.

Dewey made the cultural turn. He had come to realize the boundedness of groups within systems of shared meanings that have developed over time. But Dewey, unlike either naive cultural relativists or their transcendent-value critics, did not think this cultural limitation was unduly restrictive. He thought that cultures, particularly those that encourage diversity and deliberation, are rich in meaning and possibility, permitting their members to create even richer lives.

Louis Menand captures this Deweyan sense of the possibilities within our modern age in the closing paragraph of his review of Westbrook's book on Dewey: "Unlike almost every other writer of his time, Dewey did not regard modern life as a deprivation, a sort of cultural wound which the absence of traditional kinds of religious and civic faith made it impossible to heal. He was perfectly, almost serenely, at home in a world without certainty—much more so than his hero William James, who always seems to be fighting his way toward an accommodation with his own principles. Dewey saw that life in that world was morally deep and suffused with meaning; and in his books, as in almost no other writing of the time, we can watch the twentieth century come to recognizable life on its own terms, without being defined by comparison to ways of life it is supposed to have supplanted."[26]

Note that Menand does not say that Dewey "was perfectly, almost serenely, at home" in his own world; he is careful to say that Dewey was "at home in a world without certainty." This is correct. Dewey may not have entirely come to terms with a world that found itself embroiled in a second world war, but he did not wish for more than the world of precariousness and stability that he had described in the second chapter of *Experience and Nature*. He did not have a metaphysical complaint; his difficulty was with some of the historical developments that had occurred. Nevertheless, Menand is correct; Dewey did not regard "modern life as a deprivation," for even modern life with all of its disenchantments was, as Menand says, "suffused with meaning" and possiblity. Menand's next-to-last sentence reads: "Stylistically, I suppose, Dewey was one of the least novelistic of writers; but he had a novelist's grasp of experience." Dewey, despite his own inablility to express himself dramatically, had an imaginative "grasp of experience" and its possibilities.

"The Most Far-Reaching Question of All Criticism"

Well into the last chapter of *Experience and Nature*, "Existence, Value and Criticism," Dewey wrote: "By an indirect path we are brought to a consideration of the most far-reaching question of all criticism: the relationship between existence and value, or as the problem is often put, between the real and ideal" (LW 1:310). This relationship for Dewey was no mystery. He thought that one finds and develops value in existence through criticism or intelligence. We have or participate in various beliefs, policies, practices, or institutions. Sometimes we want to improve them. In contrast with those who say we must have a value or standard outside of the present situation in order to make some belief or practice better, Dewey insisted that we can imagine ways that are comparatively better on the basis of our experiences with or within these beliefs and practices. Then we can try out the proposed improvement, testing to see if it is in fact better. The standard is our satisfaction. We are pleased with those outcomes that meet our felt needs.

Such an answer exasperated Dewey's critics, for they regarded it as baldly hedonistic or subjectivistic. Dewey would then explain that he was not talking about the satisfaction of just any sort of need or desire, but of perceived needs that have been subjected to scrutiny. By tracing out the connections between needs and satisfactions, exploring not only the immediately satisfying but also the contextual considerations including long-term effects and the conditions necessary for the simple need-satisfaction, Dewey thought one could escape an undesirable hedonism or subjectivism.

The point of much of what Dewey did was to urge upon us the criticism of our previously uncriticized (or undercriticized) beliefs, practices, and standards. Rather than leaving things as they are or simply increasing their quantity, Dewey proposed that we transform them through criticism.[27] They are to become qualitatively better, where "better" involves a comparison between two possible ideas or courses of action. The course that, upon reflection, appears to be more satisfying of our various *considered* needs is to be preferred.

Hence the need for both intelligence and democracy. Intelligence is the consideration through criticism of alternatives. Dewey observed that "intelligence is critical method applied to goods of belief, appreciation and conduct, so as to construct freer and more secure goods, turning assent and assertion into free communication of shareable meanings" (LW 1:325). One reflects upon some practice, one that came about either by chance and was found satisfying or that is some embodied intelligence, the continuing result of previous thoughtful valuations, attempting to evaluate this practice in the light of new choices, new possibilities. Intelligence as criticism is the transformation of what is in terms of what might be preferable. Democracy in the wide sense is the public transformation of experience, the constructing of "freer and more secure goods" by means of the "free communication of shareable meanings." This deliberative, communicative, constructive process, when considered from a social psychological (or less well-defined) perspective is intelligence, but when considered from a political perspective is democracy.

Once again we see Dewey's cultural or secular orientation. He began with what is, understanding it to be the product of past constructions of physical, social, and imaginative materials. These constructions or forms can be reconstructed or transformed. The relation of existence and value is no extraordinary problem, although it may at times be a vexing one, because one is reshaping the shapes one now has in one's possession in terms of projections arising in the situation. This remaking process is enhanced by social richness, for one has not only the benefit of others' critiques, but also of their insights, insights and critiques whose values come, in part, from being qualitatively different from one's own limited experience and projections.

This is an open-ended process, but it is not without its checks. The recalcitrance of present beliefs and practices, the obduracy of the perspectives of others, and the testing of one's projections in experience all serve to limit the play of what at first glance may seem too open. Existence has a plasticity, but it is not completely amenable to the creative impulse. The limits may be physical, social, or situational, but there are limits. Despite these limits Dewey was impressed with the possiblities for growth. He thought we can stretch almost any given situation in ways that are freer and fuller—that is, in ways that not only will satisfy the present desire (or remake it), but also will lead to other future satisfactions.

Dewey was well aware that a critical, creative intelligence-democracy had its limits, but he was convinced that a "thoughtful valuation" is preferable to alternative methods, for it is the one method that can in a controlled or scientific way rework the present situation into something more desirable. It solves the problem of existence and value by showing how values developed within existence-experience can be transformed as needed. He closed *Experience and Nature* with the acknowledgement that "intelligence will [n]ever dominate the course of events," nor will it "save from ruin and destruction." Intelligence is not omnicompetent. But the reality is that we are continually faced with choices. "Some procedure has to be tried." That "intelligence" or "thoughtful valuation" is "a better method" than the other options, "authority, imitation, caprice and ignorance, prejudice and passion, is hardly an excessive claim," for "these procedures have been tried." And "the result," Dewey thinks, "is not such as to make it clear that the method of intelligence, the use of science in criticizing and re-creating the casual goods of nature into intentional and conclusive goods of art, the union of knowledge and values in production, is not worth trying" (LW 1:325–26).

This is hardly a dramatic close to Dewey's chapter on existence, value, and criticism and what many consider to be one of his more comprehensive statements of his philosophy. Dewey, "the master of the commonplace" as C. E. Ayres called him,[28] rather prosaically weighed the alternative procedures to the transformative criticism he had been advocating and concluded, given the competition, that intelligence is worth a try. But we should not expect too much. Once again, Dewey sensed the limits. There was no hard sell. Rather, there was a quiet, persistent, thoughtful urging of his preferred alternative. We know from this chapter and elsewhere why he preferred it, and he appealed to us on that basis to try it. But he did not say that it will do what some of the other procedures have promised (and failed) to do.

What Dewey believed to be thoughtful valuation or transformative criticism will allow us over time to remake those situations that trouble us not only in ways that are more satisfying, but also in ways that are instrumentally clear. We will know what cultural resources we employed and so be able to extend our instituted goods in novel situations. This practice will be neither neat nor foolproof, but it will work often enough to our advantage, Dewey thought, for us to prefer it to the other choices our culture provides.

Thus Deweyan criticism turns out to be cultural criticism, a tool Dewey did not invent, but one he improved and put to wide use. He was not only a master of the commonplace; he was also a master craftsman of those techniques of transformation of the common life that involved the deliberative, critical processes essential to the growth of the common life. He both engaged in these critical activities as a teacher and citizen and, as a public philosopher, explained the connections between these activities and the generic features of the world.

Life is a multiplicity of transactions. Some of these interactions are satisfying; some are not. But we do not have to just take what comes. We can use some activities to bring about others, ones that are satisfying. This employment of indirect action is intelligence. It adds "a new quality and dimension" to "the scene of natural interaction" (LW 4:171). Intelligence is a refinement of what naturally occurs, a making and remaking of the activities of our lives. As social individuals we employ indirect action in culturally informed ways. Although occasionally inventive, we usually make use of previously worked out procedures. Even when these are of an individual's devising, they employ cultural products. The more intelligent person is the one who "observe[s] what is going on more widely and more minutely," "select[ing] more carefully from what is noted just those factors which point to something to happen" (MW 9:153) in order to bring about what he or she wants.

Dewey's cultural instrumentalism is not dramatic, but in the context of the history of philosophy and our culture it is radical in import. Dewey did not proceed in a radical way, but the significance of his thinking was disturbing to tradition and convention. Working with the means-ends continuum, taking situations as he found them, and modifying these situations in more satisfying ways were not in themselves radical activities. Nor was his celebration of knowledge, work, rest, friendship, and other common human enterprises unusual, if taken separately. But putting these mundane activities together *and* arguing that they are sufficient for a good life constituted a disturbing challenge to traditional and conventional ways of life.

Proposing the use of criticism as "thoughtful valuation" does not seem like much of a proposal. But when one realizes that it is being put forward as a replacement for ways of life that rely primarily (or too much) on authority, coercion, caprice, ignorance, prejudice, and passion, one can grasp what a bold idea it was and is. Dewey, "the master of the common-place," recommended a series of often small, not always very noticeable, changes that over time could amount to a dramatic transformation of experience, a transformation that would make humans responsible for their choices and would locate these choices within a cultural and secular frame. Criticism was the instrument of his humanistic naturalism. But it was not just a means for Dewey; it was also an end—a way of associated living that would allow us to constantly revise the present in terms of projected better possibilties and ensuing results as simultaneously critical, intelligent, demo-cratic, humanistic, and secular.

NOTES
BIBLIOGRAPHY
INDEX

NOTES

CHAPTER 1, INTRODUCTION: DEWEY'S LIFELONG EFFORT

1. References to Dewey's works are to the critical edition edited by Jo Ann Boydston and published by Southern Illinois University Press at Carbondale. There are thirty-seven volumes in three series—*The Early Works*, *The Middle Works*, and *The Later Works*. Therefore, the citation MW 10:42 is to volume 10, page 42, of *The Middle Works*.

2. Albany: State University of New York Press, 1987, p. 22.

3. The best book on Dewey's instrumentalism and thus, in effect, his philosophy as a whole is Larry A. Hickman's *John Dewey's Pragmatic Technology* (Bloomington: Indiana University Press, 1990). By considering Dewey's work in the context of discussions on technology, Hickman displays the technical character of Dewey's philosophy. Relevant here is Hickman's observation: "Unlike most philosophers of technology, Dewey held the view that technological instruments included immaterial objects such as ideas, theories, numbers, and the objects of logic (such as logical connectives). His instrumentalist account of inquiry rejected both realism and idealism on the grounds that neither position was capable of developing an adequate understanding of the function played in knowing by tools and media of all sorts" (xii–xiii). But Hickman's placing of Dewey's instrumentalism in the context of the philosophy of technology draws the attention of all but the most determined readers to a consideration of Dewey in relation to contemporary discussions of technology. Hickman's chosen frame appears to limit the scope of his interpretation of Dewey's philosophy. My aim is to change the frame to something less definite. I intend to merge Dewey's instrumentalism into the larger Deweyan frame of culture and secularity.

4. See Joseph Ratner, "Dewey's Conception of Philosophy," in *The Philosophy of John Dewey*, ed. Paul Arthur Schilpp, vol. 1 of *The Library of Living Philosophers* (Evanston: Northwestern University, 1939), pp. 49–73, and Dewey's endorsement, "Experience, Knowledge and Value: A Rejoinder," p. 520 (LW 14:6).

5. *Culture* for Dewey, as he noted late in life, was understood by him "in its anthropological (not its Matthew Arnold) sense," designating "the vast range of things experienced in an indefinite variety of ways" (LW 1:363).

6. Robert B. Westbrook, *John Dewey and American Democracy* (Ithaca, N.Y.: Cornell University Press, 1991), p. 193. Westbrook's intellectual biography of Dewey places Dewey's social and political philosophy and activities in the foreground. In addition to its excellent treatment of Dewey's life and work, it is a rich bibliographic source. Our differences can be found lbelow and in my article "Dewey's Faith in Democracy as Shared Experience," *Transactions of the Charles S. Peirce Society* 32 (Winter 1996):11–30, and Westbrook's reply, "Democratic Faith: A Response to Michael Eldridge," *Transactions* 32:31–40, in the same issue.

7. The *first* volume of *The Library of Living Philosophers*, edited by Paul Arthur Schilpp.

8. Anne Sharpe, "Textual Commentary," LW 14:463.

9. Edited by Sidney Ratner (New York: G. P. Putnam's Sons, 1940), p. 10. Dewey's well-known address, "Creative Democracy—The Task Before Us," is in volume 14 of the *Later Works*, pp. 224–30.

10. See John Herman Randall, Jr., "The Department of Philosophy," in Randall's *A History of the Faculty of Philosophy* (New York: Columbia University Press, 1957), pp. 123–24, for a brief but useful characterization of Montague. Of interest here is Randall's comment: "Though he [Montague] found Dewey's progressivism and liberalism congenial, and learned much from him in social ethics, the intellectual gulf between the two was deep" (p. 124).

11. Charles Moritz, ed., *Current Biography Yearbook, 1966* (New York: The H. W. Wilson Company, 1967), pp. 105–106.

12. Charles Frankel, "John Dewey's Social Philosophy," in *New Studies in the Philosophy of John Dewey*, ed. Steven M. Cahn (Hanover, N.H.: Published for the University of Vermont by the University Press of New England, 1977), pp. 4–5.

13. Alan Ryan says the "basic tenet" of Dewey's "instrumentalism" or "experimentalism" is that "thought was not so much a means to action as an aspect of it" ("The Legacy of John Dewey," *Dissent* [Spring 1992]:274). Thinking is an aspect of action, but in controlling or directing action it functions as a means.

14. This is Dewey's phrase. See MW 14:152; LW 4:29 and 34, 11:45, and 14:75–79 and 89.

15. Supporting Alexander's approach is *The New Scholarship on Dewey*, ed. Jim Garrison (Dordrecht, The Netherlands: Kluwer Academic Publishers, 1995). This is a collection of articles reprinted from *Studies in Philosophy and Education* 13 (1994–95), to which Alexander contributed an essay. Garrison writes, "One theme of the new scholarship especially well represented in this volume is the tendency to place Dewey's aesthetics at the center of his thinking instead of his theory of inquiry, theory of democractic social relations, or even his philosophy of education" (p. 1).

16. In chronological order of publication, here are the books mentioned in this paragraph that have not already been cited in this introduction: James Gouinlock, *John Dewey's Philosophy of Value* (New York: Humanities Press, 1972); R. W. Sleeper, *The Necessity of Pragmatism: John Dewey's Conception of Philosophy* (New Haven: Yale University Press, 1986); Raymond D. Boisvert, *Dewey's Metaphysics* (New York: Fordham University Press, 1988); J. E. Tiles, *Dewey* (London: Routledge, 1988); Steven C. Rockefeller, *John Dewey: Religious Faith and Democratic Humanism* (New York: Columbia University Press, 1991); Tom Burke, *Dewey's New Logic* (Chicago: University of Chicago Press, 1994); James Campbell, *Understanding John Dewey: Nature and Cooperative Intelligence* (Chicago: Open Court Publishing Company, 1995); Alan Ryan, *John Dewey and the High Tide of American Liberalism* (New York: W. W. Norton and Co., 1995); and Jennifer Welchman, *Dewey's Ethical Thought* (Ithaca: Cornell University Press, 1995).

17. Deweyans disagree about the value of such a concise systematic presentation. In *Dialogue on John Dewey*, ed. Corliss Lamont (New York: Horizon Press, 1959), Lamont lamented the loss of a manuscript that had been left in a briefcase in a taxi, a manuscript that Dewey had "three-quarters" completed that would have "pulled his whole work or system—if he had a system—together." According to Lamont, Horace Kallen objected that the loss was no "tragedy," for in such a book Dewey would have had to "contradict himself." Dewey's functional approach resisted systemization (pp. 50–51). Late in life Dewey acknowledged that he had "a system" in the sense that "various problems and various hypotheses" hung together "in a perspective determined by a point of view." Thus he had to "retract disparaging remarks" he had "made in the past about the need for a system in philosophy" (LW 14:141–42).

CHAPTER 2, INTELLIGENT PRACTICE: DEWEY'S PROJECT

1. So much so as to cause many to question whether Rorty should be considered a Deweyan or a pragmatist. For sympathetic yet critical attempts to assess Rorty's pragmatist credentials, see David L. Hall, *Richard Rorty: Prophet and Poet of the New Pragmatism* (Albany: State University of New York Press, 1994) and Richard Bernstein, "American Pragmatism: The Conflict of Narratives," in *Rorty and Pragmatism*, ed. Herman Saatkamp (Nashville: Vanderbilt University Press, 1995), pp. 54–67. Three unsympathetic critiques (by Thelma Levine, James Gouinlock, and Susan Haack) are conveniently included in Saatkamp's anthology, along with Rorty's replies. Gouinlock cites several other critiques (p. 215, n. 2).

One of the more thoughtful and well-informed treatments of Rorty's interpretation of Dewey, one that correctly points out the danger for social intelligence in confusing Rorty's interpretation of Dewey with what Dewey himself thought, is that of Larry A. Hickman, "Liberal Irony and Social Reform," in

Philosophy and the Reconstruction of Culture: Pragmatic Essays after Dewey, ed. John J. Stuhr (Albany: State University of New York Press, 1993), 223–39. Hickman carefully distinguishes Dewey's understanding of philosophy's roles and the roles of art and science from Rorty's confusions. Particularly helpful are Hickman's contemporary examples of the "roles of the sciences and the arts in social reform" (p. 231) and the "important social function" of philosophy as a criticism of these other criticisms (p. 232).

2. Two recent fine summaries of Dewey's work that are worth consulting are Alan Ryan's "Overview" in *John Dewey and the High Tide of American Liberalism*, pp. 19–34, and James Campbell's *Understanding John Dewey*, "Part One: Dewey's General Philosophical Perspective," pp. 25–96.

3. *Dewey and American Democracy*, p. 539. For a contextual treatment of the renewed interest in Dewey, one that treats other contemporary philosophers as well as Rorty, see Alan Ryan, "His Reputation Revived," *Dewey and the High Tide of American Liberalism*, pp. 352–57.

4. Westbrook, in a review of James Campbell's "The Community Reconstructs: The Meaning of Pragmatic Social Thought" in *The Proceedings of the Charles S. Peirce Society* 29 (Spring 1993):259, writes, "Paleo-pragmatists might be said to be those who did not need Richard Rorty to tell them that John Dewey was one of the most important philosophers of the twentieth century and who, in turn, are uncomfortable with just about everything else Rorty had had to say about Dewey." Dewey is often a hero for Rorty, but, notably in "Dewey's Metaphysics," in *The Consequences of Pragmatism* (Minneapolis: University of Minnesota Press, 1982), he argues that Dewey, in attempting an alternative metaphysics, "came down with the disease that he was trying to cure" (p. 88); he should have stuck to cultural criticism, contends Rorty.

5. For a full, critical treatment of Dewey's "metaphysics of experience," see Alexander's third chapter, pp. 57–118. For a tempered statement of Sleeper's reservations about the usefulness of the expression "Dewey's metaphysics of experience," see *The Necessity of Pragmatism*, pp. 6–7. In the first chapter of *Necessity*, Sleeper positions his defense of Dewey's reconstructed metaphysics, epistemology, logic, and philosophy of language against Rorty, but proceeds less systematically than Alexander. His historical, deeply informed defense of Dewey is, however, not to be missed. His extensive bibliographical comments are invaluable.

6. "Comments on Sleeper and Edel," *Transactions of the Charles S. Peirce Society* 21 (Winter 1985):40. These comments were a part of a symposium, "Consequences of Pragmatism," chaired by John J. McDermott, which was held in conjunction with the annual meeting of the Eastern Division of the American Philosophical Association. McDermott's introduction and the papers by Sleeper and Edel, as well as Rorty's comments, were published in the *Transactions* 21:1–48.

7. See, for example, his distinction between irony and common sense and the public and the private in "Private Irony and Liberal Hope," which is chapter 4 of *Contingency, Irony and Solidarity* (Cambridge University Press, 1989), pp. 74 and 85. Rorty acknowledges in his response to Frank B. Farrell that he has in the past drawn contrasts too sharply (*Rorty and Pragmatism*, p. 191).

8. "Nineteenth-Century Idealism and Twentieth-Century Textualism, *The Consequences of Pragmatism*, p. 151.

9. Also, in *The Quest for Certainty*, in one of the moves that Rorty deplores, Dewey declared the relationship of real and ideal to be "the central problem of philosophy in its metaphysical aspect" (LW 4:239).

10. "Dewey's Metaphysics" in *The Consequences of Pragmatism*, p. 87. In his response to Sleeper and Edel, Rorty declared: "As far as I can see, nothing of the sort which Dewey offered us in *Experience and Nature* or in *Logic: The Theory of Inquiry* is needed to keep our culture moving, nor does the contents of either book provide anything like a map" (*Transactions* 21:40).

11. Ryan says of *Experience and Nature*: "Dewey's most 'metaphysical' work still contrived to be so thoroughly a piece of social and political criticism" (*Dewey and the High Tide of American Liberalism*, p. 239).

12. See also Rorty's introduction to LW 8, where his view is more fully developed. Also relevant here is "Pragmatism without Method," in *Objectivity, Relativism, and Truth* (Cambridge: Cambridge University Press, 1991), pp. 63–77.

13. Rorty is well aware of Dewey's discussions of this pattern, but does not think that Dewey successfully navigated between vague, recommended habits and a recipe for thinking (LW 8:xiv).

14. These three attitudes are identified and discussed in *How We Think* (LW 8:136–39).

15. My present strategy is to examine representative sections that, when pieced together, provide a coherent overview of Dewey's core project. I am trying to walk a line between reviewing whole books and stitching together fragments of Deweyan texts. The problem with my approach is that one's reconstruction may be more representative of the interpreter than of Dewey. The alternative approach has a better chance of being faithful to Dewey's various texts, but may miss the core.

16. See Tiles' third chapter, "The Emergence of Mind and Qualities," in *Dewey*, pp. 49–76, particularly pp. 59–69.

17. On the origins and associations of the prayer, see *Respectfully Quoted: A Dictionary of Quotations Requested from the Congressional Research Service*, ed. Suzy Platt (Washington: Library of Congress, 1989), p. 76. For an account of Niebuhr and Dewey's conflict regarding human activism, see Daniel F. Rice, "Diverging Views on Liberalism and Liberal Reconstruction," in *Reinhold*

Niebuhr and John Dewey: An American Odyssey (Albany: State University of New York Press, 1993), pp. 192–210.

18. Thus Dewey used *inquiry* to refer to the activity of intelligence, but when he was thinking more generally he tended to use the term *intelligence* to refer to "the power of using past experience to shape and transform future experience" (MW 11:346).

19. In the revised *How We Think* he says: "*The function of reflective thought is, therefore, to transform a situation in which there is experienced obscurity, doubt, conflict, disturbance of some sort, into a situation that is clear, coherent, settled, harmonious*" (Dewey's emphasis; LW 8:195).

20. "A Dissertation upon a Roast Pig," *The Essays of Elia*, ed. William MacDonald (London: J. M. Dent & Co., 1903), pp. 241–52.

21. In his statement announcing his possible presidential candidacy, televangelist Pat Robertson declared, "We have taken the Holy Bible from our young and replaced it with the thoughts of Charles Darwin, Karl Marx, Sigmund Freud and John Dewey" (Dudley Clendinen, "Robertson Sets Conditions for Making a Run in 1988," *The New York Times* [September 18, 1986], p. 16). Robertson and others regard Dewey as the father of progressive (which they now call humanistic) education and hold him responsible for the destruction of "Christian America's public schools." See Tim LaHaye, *The Battle for the Mind* (Old Tappan, N.J.: Fleming H. Revell Company, 1980), pp. 43–44 and 97; Homer Duncan, *Humanism: In the Light of Scripture* (Lubbock, Tex.: Christian Focus on Government, Inc., 1981), pp. 52–53; James Hitchcock, *What Is Secular Humanism?* (Ann Arbor, Mich.: Servant Books, 1982), pp. 12–13; and John Whitehead, *The Stealing of America* (Westchester, Ill.: Crossway Books, 1983), pp. 16–18 and 86–87. Almost all of the expert witnesses called by the plaintiffs in the secular humanism textbook case, tried in October 1986 in Judge W. B. Hand's federal court in Mobile, Alabama, which I attended, spoke of Dewey as the archetypal secular humanist.

22. Many have noticed that he defined philosophy there as "a criticism of criticisms" (p. 298); unnoticed has been his use of *intelligence* and *criticism* as synonyms.

23. *Dewey's Theory of Art, Experience and Nature*, p. 80. In an endnote Alexander observes: "The whole point of *Art as Experience* is, of course, how '*an* experience' develops from ordinary experience, and is itself developmental" (p. 296, n. 55).

24. *John Dewey's Pragmatic Technology*, pp. 134–39.

25. This has profound implications for Dewey's writing. He tended to write as a philosopher to specific needs, as can be readily seen in *The Public and Its Problems* and *A Common Faith*. Yet some readers thought the first was a systematic treatment of politics and the second of religion. Dewey did deal theoretically with these matters, but one must not forget the specific occasions for which

they were written. To describe them as occasional pieces would be to go too far in the other direction, but it is a mistake to regard them as Dewey's definitive statements about politics and religion.

26. In 1951, a year before his death, working on a new introduction to *Experience and Nature*, Dewey wrote: "Were I to write (or rewrite) *Experience and Nature* and the treatment of specific subject-matters would be correspondingly modified, I would abandon the term 'experience' because of my growing realization that the historical obstacles which prevented understanding of my use of 'experience' are, for all practical purposes, insurmountable. I would substitute the term 'culture' because with its meanings as now firmly established it can fully and freely carry my philosophy of experience" (LW 1:361).

27. Although Dewey's naturalism and method of inquiry are functionally absolute—that is, they had become settled matters for him—they are not absolute in the sense used by his absolutist opponents. Dewey argued for his settled, operative beliefs and practices, but he did not claim the ontological status for them that his opponents claimed for theirs. See his response to George Geiger (LW 14:77).

CHAPTER 3, TRANSFORMING SOCIETY: DEWEY'S CULTURAL INSTRUMENTALISM

1. "John Dewey and His Influence," in Schilpp, *The Philosophy of John Dewey*, p. 478.

2. "Twilight of Idols," in *The Radical Will: Selected Writings, 1911–1918*, ed. Olaf Hansen (New York: Urizen Books, 1977), pp. 343–44.

3. *The Golden Day: A Study in American Experience and Culture* (New York: Boni and Liveright, 1936), p. 138.

4. The one exception to this early and late consideration of easily refutable and more sophisticated misreadings is one of the worst (and readily shown to be so) misrepresentations of Dewey, that of John Patrick Diggins in *The Promise of Pragmatism: Modernism and the Crisis of Knowledge and Authority* (Chicago: The University of Chicago Press, 1994). I save Diggins for the last chapter, because I want to use my treatment of him to make a point relevant to that chapter.

5. Quoted in Sleeper, *The Necessity of Pragmatism*, p. 16.

6. *Dewey*, p. 22 (the footnote cited by Tiles has been omitted). Tiles has in mind primarily Dewey's analytic and realist opponents, not his idealist ones.

7. "The Common Faith," *The Nation* (October 14, 1991), p. 454.

8. Westbrook correctly takes Bourne's phrase "realistic pacificists" in "The Collapse of American Strategy" (*War and the Intellectuals: Essays by Randolph S. Bourne, 1915–1919* [New York: Harper & Row, 1964], p. 35) to be Bourne's designation of his position (see Bourne, "Conscience and Intelligence in War," reprinted in John Dewey, *The Political Writings*, ed. Debra Morris and Ian

Shapiro [Indianappolis: Hackett Publishing Company, 1993], pp. 198 and 200–201). Westbrook gives a fairly full account of the finally bitter Dewey-Bourne relationship (*Dewey and American Democracy*, pp. 186–212 231–40), but it is well complemented by Ryan in *Dewey and the High Tide of American Liberalism*, pp. 157–59 and 189–98.

9. Bourne, "Twilight of Idols," *The Radical Will*, p. 336.

10. *Public Opinion* (New York: The Macmillan Company, 1922), pp. 31–32.

11. "Dewey's Social Philosophy," in Cahn, pp. 9–10.

12. See Laski to Holmes, 13 December 1923, *Holmes-Laski Letters: The Correspondence of Mr. Justice Holmes and Harold J. Laski, 1916–35*, ed. Mark DeWolfe Howe (Cambridge: Harvard University Press, 1953), 1:571, and Richard Rorty, "Response to Gouinlock," in Saatkamp, *Rorty and Pragmatism*, p. 99.

13. Recall Dewey's statement in *The Public and Its Problems*: "The prime condition of a democratically organized public is a kind of knowledge and insight which does not yet exist. In its absence, it would be the height of absurdity to try to tell what it would be like if it existed" (LW 2:339).

14. *The Community Reconstructs: The Meaning of Pragmatic Social Thought* (Urbana: University of Illinois Press, 1992), p. 42. See also his "Democracy as Cooperative Inquiry" in Stuhr, *Philosophy and the Reconstruction of Culture*, pp. 17–35.

15. "Democracy as Cooperative Inquiry," in Stuhr (ed.), *Philosophy and the Reconstruction of Culture*, p. 29. See also chapter 6 of Campbell, *Understanding Dewey*, for a parallel but fuller critique of Mills.

16. The fullest account is Daniel F. Rice, *Reinhold Niebuhr and John Dewey: An American Odyssey* (Albany: State University of New York Press, 1993). Other recent but briefer accounts are those of Cornel West, *The American Evasion of Philosophy: A Genealogy of Pragmatism* (Madison: The University of Wisconsin Press, 1989), pp. 150–64; Larry A. Hickman, *John Dewey's Pragmatic Technology*, pp. 185–95; Steven C. Rockefeller, *John Dewey: Religious Faith and Democratic Humanism*, pp. 459–66 and 484–89; Robert B. Westbrook, *John Dewey and American Democracy*, pp. 523–32; and John Patrick Diggins, *The Promise of Pragmatism*, pp. 283–91.

Westbrook cites other accounts that are crucial for understanding this conflict and its place in American intellectual life: Arthur Schlesinger, Jr., "Reinhold Niebuhr's Role in American Political Thought and Life," *Reinhold Niebuhr: His Religious, Social, and Political Thought*, ed. Charles W. Kegley and Robert W. Bretall (New York: The Macmillan Company, 1956), pp. 126–50; Bernard Bailyn et al., *The Great Republic* (Lexington, Mass.: D. C. Heath, 1974), pp. 1151–52; and Richard W. Fox, *Reinhold Niebuhr: A Biography* (New York: Pantheon, 1985), pp. 135, 164–66, and 215–17. Westbrook regards Fox as the best corrective of the standard textbook account (Bailyn), which he says was shaped by Schlesinger (p. 524, including n. 47). A corrective to Fox, according to Rice, is Charles C. Brown, *Niebuhr and His Age: Reinhold Niebuhr's Prophetic Role in the Twentieth Century* (Philadelphia: Trinity Press International, 1992). I will also make use of Morton White's "Epilogue for 1957: Original Sin, Natural Law, and Politics," in *Social Thought in America: The Revolt Against Formalism* (Boston: Beacon Press, 1949, 1957), because it deals successfully with the issue that is of concern to me here.

17. *The Life and Mind of John Dewey* (Carbondale: Southern Illinois University Press, 1973), p. 249. Randolph Bourne, while still an admirer of Dewey, wrote the following in 1915: "Professor Dewey's thought is inaccessible because he has always carried his simplicity of manner, his dread of show or self-advertisement, almost to the point of extravagance. In all his psychology there is no place for the psychology of prestige. His democracy seems almost to take that extreme form of refusing to bring one's self or one's ideas to the attention of others. On the college campus or in the lecture-room he seems positively to efface himself. The uncertainty of his silver-gray hair and drooping mustache, of his voice, of his clothes, suggests that he has almost studied the technique of protective coloration. It will do you no good to hear him lecture. His sentences, flowing and exact and lucid when read, you will find strung in long festoons of obscurity between pauses for the awaited right word. The whole business of impressing yourself on other people, of getting yourself over to the people who want to and ought to have you, has simply never come into his ultra-democratic mind" ("John Dewey's Philosophy," *The Radical Will*, pp. 331–32).

18. "Intellectual Autobiography," Kegley and Bretall, p. 5.

19. Rice, *Niebuhr and Dewey*, p. xviii.

20. Niebuhr, *Moral Man and Immoral Society: A Study in Ethics and Politics* (New York: Charles Scribner's Sons, 1948), pp. xxiv–xxv.

21. *Dewey and American Democracy*, p. 530.

22. *The Nature and Destiny of Man: A Christian Interpretation* (New York: Charles Scribner's Sons, 1941), 1:111.

23. *Leaves from the Notebooks of a Tamed Cynic* (New York: Meridian Books, 1957; originally published in 1929), p. 62. I am indebted to West, *American Evasion*, p. 155, for this quotation.

24. Fox, *Niebuhr*, p. 145.

25. *Reflections* (New York: Charles Scribner's Sons, 1934), p. ix.

26. "Reinhold Niebuhr's Social Ethics," Kegley and Bartell, p. 49.

27. Others have concurred in this judgment. Fox, speaking of Niebuhr's criticism of Dewey in *Moral Man and Immoral Society*, observed: "Like most debaters Niebuhr was not making a close study of his opponent's thought; he was constructing an ideal-type opponent who was easy to take down" (p. 137). Rice concluded: "Niebuhr's rather selective use of Dewey's thought certainly misrepresented him, as friends of both Niebuhr and Dewey have noted" (*Niebuhr and Dewey*, p. 19). But see also n. 65, pp. 297–98, and n. 59, p. 327.

In the latter Rice contended that for all his distortions of Dewey, "Niebuhr had his finger on the pulse of Dewey's liberalism sufficiently to justify his general polemic against it." West observed that "Niebuhr's accusations against liberals—especially Dewey and [Walter] Rauschenbusch—are sweeping and often unfair" (*American Evasion*, p. 155). Hickman, after reviewing Dewey's "analyses of force, religion, and education" in the face of Niebuhr's critique, concluded that Niebuhr "misunderstood" Dewey's instrumentalism (*Dewey's Pragmatic Technology*, p. 194).

28. "The Pathos of Liberalism," *The Nation* 141 (September 11, 1935):303.

29. *The Children of Light and the Children of Darkness: A Vindication of Democracy and a Critique of Its Traditional Defense* (New York: Charles Scribner's Sons, 1944), pp. 16–17.

30. *The Nature and Destiny of Man*, 1:241.

31. For a fuller critique see White's 1957 epilogue to *Social Thought in America*, pp. 247–64.

32. Quoted in Rice, *Niebuhr and Dewey*, p. 204.

33. *Faith and History: A Comparison of Christian and Modern Views of History* (New York: Charles Scribner's Sons, 1948), pp. 11–12.

34. This remark was initially reported by his former student, Hu Shih, in the latter's contribution to S. Ratner's *The Philosopher of the Common Man*, the volume sponsored by the Conference on Methods in Philosophy and the Sciences to honor Dewey's eightieth birthday, p. 211.

35. Quoted by Hu in "Political Philosophy," p. 208; Dewey to Hu, 27 October 1939, John Dewey Papers, Special Collections, Morris Library, Southern Illinois University at Carbondale.

36. A good discussion of the development in Dewey's thought is "Against State Socialism," in Westbrook, *Dewey and American Democracy*, pp. 452–58.

37. The full text of the October 29, 1939, letter makes it clear that Dewey was responding to Hu's manuscript. The phrase "specified spatio-temporal conditions" is used by Hu (p. 209), but it is actually Dewey's (LW 12:499).

38. Tiles, whose discussion of this section of *Experience and Nature* can be usefully consulted, says, "Dewey indulges here in a piece of hyperbole which does not serve to clarify his position; he says 'external and accidental antecedents' 'are not means at all' (L1, p. 277)" (*Dewey*, p. 192). Tiles cites LW 1:277.

39. The following account duplicates, in part, my criticism of Westbrook in *Transactions of the Charles S. Peirce Society* 32 (Winter 1996):11–30. That article was drawn from my original drafts of this and other chapters. Readers may want to consult Westbrook's response, *Transactions* 32:31–40.

40. "Doing Dewey: An Autobiographical Fragment," *Transactions of the Charles S. Peirce Society* 29 (Fall 1993):499.

41. "Doing Dewey," *Transactions* 29:506.

42. Westbrook, *Dewey and American Democracy*, p. 318.

43. "Salvation through Participation: John Dewey and the Religion of Democracy," *Raritan* 12 (1993): 144–54.

44. *Transactions of the Charles S. Peirce Society* 29 (Spring 1993):262.

45. Westbrook, *Dewey and American Democracy*, pp. 251–52.

46. "Editor's Note," *Intelligence in the Modern World: John Dewey's Philosophy* (New York: The Modern Library, 1939), p. 529.

47. "Doing Dewey," *Transactions* 29:505–506.

48. For Hu Shih's account of this cultural change see "The Chinese Renaissance," which is chapter 3 of his 1933 Haskell Lectures at the University of Chicago, published as *The Chinese Renaissance* (Chicago: The University of Chicago Press, 1934). A critical account is that of Y. C. Wang, *Chinese Intellectuals and the West: 1872–1949* (Chapel Hill: The University of North Carolina Press, 1966), pp. 393–400 and 501.

49. The Consortium was an American-initiated international banking consortium for the financing of China's economic development.

50. "Dewey's Social and Political Philosophy," in Schilpp, p. 360.

51. *New Leader* (May 20, 1991):14.

Chapter 4, A Transforming Society: Democratic Means and Ends

1. *Dewey and American Democracy*, p. 317.

2. Westbrook thinks that I contradicted myself in "Dewey's Faith in Democracy as Shared Experience," *Transactions* 32:11–30, in that I allegedly acknowledged Westbrook's awareness of Dewey's balanced political approach (at the beginning of my article) but criticized Westbrook "for ignoring Dewey's appreciation for the virtues and necessity of representative democracy" ("Democratic Faith: A Response to Michael Eldridge," *Transactions* 32:39, n. 17). Yet in his response Westbrook writes, "Eldridge denies that Dewey's democratic faith found its political focus in direct forms of participatory democracy, but the hymn to local, face-to-face democracy in *The Public and Its Problems* (and much other evidence besides) demonstrates otherwise" (p. 36). Westbrook then presents in the remainder of the paragraph a more balanced view that I can mostly endorse. Still the tone is one that puts the emphasis more on direct (rather than representative) democracy than I think is warranted. He ends the paragraph with the troublesome statement about "the logic of Dewey's political theory," a statement that is narrowly true—Dewey did try to expand "agencies of direct democracy"—but misleading in that it suggests that for Dewey representative democracy was a concession.

3. *Understanding Dewey*, p. 141.

4. *Dewey and American Democracy*, p. 217.

5. Dykhuizen, *Life and Mind*, p. 170.

6. *The Communists and the Schools* (New York: Harcourt Brace and Company, 1959), p. 43.

7. David Hogan and Clarence Karier, "Professionalizing the Role of 'Truth Seekers,'" in J. E. Tiles, *John Dewey: Critical Assessments* (London: Routledge, 1992), 2:400.

8. See also James Gutmann, "Salute to Robert M. MacIver: *Academic Freedom in our Time* and the Liberal Tradition," *The Journal of Philosophy* 53 (June 7, 1956):373–77. Gutmann quotes Dewey's 1949 letter in full and makes reference to correspondence between Dewey and Sidney Hook. The aim of Gutmann's piece was to defend the mediating position of MacIver, who was being criticized for not taking Communist infiltration of education seriously enough. Gutmann's strategy was to place MacIver's position within the liberal tradition that includes John Stuart Mill, Dewey, and others.

9. Quoted in "Biography of John Dewey," ed. Jane Dewey, in Schilpp, *The Philosophy of John Dewey*, p. 18.

10. "Pragmatism Rides Again," *The New York Review of Books* (February 16, 1995), p. 33.

11. "Dewey's Social and Political Philosophy," in Schilpp, *The Philosophy of John Dewey*, p. 367.

12. "John Dewey on Democracy: The Task Before Us," in *Philosophical Profiles: Essays in a Pragmatic Mode* (Philadelphia: University of Pennsylvania Press, 1986), pp. 260–302.

13. The foregoing account is drawn from the textual commentary of Anne Sharpe (LW 14:459–66).

14. Gouinlock, *Dewey's Philosophy of Value*, p. 130.

15. *Pragmatism* (Harvard University Press, 1978; originally published in 1907), p. 37.

16. *The Journal of Philosophy* 52 (February 17, 1955):85–94.

17. Although Kennedy did not identify Morton White as one of the sympathetic critics who missed the link Kennedy identified in this article, Kennedy's essay can be taken as a response to White as well as to Bourne, whom Kennedy does mention. White had argued in a 1949 article that Dewey had made a logical error in deducing normative statements from empirical ones. This is not the place to review this charge and the responses to it. I mention this issue only to indicate that it has been a matter of controversy. My own view is that Dewey subordinated empirical claims to normative ones and that one must keep in mind the way in which norms and facts are responses to some felt need. White's essay "Value and Obligation in Dewey and Lewis" originally appeared in *The Philosophical Review* (1949), but a revised version was included in his *Pragmatism and the American Mind* (Oxford University Press, 1973), pp. 155–67. See also Sidney Hook, "The Desirable and Emotive in Dewey's Ethics," in *John Dewey: Philosopher of Science and Freedom*, ed. Sidney Hook (New

York: The Dial Press, 1950), pp. 194–216; Ralph Sleeper, "Dewey's Metaphysical Perspective: A Note on White, Geiger, and the Problem of Obligation," *The Journal of Philosophy* 57 (1960):100–115); Gouinlock, *Dewey's Philosophy of Value*, pp. 137–40, and "Dewey's Theory of Moral Deliberation," *Ethics* 88 (1978): 218–28; and Elizabeth Flower and Murray G. Murphey, *A History of Philosophy in America* (New York: G. P. Putnam's Sons, 1977), 2:869–74. White has recently responded to a previously unpublished reply by Dewey to White's original article. See Dewey, "Comments on Recent Criticisms of Some Points in Moral and Logical Theory" (LW 17:480–84), and White, "Desire and Desirability: A Rejoinder to a Posthumous Reply by John Dewey," *Journal of Philosophy* 93 (May 1996):229–42.

18. Berkeley: University of California Press, 1996.

19. Speaking of one ballot initiative that was defeated, Shaw notes: "The initiative was not the product of a broad-based discussion among key constituency groups" (p. 125).

20. In an e-mail message in response to my having sent him a version of this section in the form of a paper, "Toward a Deweyan Political Technology," Shaw acknowledged that he had "no awareness of Dewey," but that my analysis made sense (January 28, 1997).

21. There are, of course, other large areas that have yet to be addressed in a similar fashion, notably national political life. Presidential campaigns, to take an outstanding instance, are conspicious consumers of large amounts of money spent on media campaigns that are effectively antideliberative and tend to maintain socioeconomic privilege. "Education" and "deliberation" primarily take the form of slick ads that are highly selective at best and grossly distorting at worst. An active viewer/listener can, overtime, and with the help of a variety of media sources, sort through the material presented and come to an informed judgment. But this is not the norm, and few would defend the intelligence of the current highly inefficient and not very democratic campaign process.

22. At one point Shaw notes, "The Tenderloin Housing Clinic generates unrestricted funds by representing tenants in lawsuits against landlords" (p. 144).

23. Updated edition; New York: Twayne Publishers, 1994.

Chapter 5, Dewey's Religious Proposal

1. Fully aware of Dewey's faults as a writer, Alan Ryan nevertheless contends that Dewey had mastered what (according to Lewis Feuer) T. H. Huxley had called the "lay sermon." He was effectively able to address the concerns of his audience, many of whom would be simultaneously modern, liberal, and religious (p. 365). Ryan writes: "Dewey was a visionary. That was his appeal. He was a curious visionary, because he did not speak of a distant goal or a city not

built with hands. He was a visionary about the here and now, about the potentiality of the modern world, modern society, modern man, and thus, as it happened, America and Americans in the twentieth century. It was his ability to infuse the here and now with a kind of transcendent glow that overcame the denseness and awkwardness of his prose and the vagueness of his message and secured such widespread conviction. . . . He became the century's most influential preacher of a creed for liberals, reformers, school-teachers, and democrats" (*Dewey and the High Tide of American Liberalism*, p. 369).

2. John Herman Randall, Jr., "The Religion of Shared Experience," in *The Philosopher of the Common Man: Essays in Honor of John Dewey to Celebrate His Eightieth Birthday*, ed. Sidney Ratner (New York: G. P. Putnam's Sons, 1940), p. 106. This is an excellent essay on Dewey's religious proposal, for it situates the proposal in Dewey's larger philosophy. My reservations have to do with Randall's criticisms, not his exposition, of Dewey's thought.

3. Horace Friess observes that "explicit references to religion are brief and scattered in Dewey's major writings (sometimes coming as a kind of flourish or gesture toward a wide horizon near the close of a work)" ("Dewey's Philosophy of Religion," in *Guide to the Works of John Dewey*, ed. Jo Ann Boydston [Southern Illinois University Press, 1970], p. 202).

4. Jerome Paul Soneson, writes: "Dewey did not write extensively upon religious matters or integrate what he did say into his overall philosophy" (*Pragmatism and Pluralism: John Dewey's Significance for Theology* [Minneapolis: Fortress Press, 1993], p. 127).

5. *Churchmen and Philosophers: From Jonathan Edwards to John Dewey* (Yale University Press, 1985).

6. My claim in this respect is similar, then, to Soneson's: "It is possible to . argue that [Dewey] is fundamentally a religious thinker, since what informs and motivates all his thinking is his abiding concern for meaningful orientation and human fulfilment. . . . The result [of the kind of life recommended by Dewey] is an ordering and organizing of interests by a normative vision of the whole that provides unity for the self in what is taken to be a unified world of meaning" (pp. 126–27). Where I differ is in the rationale offered. I understand the religious in Dewey in terms of the strength, scope, and transformative qualities of one's life-shaping interests rather than in terms of the theological orientation, as indicated in the quotation by the phrase "normative vision of the whole." As we will see in the controversy involving Dewey and Henry Nelson Wieman, Dewey thought Wieman found more unity in reality apart from the human contribution than Dewey did. This unity, plus the human contribution, was what Wieman took to be divine. Note also the subtitle of Soneson's book: *John Dewey's Significance for Theology*.

7. *Secular* is a troublesome word to some of Dewey's interpreters, such as Steven Rockefeller, who prefer the term *naturalistic* because they take *secular* to exclude being religious, where *naturalistic* does not. I use *secular* here because,

as I will argue, Dewey's cultural instrumentalism is best understood in secular terms—that is, "this-worldly" language. But Rockefeller is correct to object, as he did in a letter commenting on my use, that Dewey thought "one could be a naturalist, accept secularization, and still be religious" (September 26, 1996). I am well aware that I am criticizing Dewey's religious proposal.

8. Campbell uses the phrase in his essay "Optimism, Meliorism, Faith," which is chapter 7 of *The Community Reconstructs: The Meaning of Pragmatic Social Thought* (p. 103); for a discussion of this cluster, see particularly pp. 102–4.

9. See, for example, his treatment of Neil Coughlan's claim regarding the possible influence of Newman Smyth on Dewey (p. 577, n. 48) and Kuklick's thesis that the Andover Seminary theologians shaped Dewey's thought (p. 581, n. 6). For a variety of reasons I was never able to get into print my objections to these assertions. Now I do not need to do so. On these and a host of other matters regarding Dewey and religion, Rockefeller has written the definitive account, freeing me to write the present book.

10. Although Rockefeller refers to Dewey's 1930 statement in "From Absolutism to Experimentalism" that begins with his declaration that "the conflict of traditional religious beliefs with opinions that I could myself honestly entertain . . . did not at any time constitute a leading philosophical problem" (LW 5:153), he does not, in his book, confront this declaration. Of course, Rockefeller recognizes that Dewey was not primarily concerned philosophically with the problems posed by "traditional religious beliefs" (see *John Dewey*, p. 75). But by framing his study of Dewey in terms of Dewey's developing faith he narrows the frame unduly. I think Rockefeller's vantage point prevents him from seeing Dewey whole—specifically the Dewey that moved beyond religious categories even as he tried to maintain the quality of being religious.

No doubt I could be criticized for failing to recognize the way in which the actual, historical Dewey never shook himself entirely free of religious forms of expression and practice. So in some ways I am engaging in a contest to discover and reveal the real Dewey. I acknowledge that the historical Dewey was more verbally religious than I think was consistent with his main philosophical convictions, but I think my secular account is closer to his proposal to intelligize practice than is Rockefeller's religiously framed one. Our differences can be readily illustrated. Note that Rockefeller chose for his book the photograph opposite the title page one of the young John Dewey (from archives at the University of Michigan). I suppose this is a photograph of Dewey when he was a member of the Michigan faculty—and a liberal Christian—in the late 1880s and early 1890s. I prefer an image of the secular, public philosopher of the 1920s and 1930s. Rockefeller could remind me that *A Common Faith* was published in 1934. The point of that book is different from Dewey's emphasis in other writings of that period. The early Dewey was clearly religious; the later Dewey had to go out of his way for people to recognize him as being so. The publication of *A Common Faith* surprised many people.

11. Three of the reminiscences were recorded by Dewey when he was age seventy and one when he was eighty, but since I am not interested as much in what happened as what he inherited this is not a problem. Biographical accounts of Dewey's early years are found in "Biography of John Dewey," ed. Jane Dewey, in Schilpp, pp. 3–45; Lewis S. Feuer, "H. A. P. Torrey and John Dewey: Teacher and Pupil," *American Quarterly* 10 (Spring 1958):34–54; Dykuizen, *Life and Mind*; Neil Coughlan, *Young John Dewey: An Essay in American Intellectual History* (The University of Chicago Press, 1975); and of course Rockefeller.

12. "Torrey and Dewey," *American Quarterly* 10:50.

13. "Some Memories of John Dewey, 1859–1952," *Commentary* 14 (1952):246.

14. Dykhuizen, p. 5. Lucina had rejected her family's inclusive form of Christianity for what Dewey calls "Evangelism." Once again, Hook reports Dewey's recollection: "I recall being told that my mother was converted to Evangelism while visiting a cousin in another city in which her father happened to be residing at the time. My grandfather's family belonged to the Universalist persuasion and my mother, originally, too. On this visit, however, she spent a great deal of time with an Evangelical friend. And my grandfather wrote warning our immediate family that unless someone took things in hand, my mother who arrived as a Universalist would return as a Partialist" ("Some Memories of John Dewey" 14:246). Jane Dewey's version of this story has Lucina's uncle warning her father back in Vermont about Lucina's impending defection from Universalism (Schilpp, p. 6).

15. *A Religious History of the American People* (New Haven: Yale University Press, 1972), pp. 780–81.

16. Ryan, *Dewey and the High Tide of American Liberalism*, pp. 100 and 102.

17. Dating the fifteen years from Dewey's introduction to Hegel in graduate school in the early 1880s puts the end of his Hegelian period in the mid- to late 1890s.

18. See Jennifer Welchman, "From Absolute Idealism to Instrumentalism: The Problem of Dewey's Early Philosophy," *Transactions of the Charles S. Peirce Society* 25 (1989):407–19.

19. See Alexander, *Dewey's Theory of Art, Experience, and Nature*, pp. xv–xvii and 1–118, and Hickman, *Dewey's Pragmatic Technology*, pp. 74–76.

20. See Hickman, *Dewey's Pragmatic Technology*, pp. 31–32.

21. In chronological order, here is a very uneven collection of articles and sections of books that treat Dewey's faith as religious in a sense unacceptable to him: Reinhold Niebuhr, "The Blindness of Liberalism," *Radical Religion* 1 (1936):4–5; John Herman Randall, Jr., "The Religion of Shared Experience," in Ratner, *Philosopher of the Common Man*, pp. 106–45; Howard B. White, "The Political Faith of John Dewey," *Journal of Politics* 20 (1958):353–67; John

Blewett, S.J., "Democracy as Religion: Unity in Human Relations," in *John Dewey: His Thought and Influence*, ed. John Blewett (New York: Fordham University Press, 1960), pp. 33–58; Georges Dicker, "John Dewey: Instrumentalism in Social Action," *Transactions of the Charles S. Peirce Society* 7 (1971):221–32; Quentin Anderson, "John Dewey's American Democrat," *Daedalus* 108 (Summer 1979):145–59; Stanley Grean, "Elements of Transcendence in Dewey's Naturalistic Humanism," *Journal of the American Academy of Religion* 52 (June 1984):263–88; William M. Shea, "John Dewey: Aesthetic and Religious Experience," *The Naturalists and the Supernaturalists: Studies in Horizon and an American Philosophy of Religion* (Macon, Georgia: Mercer University Press, 1984), pp. 117–41; Steven C. Rockefeller, *John Dewey: Religious Faith and Democratic Humanism*, pp. 527–40; James Miller, "The Common Faith," *The Nation* (October 14, 1991), pp. 450-54; and William Galston, "Salvation through Participation: John Dewey and the Religion of Democracy," *Raritan* 12 (1993): 144–54. The discussion in Rockefeller has references to other sources that find an inconsistency in Dewey between his naturalism and his religious commitment.

22. William James, *The Will to Believe and Other Essays in Popular Philosophy* (Harvard University Press, 1979 [originally published 1896]), p. 32.

23. Review of *The Community Reconstructs* in *Transactions of the Charles S. Peirce Society* 29 (1993):107–108.

24. "Doing Dewey: An Autobiographical Fragment," *Transactions* 29 (Fall 1993):506–507.

25. I have in mind Campbell's identification of the omission of consideration of significant positive professional relationships. See his review of Westbrook's *John Dewey and American Democracy* in *Transactions of the Charles S. Peirce Society* 28 (1992):599–601.

26. I am relying on the index entry on James in the Dewey critical edition (5:603). Dewey, in the text, simply says, "an American thinker" (LW 5:267). The closest I have come to a reference in James is the statement that "there is some believing tendency wherever there is willingness to act at all" (*The Will to Believe*, p. 14).

27. See Sidney Hook's introduction to the critical edition of *Experience and Nature* (LW 1:viii); Richard Rorty, "Dewey's Metaphysics," *Consequences of Pragmatism*, p. 72; and Ralph Sleeper, "Rorty's Pragmatism: Afloat in Neurath's Boat, But Why Adrift?" *Transactions of the Charles S. Peirce Society* 21 (Winter 1985):16–17.

28. In *Experience and Nature* Dewey famously defined philosophy as "a criticism of criticisms" (LW 1:298). Just as "conscience in morals, taste in fine arts and conviction in beliefs pass insensibly into critical judgments", so "the latter pass also into a more and more generalized form of criticism called philosophy" (300).

29. Earlier brief but significant treatments of religion are found in *Human*

Nature and Conduct (1922, MW 14:180–81) and *The Quest for Certainty* (1929, LW 4:243–47). The basis of the latter book was Dewey's Gifford Lectures. The topic of these lectures, by stipulation of the original bequest, was to be natural theology (LW 4:viii). Broadly conceived, Dewey's lectures were concerned with natural theology; they were an attack on the dominant traditions of philosophy and theology in their allied quests for certainty. Not to be overlooked is his essay, "As the Chinese Think" (1922; MW 13:217–27), which treats both Taoism and Confucianism in a not unappreciative manner.

30. Herbert Schneider and Horace Friess recall that they urged Dewey to speak on the subject and that there was intense interest in what he would say. Although Dewey was irritated with what subsequently happened, he continued to become involved in public discussions of religion in spite of annoying results. Schneider and Friess's recollections can be found in Rice's *Niebuhr and Dewey*, pp. 43–45.

31. "Dewey, Harper, and the University of Chicago: September, 1903–June 1904," William W. Brickman and Stanley Lehrer, *John Dewey: Master Educator* (New York: Atherton Press, 1966), p. 65f.

32. Volume 6 (May–June 1933):1–5. Dewey's friend Max C. Otto declined to sign, thinking it would "serve no sufficient purpose" (*The New Humanist* 6 [July–August 1933]:33). For a brief account of American religious humanism and Dewey's involvement in it, see Rockefeller, *Dewey: Religious Faith and Democratic Humanism*, pp. 449–52 and 456–9.

33. The phrase "morality touched by emotion" is from Matthew Arnold's *Literature and Dogma* (London: Smith, Elder and Co., 1883), p. 16. See Milton R. Konvitz's introduction (LW 9:xivf). William P. Alston, in "Religion," *The Encyclopedia of Philosophy* (New York: Macmillan Publishing Co., Inc. & The Free Press, 1967), 7:140, cites a similar statement from Arnold: "Religion is ethics heightened, enkindled, lit up by feeling."

34. *Reason in Religion*, volume 3 of *The Life of Reason* (New York: Charles Scribner's Sons, 1906), p. 179.

35. "The Religion of Shared Experience," p. 113.

36. Rockefeller (pp. 626–27) points to Edward Scribner Ames's church in Chicago, churches like it, and the Ethical Culture Societies as examples of what Dewey may have had in mind. Nevertheless, from my experience with the Baltimore Ethical Society and as an assistant leader of the New York Society for Ethical Culture (1974–77) I would have to say that, with their Sunday morning meetings and their leaders performing clergylike roles, these societies are still too churchlike and insufficiently secular to have appealed to Dewey. That is, they—like conventional churches, but less so—distract their members from secular society.

37. *Dewey and the High Tide of American Liberalism*, p. 274.

38. *Dewey: Religious Faith and Democratic Humanism*, p. 628, n. 89. Nathanson was a leader of the New York Society for Ethical Culture and per-

formed the wedding ceremony for Dewey's second marriage in 1946 (p. 544). He also was the author of *John Dewey: The Reconstruction of the Democratic Life* (New York: Frederick Ungar Publishing Co., 1951).

39. Westbrook, *Dewey and American Democracy*, p. 427.

40. "New Light on Dewey's *Common Faith*," *The Journal of Philosophy* 58 (1961):24–25.

41. In his introduction to a selection from *A Common Faith* John McDermott observes, "Dewey had a deep although unorthodox religious sensibility, best expressed perhaps in *Art as Experience*" (*The Philosophy of John Dewey: The Lived Experience* [New York: G. P. Putnam's Sons, 1973], 2:696). Referring to his friend and former colleague, McDermott, as "an astute and sympathetic critic," Ralph Sleeper quotes this sentence, then comments: "But it is surely not made explicit in *A Common Faith*" (*The Necessity of Pragmatism*, p. 183). For a suggestive discussion of the pedagogical and political possibilities of an "aesthetic sensibility," see McDermott's "From Cynicism to Amelioration: Strategies for a Cultural Pedagogy," in *The Culture of Experience: Philososphical Essays in the American Grain* (New York University Press, 1976), especially pp. 132–43.

42. "Is There Room for God in Education?" *Public Affairs Quarterly* 9 (January 1995):7. The purpose of Auxier's article is to show "teachers who believe in God" that they can "make that belief the basis of their pedagogy, and particularly of their moral standards" (p. 1).

43. "Some Memories of John Dewey," *Commentary* 14:253.

CHAPTER 6, THE SECULARITY OF DEWEYAN CRITICISM

1. The quoted words are Dewey's. In *A Common Faith* Dewey wrote: "I am not proposing a religion, but rather the emancipation of elements and outlooks that may be called religious." Then in the next paragraph he continued: "It is conceivable that the present depression in religion is closely connected with the fact that religions now prevent, because of their weight of historic encumbrances, the religious quality of experience from coming to consciousness and finding the expression that is appropriate to present conditions, intellectual and moral" (LW 9:8).

2. In *The Philosopher of the Common Man: Essays in Honor of John Dewey to Celebrate His Eightieth Birthday*, ed. Sidney Ratner (New York: G. P. Putnam's Sons, 1940), pp. 106–45.

3. *The Philosophical Review* 44 (1935):496.

4. "Dewey's Interpretation of Religion," in Schilpp, p. 397.

5. *The Role of Knowledge in Western Religion* (Beacon Hill: Starr King Press, 1958).

6. In *Guide to the Works of John Dewey*, ed. Jo Ann Boydston (Southern Illinois University Press, 1970), pp. 200–17.

7. With Herbert Schneider, *Religion in Various Cultures* (1932). Randall, in his history of the Department of Philosophy at Columbia University, writes of Friess: "Since 1944 Friess has planned, organized and been in charge of the basic cooperative graduate course in the history of religion. He has also since 1943 been editor of *The Review of Religion*, established in 1936 by the Columbia group to foster critical and philosophical scholarship in religious studies" ("The Department of Philosophy," in *A History of the Faculty of Philosophy: Columbia University* [Columbia University Press, 1957], p. 133).

8. *Journal of Religion* 34 (1954):256–66. Arnett's book, *Religion and Judgment: An Essay on the Method and Meaning of Religion* (Appleton-Century-Crofts, 1966), contains in a revised form the criticism of Dewey in the earlier article. Both the article and the book make use of Randall's critique.

9. *Pragmatism and Pluralism*, p. 126.

10. "The Religion of Shared Experience," p. 137.

11. *Purpose and Thought* (Yale University Press, 1978), p. 184. Smith's A.B. and Ph.D. degrees are from Columbia University, his B.D. from Union Theological Seminary. The latter information comes from the 1990 Herbert Schneider Award citation written by Andrew J. Reck and published in the newsletter of the Society for the Advancement of American Philosophy (June 1990).

12. "The Religion of Shared Experience," p. 143.

13. See my chapter "John Dewey's Limited Humanism: The Sectarian Stance of America's Philosopher of Holism," in *Frontiers in American Philosophy: Vol. 2*, ed. Robert W. Burch and Herman J. Saatkamp, Jr. (College Station: Texas A & M University Press, 1996), 182–91, upon which I draw in this subsection.

14. "New Light on Dewey's *Common Faith*," *Journal of Philosophy* 58 (January 5, 1961):26.

15. Along with Irving Babbit, More was a leader in the new humanism, an American movement in literary criticism that was prominent in the 1920s. Its dualistic and conservative tendencies were unacceptable to Dewey.

16. Charles Francis Potter was a former Baptist leader and later Unitarian minister who founded the First Humanist Society of New York. He was also a signer of the Humanist Manifesto.

17. Diggins declares in the introduction regarding pragmatism that he is "more struck by its limitations than by its possibilites, because I see pragmatism as having failed to fulfill many of its promises (p. 16). Again, at the end of the first chapter, he writes: "The American people, it now seems clear, played out the darker thoughts of Adams, Weber, and Veblen in living not 'for' but 'off' politics and becoming bureaucrats and consumers slouching toward suburbia, where community simply means real estate. Pragmatism sprang from native grounds, and pragmatic interpretation of life sustained America's hope in the will to believe in what satisfied belief. Yet the old promises of pragmatism remain unfulfilled, while the claims of neopragmatism remain unexamined beyond the disciplines of philosophy and literary theory" (p. 54).

18. "The Thirteen Pragmatisms," in *The Thirteen Pragmatisms and Other Essays* (Baltimore: The Johns Hopkins Press, 1963), p. 2.

19. Lovejoy's essay was reprinted in *The Thirteen Pragmatisms and Other Essays*, as well as MW 13:443–81. Dewey's response, "Realism Without Monism or Dualism," is reprinted in MW 13:40–60. Lovejoy then responded to the latter in his essay, "Time, Meaning and Transcendence" (MW 15:349–70), to which Dewey replied in "Some Comment on Philosophical Discussion" (MW 15:27–41).

20. One who does consider this interchange is Tiles. See his "Dewey and the Realists" in *Dewey* (London: Routledge, 1988), pp. 130–53, particularly pp. 130–7.

21. *John Dewey: An Intellectual Portrait* (New York: The John Day Company, 1939).

22. *Guide to the Works of John Dewey*, ed. Boydston, pp. 83–85.

23. Review in *The Journal of American History* 82 (June 1995):170.

24. Westbrook and other reviewers complain of Diggins's loose style: "This is a big and baggy book—loosely argued, repetitive, and filled with annoying errors of typography and fact" (Westbrook 82:170). Even harsher is Alan Wolfe: "The shoddy workmanship, the intellectual inconsistencies and the conceptual confusion that mark Diggins's otherwise thought-provoking book have one final consequence. By surrendering to postmodern methods, Diggins undermines any claim that he himself might have to speak with authority" ("The End of Essences," *The New Republic* [August 8, 1994], 38).

25. *Troubled Philosopher: John Dewey and the Struggle for World Peace* (Port Washington, N.Y.: Kennikat Press, 1977).

26. "The Real John Dewey," *New York Review of Books* 39 (June 25, 1992):55.

27. Dewey, in *The Quest for Certainty*, notes that "the greater part of the activities of the greater number of human beings is spent in effort to seize upon and hold onto such enjoyments as the actual scene permits." His adverse judgment regarding this is clearly revealed in the next sentence: "Their energies and their enjoyments are controlled in fact, but they are controlled by external conditions rather than by intelligent judgment and endeavor" (LW 4:227–28).

28. The full sentence is: "In the bedlam of tragedy, melodrama and light opera in which we live, Dewey is still the master of the commonplace" ("Dewey: Master of the Commonplace," *The New Republic* 97 [January 18, 1939], p. 306). This is an article well worth reading. Ostensibly an article in the series "Books That Changed Our Minds," about Dewey's 1938 *Logic*, it turns out to be not only that, but also a good, brief overview of Dewey's commonplace philosophy and its cultural status at the end of the 1930s. I am indebted to Alan Ryan, *Dewey and the High Tide of American Liberalism*, p. 344, for this reference. His discussion is also worth consulting.

❖
BIBLIOGRAPHY

Ahlstrom, Sydney E. *A Religious History of the American People*. New Haven: Yale University Press, 1972.

Alexander, Thomas M. *John Dewey's Theory of Art, Experience, and Nature: The Horizons of Feeling*. Albany: State Univeristy of New York Press, 1987.

Arnett, Willard E. *Religion and Judgment: An Essay on the Method and Meaning of Religion*. New York: Appleton-Century-Crofts, 1966.

Auxier, Randall. "Is There Room for God in Education?" *Public Affairs Quarterly* 9 (January 1995):1–13.

Ayres, C. E. "Dewey: Master of the Commonplace." *The New Republic* 97 (January 18, 1939):303–6.

Bernstein, Richard J. *John Dewey*. New York: Washington Square Press, Inc., 1967.

———. *Philosophical Profiles: Essays in a Pragmatic Mode*. Philadelphia: University of Pennsylvania Press, 1986.

Blewett, John, S. J., ed. *John Dewey: His Thought and Influence*. New York: Fordham University Press, 1960.

Boisvert, Raymond D. *Dewey's Metaphysics*. New York: Fordham University Press, 1988.

Bourne, Randolph. *The Radical Will: Selected Writings, 1911–1918*. Ed. Olaf Hansen. New York: Urizen Books, 1977.

Boydston, Jo Ann, ed. *Guide to the Works of John Dewey*. Carbondale: Southern Illinois University Press, 1970.

———. *John Dewey: The Early Works: 1882–1898*. Five volumes. Carbondale: Southern Illinois University Press, 1967–72.

———. *John Dewey: The Later Works: 1925–1953*. Five volumes. Carbondale: Southern Illinois University Press, 1967–72.

———. *John Dewey: The Middle Works: 1899–1924*. Fifteen volumes. Carbondale: Southern Illinois University Press, 1976–83.

Brickman, William W., and Stanley Lehrer. *John Dewey: Master Educator*. New York: Atherton Press, 1966.

Brown, Charles C. *Niebuhr and His Age: Reinhold Niebuhr's Prophetic Role in the Twentieth Century*. Philadelphia: Trinity Press International, 1992.

Burch, Robert W. and Herman J. Saatkamp, Jr., eds. *Frontiers in American Philosophy*. Two Volumes. College Station: Texas A & M University Press, 1992 and 1996.

Burke, Tom. *Dewey's New Logic*. Chicago: University of Chicago Press, 1994.

Cahn, Steven M., ed. *New Studies in the Philosophy of John Dewey*. Hanover, N.H.: Published for the University of Vermont by the University Press of New England, 1977.

Campbell, James. *The Community Reconstructs: The Meaning of Pragmatic Social Thought*. Urbana: University of Illinois Press, 1992.

————. Review of Robert B. Westbrook, *John Dewey and American Democracy*. *Transactions of the Charles S. Peirce Society* 28:593–601.

————. *Understanding John Dewey: Nature and Cooperative Intelligence*. Chicago: Open Court Publishing Company, 1995.

Coughlan, Neil. *Young John Dewey: An Essay in American Intellectual History*. Chicago: The University of Chicago Press, 1975.

Dewey, John. John Dewey Papers. Special Collections/Morris Library. Southern Illinois University, Carbondale, Ill.

DeWolfe, Mark, ed. *Holmes-Laski Letters: The Correspondence of Mr. Justice Holmes and Harold J. Laski, 1916–35*. Cambridge: Harvard University Press, 1953.

Diggins, John Patrick. *The Promise of Pragmatism: Modernism and the Crisis of Knowledge and Authority*. Chicago: The University of Chicago Press, 1994.

Dykhuizen, George. *The Life and Mind of John Dewey*. Carbondale: Southern Illinois University Press, 1973.

Eldridge, Michael. "Dewey's Faith in Democracy as Shared Experience." *Transactions of the Charles S. Peirce Society* 32 (Winter 1996):11–30.

Feuer, Lewis S. "H. A. P. Torrey and John Dewey: Teacher and Pupil." *American Quarterly* 10 (Spring 1958): 34–54.

Fisher, Robert. *Let the People Decide: Neighborhood Organizing in America*. Updated edition. New York: Twayne Publishers, 1994.

Flower, Elizabeth, and Murray G. Murphey. *A History of Philosophy in America*. Two volumes. New York: G. P. Putnam's Son's, 1977.

Fox, Richard W. *Reinhold Niebuhr: A Biography*. New York: Pantheon, 1985.

Galston, William. "Salvation through Participation: John Dewey and the Religion of Democracy." *Raritan* 12 (1993):144–54.

Garrison, Jim, ed. *The New Scholarship on Dewey*. Dordrecht, The Netherlands: Kluwer Academic Publishers, 1995.

Gouinlock, James. *John Dewey's Philosophy of Value*. New York: Humanities Press, 1972.

Gutmann, James. "Salute to Robert M. MacIver: *Academic Freedom in Our Time* and the Liberal Tradition." *The Journal of Philosophy* 53 (June 7, 1956): 373–77.

Hall, David L. *Richard Rorty: Prophet and Poet of the New Pragmatism.*
    Albany: State University of New York Press, 1994.

Hickman, Larry A. *John Dewey's Pragmatic Technology.* Bloomington: Indiana
    University Press, 1990.

Hook, Sidney. *John Dewey: An Intellectual Portrait.* New York: The John Day
    Company, 1939.

————. *John Dewey: Philosopher of Science and Freedom.* New York: The Dial
    Press, 1950.

————. "Some Memories of John Dewey, 1859–1952." *Commentary* 14
    (1952):245–53.

Howe, Mark DeWolfe, ed. *Holmes-Laski Letters: The Correspondence of Mr.
    Justice Holmes and Harold J. Laski, 1916–35.* Cambridge: Harvard
    University Press, 1953.

Howlett, Charles F. *Troubled Philosopher: John Dewey and the Struggle for
    World Peace.* Port Washington, N.Y.: Kennikat Press, 1977.

Iversen, Robert W. *The Communists and the Schools.* New York: Harcourt Brace
    and Company, 1959.

James, William. *Pragmatism.* Cambridge: Harvard University Press, 1978; orig-
    inally published in 1907.

————. *The Will to Believe and Other Essays in Popular Philosophy.*
    Cambridge: Harvard University Press, 1979; originally published in 1896.

Kegley, Charles W., and Robert W. Bretall, eds. *Reinhold Niebuhr: His
    Religious, Social, and Political Thought.* New York: The Macmillan
    Company, 1956.

Kennedy, Gail. "The Hidden Link in Dewey's Theory of Evaluation." *The
    Journal of Philosophy* 52 (February 17, 1955):85–94.

Kuklick, Bruce. *Churchmen and Philosophers: From Jonathan Edwards to John
    Dewey.* New Haven: Yale University Press, 1985.

Lamont, Corliss, ed. *Dialogue on John Dewey.* New York: Horizon Press, 1959.

————. "New Light on Dewey's *Common Faith.*" *The Journal of Philosophy* 58
    (1961):21–28.

Lippmann, Walter. *Public Opinion.* New York: The Macmillan Company, 1922.

Lovejoy, Arthur O. *The Thirteen Pragmatisms and Other Essays.* Baltimore:
    The Johns Hopkins Press, 1963.

MacDonald, William, ed. *The Essays of Elia.* London: J. M. Dent & Co., 1903.

McDermott, John J. *The Culture of Experience: Philosophical Essays in the
    American Grain.* New York: New York University Press, 1976.

Menand, Louis. "The Real John Dewey." *The New York Review of Books* 39
    (June 25, 1992):50–55.

Miller, James. "The Common Faith." *The Nation* (October 14, 1991):450–54.

Moritz, Charles, ed. *Current Biography Yearbook, 1966.* New York: The H. W.
    Wilson Company, 1967.

Mumford, Lewis. *The Golden Day: A Study in American Experience and Culture*. New York: Boni and Liveright, 1936.

Nathanson, Jerome. *John Dewey: The Reconstruction of the Democratic Life*. New York: Frederick Ungar Publishing Co., 1951.

Niebuhr, Reinhold. "The Blindness of Liberalism." *Radical Religion* 1 (1936):4–5.

————. *The Children of Light and the Children of Darkness: A Vindication of Democracy and a Critique of Its Traditonal Defense*. New York: Charles Scribner's Sons, 1944.

————. *Faith and History: A Comparison of Christian and Modern Views of History*. New York: Charles Scribner's Sons, 1948.

————. *Leaves from the Notebooks of a Tamed Cynic*. New York: Meridian Books, 1929, 1957 (originally published in 1929).

————. *Moral Man and Immoral Society: A Study in Ethics and Politics*. New York: Charles Scribner's Sons, 1948.

————. *The Nature and Destiny of Man: A Christian Interpretation*. New York: Charles Scribner's Sons, 1941.

————. "The Pathos of Liberalism." *The Nation* 141 (September 11, 1935):303–304.

————. *Reflections on the End of an Era*. New York: Charles Scribner's Sons, 1934.

Otto, Max. Review of John Dewey, *A Common Faith*. *The Philosophical Review* 44 (1935):496–97.

Platt, Suzy, ed. *Respectfully Quoted: A Dictionary of Quotations Requested from the Congressional Research Service*. Washington: Library of Congress, 1989.

Randall, John Herman, Jr. *A History of the Faculty of Philosophy*. New York: Columbia University Press, 1957.

Ratner, Joseph, ed. *Intelligence in the Modern World: John Dewey's Philosophy*. New York: The Modern Library, 1939.

Ratner, Sidney, ed. *The Philosopher of the Common Man: Essays in Honor of John Dewey to Celebrate his Eightieth Birthday*. New York: G. P. Putnam's Sons, 1940.

Resek, Carl, ed. *War and the Intellectuals: Essays by Randolph S. Bourne, 1915–1919*. New York: Harper & Row, 1964.

Rice, Daniel F. *Reinhold Niebuhr and John Dewey: An American Odyssey*. Albany: State University of New York Press, 1993.

Rockefeller, Steven C. *John Dewey: Religious Faith and Democratic Humanism*. New York: Columbia University Press, 1991.

Rorty, Richard. "Comments on Sleeper and Edel." *Transactions of the Charles S. Peirce Society* 21 (Winter 1985):39–48.

————. *Consequences of Pragmatism*. Minneapolis: University of Minnesota Press, 1982.

———. *Contingency, Irony and Solidarity*. Cambridge: Cambridge University Press, 1989.

———. *Objectivity, Relativism, and Truth*. Cambridge: Cambridge University Press, 1991.

Ryan, Alan. *John Dewey and the High Tide of American Liberalism*. New York: W. W. Norton and Co., 1995.

———. "The Legacy of John Dewey." *Dissent* (Spring 1992):273–78.

Saatkamp, Herman J., Jr., ed. *Rorty and Pragmatism: The Philosopher Responds to His Critics*. The Vanderbilt Library of American Philosophy. Nashville: Vanderbilt University Press, 1995.

Santayana, George. *The Life of Reason*. Five Volumes. New York: Charles Scribner's Sons, 1905–1906.

Schilpp, Paul Arthur, ed. *The Philosophy of John Dewey*. The Library of Living Philosophers. Vol. 1. Evanston: Northwestern University, 1939.

Shaw, Randy. *The Activist's Handbook: A Primer for the 1990's and Beyond*. Berkeley: University of California Press, 1996.

Shih, Hu. *The Chinese Renaissance*. Chicago: The University of Chicago Press, 1934.

Sleeper, R. W. *The Necessity of Pragmatism: John Dewey's Conception of Philosophy*. New Haven: Yale University Press, 1986.

———. "Rorty's Pragmatism: Afloat in Neurath's Boat, But Why Adrift?" *Transactions of the Charles S. Peirce Society* 21 (1985):9–20.

Smith, John E. *Purpose and Thought*. New Haven: Yale University Press, 1978.

Soneson, Jerome Paul. *Pragmatism and Pluralism: John Dewey's Significance for Theology*. Minneapolis: Fortress Press, 1993.

Stuhr, John J., ed. *Philosophy and the Reconstruction of Culture: Pragmatic Essays after Dewey*. Albany: State University of New York Press, 1993.

Tiles, J. E. *Dewey. The Arguments of the Philosophers* series. Ed. Ted Honderich. London: Routledge, 1988.

Tiles, J. E., ed. *John Dewey: Critical Assessments*. Four volumes. London: Routledge, 1992.

Welchman, Jennifer. *Dewey's Ethical Thought*. Ithaca: Cornell University Press, 1995.

———. "From Absolute Idealism to Instrumentalism: The Problem of Dewey's Early Philosophy." *Transactions of the Charles S. Peirce Society* 25 (1989): 407–19.

West, Cornel. *The American Evasion of Philosophy: A Genealogy of Pragmatism*. Madison: The University of Wisconsin Press, 1989.

Westbrook, Robert B. "Democratic Faith: A Response to Michael Eldridge." *Transactions of the Charles S. Peirce Society* 32 (Winter 1996):31–40.

———. "Doing Dewey: An Autobiographical Fragment." *Transactions of the Charles S. Peirce Society* 29 (Fall 1993):493–511.

————. *John Dewey and American Democracy*. Ithaca: Cornell University Press, 1991.

————. Review of James Campbell, *The Community Reconstructs: The Meaning of Pragmatic Social Thought. Transactions of the Charles S. Peirce Society* 29 (1993):259–63." Should that be "Transactions" intead of "Proceedings"?

————. Review of John Patrick Diggins, *The Promise of Pragmatism. The Journal of American History* 82 (1995):170–71.

White, Morton. *Social Thought in America: The Revolt Against Formalism*. Boston: Beacon Press, 1949, 1957.

Wolfe, Alan. "The End of Essences," *The New Republic* (August 8, 1994):34–38.

INDEX

MICHAEL ELDRIDGE holds undergraduate degrees from
Harding College and from Yale, an M.A. from Columbia, and a
Ph.D. from the University of Florida. In addition to life as a scholar, having contributed a number of essays to collections in the field
of philosophy, he has worked as a community and political organizer and as a religious professional. He currently teaches philosophy at the University of North Carolina at Charlotte.